AMERICAN WAYS

A History of American Cultures

AMERICAN WAYS

A History of American Cultures, 1865–Present
Volume II
Second Edition

BENJAMIN G. RADER

University of Nebraska at Lincoln

THOMSON

WADSWORTH

Australia • Canada • Mexico • Singapore • Spain
United Kingdom • United States

THOMSON

WADSWORTH ™

Publisher: *Clark Baxter*
Senior Acquisition Editor: *Ashley Dodge*
Editorial Assistant: *Lucinda Bingham*
Technology Project Manager: *Dave Lionetti*
Marketing Manager: *Lori Grebe Cook*
Marketing Assistant: *Teresa Jessen*
Marketing Communications Manager: *Laurel Anderson*
Project Manager, Editorial Production: *Candace Chen*
Art Director: *Maria Epes*
Print Buyer: *Lisa Claudeanos*
Permissions Editor: *Joohee Lee*
Production Service: *Cadmus Professional Communications*
Photo Researcher: *Stephen Forsling*
Copy Editor: *Tamara Marshall-Keim*

Cover Designer: *Janet Wood*
Cover Image: Charles Darwin, © Bettmann/Corbis; Acoma Pueblo, Edward S. Curtis/Library of Congress; Factory scene, Lynne, MA, 1888, © Schenectady Museum/Corbis; John Dewey and Margaret Sanger, © Bettmann/Corbis; Ludacris and posse, Miami, FL, 2001, © Reuters/Corbis; Mexican American parishioners praying, © Bob Daemmrich/The Image Works; Victorian mansion, © G. E. Kidder Smith/Corbis; Beat writers, San Francisco, CA, 1956, © Allen Ginsberg/Corbis
Cover/Text Printer: *Transcontinental Printing/Louiseville*
Compositor: *Cadmus Professional Communications*

Printed in Canada
1 2 3 4 5 6 7 09 08 07 06 05

For more information about our products, contact us at:
Thomson Learning Academic Resource Center
1-800-423-0563

For permission to use material from this text or product, submit a request online at
http://www.thomsonrights.com.
Any additional questions about permissions can be submitted by email to
thomsonrights@thomson.com.

Library of Congress Control Number: 2004117039

ISBN 0-495-03009-0

Thomson Higher Education
10 Davis Drive
Belmont, CA 94002-3098
USA

Asia (including India)
Thomson Learning
5 Shenton Way
#01-01 UIC Building
Singapore 068808

Australia/New Zealand
Thomson Learning Australia
102 Dodds Street
Southbank, Victoria 3006
Australia

Canada
Thomson Nelson
1120 Birchmount Road
Toronto, Ontario M1K 5G4
Canada

UK/Europe/Middle East/Africa
Thomson Learning
High Holborn House
50–51 Bedford Row
London WC1R 4LR
United Kingdom

Latin America
Thomson Learning
Seneca, 53
Colonia Polanco
11560 Mexico
D.F. Mexico

CONTENTS

THE WAYS OF OTHERS 221

THE ORIGINS OF MODERN WAYS 255

THE COMING OF AGE OF MODERN WAYS 285

THE CULMINATING MOMENT OF MODERN WAYS 321

INTRODUCTION

In the older neighborhoods of countless American towns and cities today, one can observe refurbished gingerbread houses with turrets, cupolas, and extended verandas. Built in the nineteenth or early twentieth centuries, these houses serve as vivid monuments of a past age. They convey to our time a message of white, Protestant, middle-class respectability; of stern, bearded fathers; of sweet, caring mothers; of obedient, well-mannered children; of the saying of grace before meals; of sumptuous Sunday family dinners; and, above all else, of familiar routines. It was these routines, recalled Henry Seidel Canby when describing his family life in the Wilmington, Delaware, of the 1890s, "that inspired confidence in a patterned universe," a confidence that Canby found sorely wanting in the twentieth century.

It is the ways of the American past, such as those represented by the middle-class Victorian families in their gingerbread houses, that are the subject of this book. Rather than recounting the horrors and heroics of wars, pivotal presidential elections, or stunning technological breakthroughs, this book looks beneath the surface of American history. It examines those fundamental customs, beliefs, values, and practices that are, or have been, characteristic of Americans or of various groups of Americans. In particular, *American Ways* looks at religious, social (including class, gender, race, and ethnicity), family, political, work, and leisure ways. Frequently such ways are related to one another. Together, they comprise what may be described as a *culture*.

The recurring tensions between the individual, with her or his interests on the one side, and community, with ties and obligations that exist beyond the self on the other, constitute the major theme of this book. While individualism has long been at the very core of American society and culture, it always has been caged in by widely agreed upon constraints. For example, the founders of the republic loudly proclaimed the principles of individual freedom, but at the same time they insisted that a virtuous citizenry—a citizenry that exercised self-restraint—was essential to the new republic's survival. Similarly, each of the nation's major religious communities defended individual freedom, but they invariably justified such freedom only within the limits imposed by obligations to God, the community, and a divinely ordained system of personal morality. Hence, the pursuit of material welfare, for example, never exempted an individual from obeying the Ten Commandments. In addition, the unequal rights and obligations embedded in the nation's social ways long limited the individual freedom of women, African Americans, Native Americans, and working-class people.

American Ways also explores the historical relationships of American ways to the political, social, and economic forces that shaped them. For example, the physical environment, including soil and weather, played a large role in determining the ways of Native Americans and the first European settlers in the Americas. So did the War for Independence and the Industrial Revolution trigger significant departures from traditional ways. In the twentieth and twenty-first centuries, no outside forces have been more important than mass consumption and mass media in shaping American values and behaviors. In turn, the adoption of new ways affected social, economic, and political history. For example, the ethos of self-control adopted by the middle class in the nineteenth century helped to create a more efficient workforce, one that expedited industrialization, while the spirit of self-fulfillment in the twentieth century encouraged the growth of a mass-consumption society.

In addition, this book represents one way—certainly not the only one—of generalizing about the history of American cultures. The first part of this volume begins with an examination of the middle-class ways (sometimes also described as Victorian or bourgeois) of the nineteenth and early twentieth centuries. Mostly Protestant in faith, materially ambitious, and concerned with the consequences flowing from the destruction of traditional social ties, the middle class gave special attention to self-control. In constructing its own set of ways, the middle class even emptied some of the other groups of some of their vitality. By appropriating from the working class the value of work, from the aristocracy the value of genteel refinement, and from evangelical Protestants the value of personal morality and high moral purpose, the middle class claimed (and to a substantial degree gained) the cultural leadership of the entire nation.

Yet as powerful as these ways were, Part VIII reveals that the middle class never achieved a complete hegemony over American life. Though they succeeded in subduing the Native American population militarily, efforts by white middle-class Americans to erase the distinctive identities of Indians and to assimilate them into middle-class society went mostly for naught. The Industrial Revolution created a distinctive working class, one whose ways were frequently at odds with those of both the upper and middle classes. The arrival of millions of immigrants from Europe, Canada, Mexico, and Asia added yet another challenge to middle-class supremacy. Finally, in the nineteenth century and beyond, neither the Civil War (1861–65) nor Reconstruction (1865–76) bridged the great regional chasm that separated the North and the South.

Part IX treats the origins of modern ways, those ways with which we are most familiar today. Between the 1880s and the 1930s, large numbers of Americans began to retreat from middle-class Victorian ways. The rise of a mass-consumption economy, the development of a mass media, and the creation of a new middle class encouraged the adoption of values and behaviors more conducive to consumption than to production. For more and more Americans, self-control—at least in one's leisure time—gave way to greater self-indulgence and a quest for greater excitement. Simultaneously, ever larger spheres of American life were slipping away from religious influence and control. By the 1920s, the nation was in the midst of a new cultural era, one that scholars frequently label as "modern."

Part X examines the "coming of age" of modern ways. In the decades between World War I (1914–18) and the turbulent 1960s, large numbers of Americans experienced a profound shift in sensibility. They began to look more to expertise and personality than to character, to place more faith in science than in folk wisdom, to accept moral relativism more than absolute notions of right and wrong, and, above all else, to place less emphasis on self-control and more on self-fulfillment than their nineteenth-century predecessors. Yet the proponents of modern ways never achieved a complete triumph. Far from it. In the 1920s, traditionalists launched a massive counterattack. In the face of the Great Depression of the 1930s, Americans were torn between visions of the future and impulses leading them back to the ways of the past. Confronted with powerful ideological enemies during World War II and the early Cold War, American sought to create an united front, an "American Way of Life" that contained aspects of both modern and traditional ways.

Part XI deals with the "long sixties" (the decade of the 1960s and early 1970s) as the culminating moment of modern ways. It was then that the modern values of cultural pluralism and toleration found expression in a rights revolution. As in no previous era in American history except perhaps the 1920s, the long sixties challenged all traditional sources of cultural authority. While rejecting nearly all authority except that arising from the self or from within their own ranks, many of the nation's rebellious youth yearned for and experimented with new kinds of community. But in the end the most enduring result of this aspect of the long sixties cultural rebellion was a new individualism, one that placed individual happiness before concern for character or community and prized a view of life as one long array of unrestrained and ever-changing individual choices.

Coming to terms with the momentous cultural upheavals of the long sixties and an expanding consumer capitalism is the subject of Part XII. During the last quarter of the twentieth century and the first years of the twenty-first century, most Americans continued to embrace the new individualism. Believing that the chief end in life was personal happiness, older social ties built around voluntary associations, political participation, marriage and families, and personal friendships weakened. Neither did the nation's core or common culture hold firm. Everywhere and in all aspects of American life, it seemed, divisions along religious, regional, racial, gender, and ethnic lines sharpened. Yet the nation had persevered through deep social divisions before and there was evidence that it might be able to do so in the future.

These are in brief the major sets of ways examined in this book. The divisions between them are not meant to be hard and fast. To this day, aspects of earlier cultures obviously remain important. Strong echoes of earlier cultures may still be heard in the nation's speech dialects, in its regional patterns of life, in its political behavior, in its religious practices, and even in its family life. Furthermore, each of the cultures was evolutionary rather than discrete; each enveloped and expanded upon earlier ones. Hence, the beginning of one culture closely resembled the end of the preceding one. Indeed, a central point of this book is that the legacy of earlier ways remains a key determinant of our ways today. It is for this reason that many modern Americans find comfort in viewing and living in the Victorian houses that still stand in our midst. They recognize, even if only half-consciously, what Abraham Lincoln once described so eloquently as the "mystic chords of memory."

A BRIEF NOTE TO THE READER

This book has been shaped by my conviction that there is a special need for a book presenting the broad outlines of the history of American ways. Knowledge of this history is, I believe, essential to understanding more fully the world about us. It will assist you, the reader, in comprehending what you read in the serious press, what you encounter in major literary and scientific texts, what you see in museums, and what you see and hear on television. In short, by reading this book, you will gain a familiarity with the key cultural paradigms that shape much of the discourse in contemporary life.

Here, rather than an encyclopedic rendering of American history, I have emphasized major themes and important ideas. *American Ways* seeks to provide a coherent and interpretive narrative of the most fundamental changes and continuities in the nation's past. Coherence arises principally from a focus on the tension between the contradictory impulses toward individualism and toward community that run throughout the course of American history. *American Ways* may also be thought of as a road map. You will not find here a discussion of every road, only the major highways into the American past. Without such a guide, none of us can travel far in our quest for understanding what the past has to teach us.

Readers familiar with the first edition will find in this revision a new organizational format and a considerable body of new material. Each volume now contains six parts, with each part divided into two chapters. While more numerous, the chapters are shorter in length. New material in this volume includes a discussion of the civic life of the middle class in the late nineteenth and early twentieth centuries, a consideration of the West in the American imagination, and a vastly expanded treatment of developments in American culture since about 1960. In particular, I have reformulated and elaborated my treatment of how Americans have sought to come to terms with modern ways. Finally, in accordance with the findings of recent scholarship, I have taken this opportunity to make other revisions throughout the text.

ACKNOWLEDGMENTS

Direct contributions to the completion of this book came from many quarters. Both the first and second editions' contents and organization owe a large debt to the questions, papers, and comments of literally dozens of students. For the first edition, Drake Bush offered invaluable direction and support. That edition also benefited from reviews of specific chapters by Robert Becker, Bruce J. Dierenfield, Van Beck Hall, Elizabeth Van Beeck, Jessica Coope, Heather Furnas, Thomas Jundt, Wendy Katz, Dane Kennedy, Timothy Mahoney, Christin Mamiya, Susan Miller, Charlene Porsild, Kenneth Winkle, and Sharon Wood. For this edition, I also benefited from suggestions or help from Carolyn Biltoft, Tim Borstelmann, Heather Furnas, James Garza, Joe Harder, Jonathan Herzog, Wendy Katz, Renee Laegreid, Timothy Mahoney, Bruce Pauley, Guillaume Ratel, Walter Rucker, Preston Shires, and Victoria Smith, and reviews of Chapters 23 and 24 by Jessica Coope and Thomas Jundt, as well as by members of an informal interdisciplinary reading group of the University of Nebraska—Lincoln, who offered criticism, encouragement, and intellectual stimulation. For contributions in rendering this edition into final shape, my special thanks go to Lucinda Bingham, M.R. Carey, Candace Chen, Ashley Dodge, and Stephen Forsling. Words are inadequate to describe the contributions of Barbara Koch Rader, not only to this revision but to my life more generally.

VII

THE WAYS OF THE MIDDLE CLASS

The fifty-three years between 1865, the end of the Civil War, and 1918, the end of World War I, were momentous ones for the United States. These were years in which the nation tried to reconstruct itself after a bloody civil war. It was an era of armed conflict, including the final phase of a four-hundred-year war with the American Indians, the Spanish-American War, the suppression of the Filipino uprising, and World War I. These were the years that the new republic acquired a far-flung overseas empire, including Alaska, Hawaii, Puerto Rico, and the Philippines. Abetted by massive waves of immigration, the nation's population also soared, from about 35 million people in 1865 to 106 million in 1920. The economy grew even more rapidly. Still predominately an agricultural republic in 1865, by 1920 the United States had grown into the greatest industrial giant the world had ever seen. By 1920, for the first time according to the Census, more Americans lived in urban than in rural areas.

Accompanying these seismic changes was the development within the United States of great social cleavages. Between 1865 and 1920 the nation became essentially a three-tiered society. At its apex were the super wealthy, the top 5 percent of the population who owned some 60 percent of all the property in the nation. Their numbers included the nation's major landholders, bankers, merchants, and manufacturers. At the bottom of society were those who owned little if any property. In between was the emerging middle class; its members comprised some 30 to 35 percent of the population and owned most of the remaining property.

Middle-class ways are the subject of the following two chapters. (Nineteenth- and early twentieth-century middle-class culture is also sometimes labeled *Victorian* or *bourgeois*, thereby implying that the middle classes throughout the Western world shared a common set of values, attitudes, and behaviors.) Occupationally, the middle class included farmers, merchants, professionals (whose numbers increased rapidly in the late nineteenth and early twentieth centuries), independent artisans, and small manufacturers. Frequently comprised of self-made men and located mostly in the northern half of the nation, this middle group was overwhelmingly white and Protestant. While not exclusively a party of the middle class, the long-term successes of the Republican party were not only a reflection of that class's stunning power in politics but also in American life more generally. Between the election of Abraham Lincoln in 1860 and Franklin D. Roosevelt in 1932, eleven Republicans and only two Democrats won the presidency.

With the breakdown of the eighteenth century's hierarchical order and the opening up of new opportunities for ordinary white people in the nineteenth century, white middle-class Protestants claimed for themselves and their culture the moral leadership of the new nation. Such a claim rested on their supreme confidence that they, and they alone, represented the nation's "best" and most "respectable" people. After all, it was their undeviating attention to self-control, they concluded, that had brought them material success and had distinguished them from the nation's more "dissolute" peoples.

13

MIDDLE-CLASS FAMILY WAYS

With the authority of traditional hierarchies, churches, and local communities in retreat or disarray, no institution was more important to the nineteenth- and early twentieth-centuries middle class than the family. The family took over tasks that earlier had been shared with others. The most important of these was the obligation to mold in each child a sturdy moral conscience. Once a set of simple moral truths had been firmly embedded in each child's personality, he or she would no longer require external restraints. *Self-control* would then come automatically. The middle class also looked to the family as a resource for bringing greater order, stability, and warmth into their lives. To

A Middle-Class Victorian Family at Home. Nothing of the trials and cares of the outside world intrude on this idyllic family scene from the 1869 publication *The American Home*, by Catharine Beecher and Harriet Beecher Stowe. For the middle class, the home assumed many of the cultural and social responsibilities earlier assigned to churches, communities, and the upper classes.

New York Public Library

189

counter the disintegrative forces arising from the rapidly changing world of business and industry, the Victorian family invented its own rich world of symbols, rituals, and myths.

THE INVENTION OF THE VICTORIAN FAMILY

In countering the psychic ravages of their time and in making the home more effective as an agency promoting self-control, the middle class invented a new kind of family. It was an institution with a strong sense of its own existence. Each family constructed for itself a past, one similar to that which elite families had always possessed. To bolster claims for their families as historical entities, the middle class began as never before to invest with deeper meanings material objects that had been handed down from earlier generations. Furniture, silver, and quilts that formerly had had only economic significance now became priceless family heirlooms. As never before, families began to preserve photograph albums, diaries, letters, and other memorabilia.

Courtship, the first step in the creation of a new family, became a far more important ritual than in the past. In the more prolonged courtships of the middle class, the family's parlor was a special site. In this feminized enclave where the family took special care to exhibit its claims to respectability, the young woman might offer her beau cakes and tea and sing and play the piano for him. The couple might also recite poetry and read aloud to one another. While typical couples engaged in some touching and kissing during courtship, other physical intimacies were less likely. The plunge in the incidence of premarital pregnancies (especially within the middle class) in the nineteenth century reflected the effectiveness of prohibitions against the physical expression of sexual passion.

For the middle class, weddings likewise grew in symbolic significance. In her marriage to Prince Albert in 1840, Queen Victoria herself popularized a newly invented wedding costume. The luminous white gown, veil, and bouquet dramatically set the bride apart from all the other women present and vividly dramatized the fact that weddings had become the foremost rite of passage for middle-class females. Weddings were increasingly familial rather than communal ceremonies; invitations were sent out only to family members and to close friends. Wedding anniversaries, once rarely celebrated, now became a special occasion for acknowledging the solemn bond that had inaugurated the formation of a new family.

Set aside at a separate time in a special "dining room," the evening meal now became far more formal and ceremonial than in the past. It "was a ritual," recalled Henry Seidel Canby of family dinners during his boyhood in Wilmington, Delaware, in the 1890s. The saying of grace before the meal and the rite of sharing food reinforced family bonds. "It was this familiar movement," Canby contended, "this routine with a certainty of repetition, that inspired confidence in a patterned universe," a confidence that he found sorely wanting in the twentieth century.

Once primarily a day for religious and public activities, Sundays became a special middle-class family holiday. With far more success than their Sabbatarian predecessors, the middle classes in both Great Britain and the United States succeeded in shutting down trade and public leisure activities on Sunday. While proper Victorians attended church services, much of the remainder of the day was spent in ritualistic family activities. It was then that the middle classes gathered for a special ceremonial feast, the Sunday family dinner.

Christmas underwent a roughly similar transformation. The traditional Christmas had been an unruly rite of communal renewal. In practices such as wassailing and mumming, the ordinary people took to the streets; they dressed in wild attire, sometimes donned masks, sang rude songs, made mocking and obscene gestures, and insisted that their superiors treat them with food and drink. Never endorsed by evangelical Protestants, who considered the traditional celebration to be both pagan and papist, the older Christmas practices nearly died out in both Britain and America.

But in the middle decades of the nineteenth century, the middle classes in the English-speaking world invented an almost entirely new way of celebrating Christmas. The popular English novelist, Charles Dickens, who wrote *A Christmas Carol* in 1843, seems to have almost singlehandedly transformed Christmas into a mostly family affair. Families sent out special cards to relatives and close friends; they brought a tree (once considered a pagan practice) indoors and decorated it; they invented the modern Santa Claus as a benevolent, fun-loving, avuncular figure; they gave and received gifts; and they shared a special meal on Christmas day. The ritualized nature of the holiday, with its emphasis upon doing things as they had always been done, symbolically linked present families with their predecessors.

The creation of a set of special times helped the middle class to compensate for the weakening of traditional communal and religious senses of time. The numerically standardized clock time of the office and the factory had robbed traditional time of its rich associations with the natural rhythms of night and day and the seasons as well as the traditional church calendar. Alongside clock time, middle-class families created their own special times, which, as we have seen, they sought to stock with an abundance of powerful symbolic meanings.

THE MIDDLE-CLASS HOME

"A man is not a whole or a complete man," wrote poet Walt Whitman, "unless he owns a house and the ground it stands on." In the eighteenth century, the "middling ranks" had frequently lived in structures of unpainted wooden planks or in log cabins, but nineteenth-century aspirants to respectability strove to acquire larger houses and to make them more attractive. Sturdy red brick or stone became the building material of choice for the upper end of the middle class while the remainder usually settled for white, balloon-framed houses with green shutters. (Still standing in many communities today are recently refurbished gingerbread houses. With turrets, cupolas, and extended verandas, they are revealing statements of their age.) Whether red, white, or another color, the new houses literally blazed to the outside world a message of middle-class respectability.

A Nineteenth-Century Victorian Mansion, Eureka, California. "A man is not a whole or a complete man," wrote poet Walt Whitman, "unless he owns a house and the ground it stands on." Set off from the street by a fence and yard, the soaring gothic houses of the middle class were both monuments to individual achievement and to family respectability. Even today, they continue to evoke feelings of tranquility and stability.

No longer did middle-class families build their houses next to the streets or in neighborhoods that included the poor. By insisting on front yards that were artfully decorated with trees, shrubs, and flowers and enclosed by a white picket fence, middle-class families created attractive barriers between themselves and the squalor of the streets.

More highly differentiated spaces within the home also reflected the middle-class quest for respectability. While in modest homes working, cooking, eating, and sleeping might all take place in the same room or set of rooms, space in Victorian homes became far more specialized. Ideally, each house contained separate rooms for each major activity. With a higher value placed on modesty and privacy than in the past, the family no longer slept together in the same room or in the same bed. In middle-class houses, hallways and separate bedrooms segregated the parents from the children and the children from one another.

Rather than an indicator of aristocratic pretensions, to the middle class the tasteful decoration of rooms was an important index of the family's civility and personal morality. "We are sure to judge a woman in whose house we find ourselves for the first time, by her surroundings," explained Elsie de Wolfe in a treatise entitled *The House in Good Taste* (1913); "We judge her temperament, her habits, her inclinations, by the interior of her home." "Taste is not only a part and an index of morality," wrote Englishman John Ruskin, who was widely read on both sides of the Atlantic, "it is the ONLY morality. . . . Tell me what you like, and I will tell you what you are." A huge middle-class market developed in the nineteenth century for New Haven clocks, Waltham watches, Lowell carpets, machine-pressed glassware, upholstered sofas, mahogany bureaus, and dozens of other mass-produced imitations of costly luxuries that were beyond the budgets of the typical working-class family. None of the furnishings was more important than mirrors. Mirrors could be found nearly everywhere—on walls, on doors, over mantles, and on chests of drawers. The proliferation of mirrors reflected a growing concern for how one presented one's self to others.

In publicly displaying their refinement, the middle class gave special attention to parlors. Emptied of tools and beds, it was in the parlor that the middle-class family represented an ideal version of itself to itself and to others. In order to avoid harshness, angularity, and sharp lines, middle-class families decorated their parlors with a profusion of soft, warm fabrics. Carpets covered the floors, thick draperies shrouded the windows, and mountains of pillows were deposited everywhere. Ideally, each parlor contained a piano or a parlor organ and a well-stocked bookcase. In the creation of the parlor, historian Richard Bushman has trenchantly observed, "people implicitly claimed the right to live like rulers."

THE SEPARATE SPHERE OF WOMEN

In principle, the middle class promoted the idea of "separate spheres." According to this doctrine, women should occupy the private sphere of the home while men should occupy the public sphere of work. Within the home, the woman was to care for children, manage the household, and comfort her husband. Within the public sphere, the husband was to be the family's bread-winner. Contrary to the imagery conjured up by the phrase "separate spheres," the proponents of the doctrine never intended that the occupants remain exclusively within these respective spheres. For example, the mother/wife could—indeed, even should—venture into the public realm to do church and philanthropic work while the husband/father was expected to perform specific family rituals within the home.

Neither was the ideology of separate spheres entirely new. By arguing that women should assume a special responsibility for the rearing of a vir-tuous citizenry, the founders of the new republic had anticipated the nine-teenth century's enthusiasm for the separate sphere doctrine. But the great economic upheavals of the nineteenth century were more important cata-lysts for drawing sharper boundaries between the lives of middle-class women and men. Furthermore, these revolutions relocated some forms of work from the home to the office building and the factory. No longer was the home a major production site; household items ranging from bread to cloth-ing were increasingly made outside the home. While many middle-class housewives continued to perform unpaid reproductive and household chores, the better-off increasingly employed domestic servants for cooking and cleaning.

As the home was emptied of many of its earlier productive functions, in principle it became a place devoted more exclusively to the family and to culture. Here, the woman was expected to construct a refuge, "an elysium," as one writer put it, "to which [the husband] can flee and find rest from the stormy strife of a selfish world." Here, as in Charles Dickens's *A Christmas Carol*, one escaped from the cold, domineering office of Scrooge to the warmth of the Cratchett's family hearth. The ideal Victorian home was not only a shelter from the anxieties of modern life, as literary historian Walter Houghton has observed, but also "a shelter for those moral and spiritual val-ues which the commercial spirit" was "threatening to destroy."

Proponents of the separate spheres doctrine urged mothers to take on an expanded role in parenting. Indeed, fulfilling the obligations of motherhood now became a middle-class woman's major lifework. A mother's warm love, her tender voice, and her sweet smile became powerful Victorian symbols. It was now the mother rather than the father who was primarily responsible for a child's success or failure in life. Consistent with the new role of women in parenting, by the 1850s the courts had begun to make mothers rather than fathers the custodial parent of minor children in divorce cases.

As suggested by the changing conceptions of motherhood, the middle class sharpened gender distinctions. In the past, part of the rationale for patriarchy had rested on the assumption that men possessed superior reasoning powers and were less given to passion than women. But, in the nineteenth century, confronted by the perils and opportunities of the new economy and the specter of social disorder, attitudes toward gender differences changed. Men now became increasingly thought of as the more aggressive and impulsive sex. The most admired men were those who exercised self-control while channeling their volcanic passions into their work.

Women, on the other hand, were now thought to come by self-control and self-sacrifice more naturally than men. Innately gentler, less selfish, more pious, and more refined than men, they could, by example and instruction, influence positively the moral lives of their beaus, their husbands, and their children. Hence, while men's work was being thought of as a career or a job, women's work retained the older meaning of a "calling," an occupation defined in terms of its contribution to a larger good. Walter Houghton has compared the role of the Victorian mother to that of a priestess. "On the shoulders of its priestess, the wife and mother," he has written, "fell the burden of stemming the amoral and irreligious drift of modern industrial society." While such thinking placed women on a higher moral plane than men, it at the same time reinforced other pressures that were confining women's activities to the home. In other words, the idea of female moral superiority served to firm up the walls that excluded women from those centers of economic and political power that existed outside the home.

REARING CHILDREN

Before the great economic revolutions of the nineteenth century, land had been the basic resource of society. But with growing numbers of families detached from farms, bequeathing a legacy in land was no longer practicable. Instead of a landed inheritance, middle-class families now sought to equip their children for the future with superior moral and intellectual resources.

The most important of these was self-control. "The *child* must be *treated* as a *free, self-guiding, self-controlling being*," wrote Bronson Alcott. "He must be allowed to feel that he is under his own guidance." Gaining a self-command of feelings and impulses required a more regimented childhood than in the past; consequently, middle-class families employed more rigid schedules for feeding, toilet training, play, religious instruction, and school than their predecessors. Rather than the rod for discipline, parents resorted more frequently to the withdrawal of affection and the inculcation of guilt. Obtaining control over the self was no easy task. After having lost her temper, a nine-year-old Louisa May Alcott resolved to do better. "If I only *kept* all [of the resolutions] I make," she wrote in her diary, "I should be the best girl in the world. But, I don't, and so am very bad." In a notation beneath the entry, one she wrote much later upon reviewing the diary for use in an autobiography, Alcott wrote: "Poor little sinner! She says the same at fifty [years old]—L. M. A."

Consistent with the ideology of separate spheres, middle-class boys and girls were reared differently. Mothers urged their sons to strive for "manly independence" while daughters were told to aspire to "moral purity" and "true womanhood." Yet middle-class families encouraged intense emotional bonds between mothers and sons, hoping that sentimental attachments would help boys to internalize self-control and lead them to look to their mothers rather than their peers for a proper standard of moral conduct. While there was less concern about the likelihood of young women achieving true womanhood than young men achieving manly independence, a large outpouring of advice literature told girls how to develop good manners, morals, and domestic skills.

The increased importance attached to the development of self-control placed heavier demands and expectations on formal education. The "primary objective" of education was not the cultivation of the intellect, explained educational reformer Henry Barnard at mid-nineteenth century, but "the regulation of feelings and dispositions [and] the extirpation of vicious propensities." Along with the family, the public schools sought through Bible readings, didactic tales, commentaries, and simplistic aphorisms to hammer into each child's personality a few general but immutable moral absolutes. Once these moral imperatives had been internalized, they would, as one educator said, "endure as long as life endures." With this legacy, each child was ready, upon achieving adulthood, to make his or her own way in the world.

In time, middle-class parents sought even more from education. To obtain training and formal certification for well-paid jobs in bureaucracies and in the professions, they sent their sons to high schools, professional schools, and colleges. Seeking to shield them from seduction, economic exploitation, and mental overstimulation and to prepare them for lives as wives and mothers, middle-class parents also prolonged the formal education of their daughters.

MIDDLE-CLASS SEX WAYS

When we think of the Victorian age today, sexual repression is the first thought that is likely to leap to our minds. This is partly because of a striking absence of candor (compared to today) that characterized both public and private discussion of sexuality in the nineteenth century. The use of sexual euphemisms abounded. Rather than speaking of a woman's arms or legs—both terms suggested an untoward familiarity—refined people spoke of her "limbs." "Bosom" was the polite name for breasts, "the secret vice" meant masturbation, "the social evil" referred to prostitution, and "fallen doves" was a polite term for prostitutes.

Our view of Victorian sexuality has been further shaped by the campaigns in the late nineteenth and early twentieth century against obscenity and birth control. The name of Anthony Comstock, a former Connecticut dry-goods salesman who made it his lifework to suppress obscenity, has become virtually synonymous with sexual repression. Comstock's crowning achievement came in 1873 when Congress passed without debate the so-called Comstock Law, a statute that barred all "obscene" materials from the mails. Supervising enforcement of the new law fell to none other than Comstock himself. In a well-financed campaign—again led by Comstock—state and local governments across the country tightened up and more strictly enforced their laws against pornography and the sale of contraceptives. Perhaps it was little wonder then that British playwright George Bernard Shaw coined the term "Comstockery" to sum up America's constrictive sexual attitudes and practices.

While most Americans were less zealous than Comstock in cracking down on obscenity and contraceptives, his campaign *did* rest on wide public support. Profoundly influenced by the chivalric notions of love popularized by the romantic poets and the sentimental novelists of the day, the middle-class Victorians saw romantic love and raw sexual lust as incompatible feelings. Love represented a far more refined and elevated attraction to another person than did lust. Indeed, love was a powerful force for sexual restraint and purity; by strengthening their resolve to resist temptation, love of an angelic woman could even save men from capitulating to their baser, carnal yearnings. Ideally, then, sex should be reserved exclusively for marriage, and even then it should remain subordinated to, and thoroughly immersed in, powerful feelings of romantic love.

Apart from the popularity of romantic love, a burgeoning body of sexual advice literature tied good physical health to the practice of sexual restraint. Influenced by the theory that the body was a closed energy system, whose sexual resources were depleted with each use, the reformers insisted that sexual indulgence jeopardized one's bodily well-being. It could result in such calamities as "seminal weakness, impotence, . . . pulmonary consumption, hypochondriasis, loss of memory, . . . and death." In particular, doctors and health reformers railed against masturbation; the "solitary vice" not only could cause illness and insanity, they said, but also its practice drained women's bodies of vital psychic energy and men's of a portion of their lifetime endowment of sperm.

The middle-class preoccupation with sexual restraint arose from something more than concern for good health, though indeed much of the day's conventional medical wisdom attributed frightening consequences to sexual excesses. It entailed something more than enhancing one's prospects for material success, albeit this was no insignificant consideration. Dr. John Cowan, for example, explained that "a continent life . . . surely guides to success in all business undertakings." It also entailed something more than a strategy for establishing a family's respectability and its credentials for moral leadership, although these considerations, too, undoubtedly influenced the sexual attitudes and behavior of countless middle-class families.

Ultimately, the driving force behind the campaign for repression arose from profound middle-class anxieties. The principle of equality and the opening up of opportunities for getting ahead materially had released sexuality from its traditional moorings, as it had removed other restraints on the individual. For example, neither parents nor clergy any longer had the authority to enforce marriage in the event of an unwanted pregnancy. A host of sexual radicals—Robert Dale Owen, Fanny Wright, John Humphrey Noyes, and Victoria Woodhull, among others—proposed daring alternatives to the confinement of sexuality within monogamous marriages. Perhaps even more disturbing to the middle class was the apparent rise in the practice of birth control, the increasing numbers of surgical abortions, the burgeoning market for pornography, and the growth of prostitution. Dammed up behind a wall of Victorian propriety and prudery was a separate world of seething sexuality, one that might at any moment burst through the floodgates and inundate the middle-class family and the entire nineteenth-century social order.

A part of middle-class erotic anxiety may have also arisen from their own changing sexual ways. As historians John D'Emilio and Estelle Freedman have shown in their history of American sexuality, middle-class families took steps, albeit frequently halting ones, that gradually unlinked the ages-old connection between reproduction and sexuality. Rather than anchoring sexual experience in reproduction, they increasingly tied it to love, intimacy, and even personal pleasure. From such surviving sources as diaries and private correspondence, we know that growing numbers of middle-class couples believed that having sexual intercourse (apart from any consideration of reproduction) strengthened their marriages. By the late Victorian era, even physicians and health reformers were beginning to endorse this position. "The sexual relationship is among the most important uses of married life," reported a medical text in 1883. "It vivifies the affection for each other, as nothing else in the world can, and is a powerful reminder of their mutual obligation to each other and to the community in which they live."

Additional wealth, more leisure time, and greater control over fertility facilitated the severance of sex from reproduction. A falling birthrate for white women—from an average of seven children in 1800 to less than four in 1900—suggested that married couples might have been exploring the possibilities of erotic experiences that were unconnected to reproduction. It is more likely, however, that this "fertility revolution" arose more from a recognition (perhaps unconsciously) by urban middle-class families that children were no longer economic assets. Having fewer children not only meant more disposable income but also allowed the family to invest more of its resources in each individual child (especially in their sons). With smaller families each child could receive additional financial assistance in preparing them for jobs that required more advanced skills. Reducing the number of children may have also represented an assertion of female autonomy, for it relieved the wife of burdens associated with reproduction and allowed her to wield more control over her own sexuality.

In nineteenth century America, curtailing the incidence of unwanted pregnancies was not an easy or simple matter. Couples rarely used condoms or diaphragms; these mechanical prophylactics were difficult to obtain and frowned upon by public opinion. Some women employed sponges and douches, neither of which were highly effective in preventing conception. Neither did coitus interruptus (male withdrawal before ejaculation) or the rhythm method (trying to time intercourse only during a woman's infertile period) guarantee exemption from unwanted pregnancies. Some women took "female pills," which contained poisons that could abort a fetus, especially during early pregnancy, as well as jeopardize a woman's health. As many as one in four pregnancies may have been terminated by surgical abortion. But the most popular and successful of all forms of birth control was probably sexual abstinence. After having achieved the desired family size, middle-class wives frequently retreated from the marital bed to a separate bedroom. Here, they might remain for the rest of their lives.

UPPER-CLASS FAMILIES

The rise to supremacy of middle-class ways placed the nation's wealthiest citizens in an awkward position. While there had always been Americans with aristocratic pretensions, the nation had never had a hereditary upper class in the European sense. Without a hereditary aristocracy, it was frequently not an easy matter to distinguish the upper from the middle class. In addition, republican ideology and the opening of the doors of opportunity for ordinary white men had combined in the early nineteenth century to weaken traditional elite authority. Nevertheless, by mid-nineteenth century, wealthy families in every major city and throughout the slave-owning South sought to distinguish themselves from the middle class by aping the ways of the European aristocracy.

Fed by the spectacular transfusions of new wealth arising from the Industrial Revolution and the creation of huge corporations, by the 1880s and 1890s the efforts to create an American aristocracy had, in the words of historian Robert Wiebe, "the look of a formidable enterprise." Each city had its fashionable residential area of the super rich: In Chicago it was the Gold Coast, in Manhattan Fifth Avenue, in San Francisco Nob Hill, and in Denver Quality Hill. On the hillsides above the humid city of Cincinnati, a traveler observed in 1883, "the homes of Cincinnati's merchant princes and million-aires are found . . . elegant cottages, tasteful villas, and substantial man-sions, surrounded by a paradise of grass, gardens, lawns, and tree-shaded roads." The wealthy escaped summer's heat by building lavish "cottages" in such cooler spots as Newport, Rhode Island, and Bell Harbor, Maine, and, when wintry winds began to blow, they made their way to resorts in the Carolinas, Georgia, and eventually Florida. They engaged in conspicu-ous consumption, sent their sons to the colleges that catered only to the nation's most affluent, formed socially exclusive clubs, and patronized expensive sports.

But neither the accumulation of great fortunes nor the adoption of aristo-cratic lifestyles necessarily led to high social standing. Older established elites frequently shut out the nouveau riche. In the East, the Boston Brahmin and Philadelphia Main Line families, who had acquired their wealth in the colonial and Revolutionary eras, created close-knit, virtually impenetrable family dynasties. Even such relatively raw and open cities as San Francisco and Denver had their established elites. In New York, a flood of moneyed newcomers overwhelmed the city's older elite. Led by Ward McAllister, a southern-born lawyer who had made a fortune in the California gold rush, New York's wealthy sought to construct a distinctive upper class. They set up rules of conduct and developed a careful list of those whom they deemed eli-gible for New York's high "society." McAllister's *Social Register*, first pub-lished in 1888, contained a list of the "Four Hundred"—the cream of New York's society—based on the invitation list to Mrs. William Astor's great ball on February 1, 1892. Late in the nineteenth century, numerous smaller cities claimed their own local Four Hundreds.

Yet, as hard as they tried, American plutocrats never succeeded in con-structing an upper class in the European sense. Each city had its own rich, its own Four Hundred, but they rarely interacted much with the nabobs from other cities and even when they were lumped together failed to constitute a nationally coherent class. Neither did the super rich win the admiration nor the full approval of the nation's middle class. While embracing genteel refine-ment, most of the middle class disliked the wealthy's relaxation of self-control and their unproductive use of leisure. Both Thorstein Veblen in his *The Theory of the Leisure Class* (1899) and middle-class cartoonists mercilessly lampooned the ways of the upper class, in particular their un-aristocratic inclination to ostentatiously display their wealth or to accumulate ever more wealth, inclinations more easily resisted by Europe's landed aristocracy than by America's entrepreneurial buccaneers. While possessing "the loftiest pretensions to 'aristocracy,'" sneered British counsel Thomas Grattan, America's very rich frequently descended "to very low methods of money-making." Finally, great waves of new wealth regularly overwhelmed those who sought to build an American aristocracy. Money, as Robert Wiebe has observed, purchased luxurious goods "but not class position."

North Wind Picture Archives

A Summer Ride on the Beach, 1889. The families of the wealthy frequently spent their summers at fashionable spas. While middle-class Victorians saw leisure in terms of renewing one's self for work and other important duties, the wealthy were inclined to enjoy spare-time activities for their own sake. Furthermore, conspicuous and expensive leisure activities provided a means by which the upper class could distinguish itself from the nation's other social classes.

CONCLUSION

No institution was more important to middle-class Americans of the late nineteenth and early twentieth centuries than the family. Seeing the family as the primary agency in shaping the character of the young, as a source of social stability, and as a refuge from the travails of modern industrial society, the middle class invested enormous amounts of time, money, and emotional energy into the invention and perpetuation of a new kind of family. The new family nurtured a strong sense of its own existence as a historic entity, encouraged an adherence to routines and rituals, and in other respects took on functions earlier assigned to churches and local communities. In the idealized version of the middle-class family, one that traditionalists yearn for even today, women and men occupied separate spheres, motherhood was revered and sentimentalized, and children were obedient and unspoiled.

14

MIDDLE-CLASS CULTURAL AND CIVIC LIFE

The middle-class effort to acquire control over themselves and others entailed more than attention to the self. It also led to a turning outward. In particular the middle-class sought to promote in the general society what it called "culture." Indeed, after the Civil War, as the middle class was losing some of its religious zeal, culture began to occupy a place along side the Puritan City on a Hill, the Revolution's virtue, and the antebellum era's Kingdom of God on Earth as expressions of the nation's highest aspirations. At the turn of the twentieth century, middle-class Americans also embarked upon a remarkable era of social inventiveness. Through the establishment of a dense network of voluntary associations and the use of state power, they began a massive effort to refurbish the nation's civic life.

THE MIDDLE-CLASS CONCEPTION OF CULTURE

The term *culture* meant something decidedly different in the nineteenth century than it means to us today (and as the word is employed throughout this book). Today *culture* usually refers to those resources that humans call upon to aid them in coping with the world about them. Therefore, culture includes virtually all customs and institutions. As an example of this usage, we have examined in Chapter 13 such topics as middle-class ways of work, gender, family, sex, child rearing, and religion. We have considered each of these ways as an integral component of a larger middle-class culture. Put somewhat differently, the modern definition of culture embraces the entire complex of values and practices that shape and guide human behavior.

The Victorian conception of culture, on the other hand, was less a matter of describing how people behaved than *how they ought to behave.* Culture should be didactic; it should teach people how to behave morally. Moreover, it should elevate them from the everyday world of the "trivial and the sordid" (in the words of American Ralph Waldo Emerson) into a realm of "sweetness and light" (in the words of Englishman Matthew Arnold). More specifically, culture referred to a Euro-American heritage of good manners, a knowledge of great literature, and a respect for the fine arts. Sometimes labeled as genteel, high, or polite, this notion of culture, in its most restrictive and exquisite form, entailed in Arnold's oft-quoted words "the best that has been thought and said in the world."

This conception of culture rested on a set of bedrock assumptions, all of which were coming under increasing assault even as they were uttered. One of these was a belief in an orderly universe, one presided over by a benevolent God and governed by immutable natural laws. Ultimate truths existed not only in nature, the Victorians believed, but also in religion, ethics, politics, economics, and the arts. Therefore, nothing—not literature, religion, or politics—was immune from moral judgment. Such thinking not only offered the comfort of belief in a set of transcendental certainties, but also eased the difficulties of reaching correct moral judgements. A second bedrock Victorian assumption was a deep faith in the capacity of the human mind, either through reason or intuition, to perceive these ultimate truths.

Conceptual polarities helped the middle-class Victorians to mentally order their experiences. On one side was "right," and on the other "wrong." On one side was the "human" or the "civilized" while on the other was the "animal" or the "savage." The list could be expanded indefinitely: men/women, adults/children, whites/blacks, heroes/ordinary mortals, the refined/the crude, and the worthy/the unworthy. To the Victorians, such dichotomies were *not* merely mental constructs invented by humans for simplifying reality so that it could be more easily understood. These dichotomies had a real and permanent existence apart from how humans thought about them.

ACQUIRING REFINEMENT

To the middle class, culture and refinement were virtually synonymous terms. Earlier, in the more rank-ordered, hierarchical society of the eighteenth century, refinement was for the most part reserved for the gentry. Only the great southern planters and wealthy northern merchants had the financial wherewithal to build and furnish stately mansions. They were the only people to dress and behave like the European aristocracy. Everyone else—or so it was presumed by the gentry—had inferior tastes and sensibilities.

At first glance, republican America would not seem to offer fertile ground for the growth of refinement. After all, according to America's revolutionary theorists, a successful republic required the rejection of the European aristocracy's fopperies and extravagances. Furthermore, refinement, which envisioned an existence devoted to leisure and art, seemed to run counter to the self-denial and hard work that were at the heart of middle-class

Strong Museum, Rochester, NY

Strong Museum, Rochester, NY

"Ungraceful Positions" versus "Gentility in the Parlor." Taken from a manual on good manners, the top drawing constitutes an inventory of improper etiquette, while all the errors are corrected in the bottom drawing. These lessons in etiquette reflect the increasing importance that the middle class attached to good manners and proper dress.

Protestant life. Aristocratic idleness had to be exorcised if the individual and society were to be saved. Nonetheless, in the nineteenth century the expanding middle class of merchants, professionals, prosperous farmers, small manufacturers, and skilled artisans claimed for themselves the refinement that had formerly been monopolized by the gentry. Awash with large infusions of new purchasing power and the proliferation of mass-produced, cheaper goods, refinement spread downward from the elite to the sprawling middle class.

Refinement began with proper dress and the acquisition of good manners. With traditional hierarchies broken up or in disarray, it was increasingly difficult to identify people socially. Strange faces replaced familiar ones, especially in the flux of the rapidly growing cities. Amidst this social confusion, manners and dress assisted the respectable people in locating and assessing one another. Exhibitions of good manners and fashionable dress even provided strangers with passports into local circles of respectability and extended to them additional opportunities for advancing their material fortunes.

Until the nineteenth century, refined manners had been mostly a concern of the gentry. The lower social ranks of American society paid little attention to etiquette. They frequently ate with their hands and drank from a common cup. Coughing, spitting, scratching, nose blowing, farting, and urinating in public places were not uncommon. Emotions were by later standards freely expressed; loud, blunt talk and boisterous laughter frequently punctuated the social intercourse of the ordinary people.

The nineteenth century witnessed a seismic shift in manners, one in which the middle classes throughout the Western world appropriated the etiquette of the gentry. Courtesy books, many of whose rules could be traced back to the courts of the Italian Renaissance, flooded into middle-class homes. In his novel *The Rise of Silas Lapham* (1885), William Dean Howells had the self-made Lapham family from rural New Hampshire anxiously consult a book on manners before they dined with the patrician Corey family of Boston. By learning proper manners, the manual promised the Laphams, as well as countless others, that they could avoid social mortification.

Conduct manuals offered readers seeking middle-class respectability a complex set of directions for presenting themselves effectively in public places. Readers should above all else avoid picking their noses, passing gas, clearing their throats, yawning, or scratching themselves in public. Even the popular American practice of chewing and spitting tobacco came under assault. "In public," as John Kasson has perceptively observed, "the individual uneasily pretended to be in private." When confronted with strangers, maintenance of physical distance, aversion of eye contact, and sober facial expressions helped to preserve one's sense of privacy and dignity. Acquaintances, lovers, even husbands and wives, were warned never to embrace or kiss in public. "Happily," unlike in Europe, added one writer on manners, "kissing and embracing among men are never seen in this country."

Avoidance of conspicuous public display included dress. In the eighteenth century, men in the upper ranks frequently dressed as flamboyantly as women. Properly dressed gentlemen donned powdered wigs, brightly hued jackets, silk cuffs, ruffles, tightly fitted breeches, and knee-length, white silk stockings. In the nineteenth century men's dress underwent a fundamental shift. The dark, sober suit became the standard uniform of business and professional men throughout the Western world. Its full-cut coat, "great" overcoat, and loose-fitting pants disguised the true shape of the man's body while exaggerating the size of his shoulders and his girth. The fashion of full beards and mustaches, popular in the second half of the nineteenth century in both Europe and America, also aided men in presenting themselves as persons of substance, gravity, and maturity.

Fashionable women's dress likewise underwent important changes. During the daylight hours, no proper woman exposed to public gaze more of her skin than her face. Gloves, cuffs, long sleeves, high collars, leggings, stockings, shoes, "a sea of petticoats," and floor-length dresses ensured the sartorial modesty of women. As with men, women's street clothes steadily darkened over the nineteenth century. Yet female dress simultaneously highlighted sexual differences. A prominently protruding bustle and a corset that pushed the breasts upward and tightly constricted the waist left no doubts about a woman's sexual identity.

The act of eating provided one of the most demanding tests for assessing one's mastery of the body and the emotions. In earlier times (except among the gentry) etiquette in eating was by today's standards astonishingly crude. People not only ate with their hands but also slurped soup and sauces directly from their plates, dipped their fingers and hands into common bowls, and drank from common goblets. But as early as the eighteenth century, the middling ranks began to adopt far more refined eating ways, including for the first time the use of forks. While opponents complained that eating peas with a fork was like "eating soup with a knitting needle," skillful handling of the new eating instrument helped to verify one's proficiency in the acquisition of genteel table manners.

REFINING PROTESTANT CHRISTIANITY

While many Catholics, Jews, and secular-oriented intellectuals embraced at least some if not all of the middle-class Victorian ways, Protestantism was at the core of the new culture. Indeed, the new culture's supremacy arose in part from the sweeping successes of the great religious revivals of the nineteenth century. Evangelical faith reinforced and fortified the middle class's quest for self-control. By equating religious duty and morality with success in money-making, religious faith could also offer a potential rationale for the accumulation of personal wealth. Finally, a commitment to church, family, and community and a reputation for temperance and hard work—all of these provided visible markers of middle-class respectability.

Yet the relationship between Protestantism and refinement was an uneasy one. Traditionally, many Protestant groups, especially those with Calvinistic antecedents, had condemned the refinement of the upper classes. Refinement, they insisted, represented an alluring secular alternative to Christianity. It diverted attention from God and his commandments. Lorenzo Dow, a popular antebellum evangelist, warned that the "Schools of Babylon" included the "dancing school," the "school of music," and the school for the "promotion of polite literature." Furthermore, renunciation of an earlier life devoted to imitating the behavior of the European aristocracy was a standard episode in nineteenth-century American conversion narratives.

Yet, in the end, the allure of respectability and refinement proved difficult if not impossible for middle-class Protestants to resist. At first, the Baptists and the Methodists, the two most successful evangelical denominations, held out; they stood firm against genteel refinement. But as early as the 1830s the Congregationalists, the Presbyterians, and the Unitarians began to embrace gentrification. In time, spokesmen and women for these denominations began to virtually equate good manners and proper dress with godly morality.

By mid-nineteenth century, in the more prosperous urban churches, the evangelical fires that had fed the millennial vision of the United States as a future heaven on earth had noticeably slackened. Emotionally searing revivals were less common. Ministers in these churches toned down their insistence upon a sudden, apocalyptic conversion experience. In his popular book *Christian Nurture* (1847), Horace Bushnell even went so far as to propose a gradual, step-by-step process of conversion, one that began with the spiritual nurture of the young. Though hotly contested by traditional evangelicals, such a view won increasing favor among middle-class Protestants. Urban, middle-class church services also grew more formal and liturgical. Disregarding earlier objections to the use of musical instruments in worship services, urban Protestant churches even began to feature great organs and robed choirs.

Nothing reflected more tangibly the growing refinement of nineteenth-century Protestantism than a revolution in church architecture. Until the nineteenth century, Calvinistic Protestant groups had associated elegant church buildings with the hated Roman Catholics or with the almost equally despised Church of England (or the Protestant Episcopal Church as it was known in America after the Revolution). The lavish churches of the Catholics and the Episcopalians, according to Puritans (Congregationalists), Quakers, Baptists, Methodists, and Presbyterians deflected attention from God and encouraged the worship of false idols. In keeping with the principle of simplicity, these Protestant denominations usually held services in unpainted, unadorned, box-shaped "meetinghouses."

Except among the Quakers and the more radical of the evangelicals, such attitudes toward church architecture completely flip-flopped during the nineteenth century. Protestant church buildings, especially those in the cities, increasingly imitated the latest styles of the Church of England. Massive gothic structures became the style of choice; as early as 1858, even the Methodists, a denomination that once took pride in its plebeian origins, built St. Paul's, a large gothic-style church in New York City. While without the financial means to duplicate the grandeur of their larger urban counterparts, the towns of New England also upgraded the appearance of their churches. Everywhere they replaced their older, unpainted meetinghouses with white rectangular buildings. A towering spire and belfry at the church entrance vividly testified to how far the nineteenth-century Congregationalists had departed from their more austere seventeenth-century Puritan ancestors.

By the latter half of the nineteenth century the rising tide toward a more refined Protestantism could not be stopped. Across the land on Sunday mornings well-dressed worshipers sat in the cushioned pews of elegant church buildings where they listened to the soaring swells of great organs, the voices of trained choirs, and the polished sermons of educated ministers. Such refinement had its costs, for it drove the working class out of the great middle-class-dominated urban Protestant churches. "The Protestant Church is too aristocratic for the clothes [the working people] are able to wear," explained a manufacturer. Working-class Protestant families either rejected formal ties to churches altogether or they embraced new evangelical groups who welcomed them as social equals and who rejected conspicuous displays of gentility.

ACQUIRING CULTURE

To a degree that astonishes us today, millions of Americans in the nineteenth century sought not only to acquaint themselves with the best that had been thought and said but also with the best music and the best paintings the world had ever produced. The operas "*Lucretia Borgia* and *Faust, The Barber of Seville* and *Don Giovanni,* are everywhere popular," reported George Makepeace Town in 1870; "you may hear their airs in the drawing rooms and concert halls, as well as whistled by the street boys and ground out on the hand organs." In towns both small and large opera houses sprang up across the nation. By the end of the century, no parlor was complete without a piano, and nearly every middle-class woman enjoyed at least rudimentary skills in playing the instrument. Piano music promoted refined behavior, even among males. "Husbands and brothers may be made almost domestic by one cheerful note," observed an advice manual of the 1890s. Millions purchased color reproductions of original paintings in the form of lithographs and hung them on their parlors or in their hallways.

Yet all of these signs of the popularity of culture paled beside that of reading. Abetted by the public schools and library movements and an explosion in the publication of newspapers, magazines, and books, reading became virtually a national obsession. Everyone was urged to read. Americans read alone, they read aloud to one another, they read to improve themselves morally and materially, and they read to acquire culture. "A book case filled with well selected and well bound volumes"—this was the "one luxury," according to Catharine Maria Sedgwick in her novel *Home*, "which long habit

The Influence of Music. Taken from the cover of a popular nineteenth-century periodical and entitled "Influence of Music," this 1869 lithograph suggests that playing and listening to refined music tamed the "savage" impulses of men. The beaux arts, middle-class Victorians believed, elevated the human spirit, encouraged an inward grace, and improved personal morality.

and well cultivated taste [have] rendered essential to happiness." No activity for the promotion of self-culture, especially among women, equaled the importance of reading.

Authors were among the nation's most celebrated heroes. Several were imports from other parts of the English-speaking world. William Shakespeare, Charles Dickens, and Sir Walter Scott were more than household names in America; millions of Americans could quote from Shakespeare at length or summarize the plots of Scott's *Ivanhoe* or Dickens's *A Tale of Two Cities*. Almost equally revered were such American writers as Henry Wadsworth Longfellow, Ralph Waldo Emerson, and Louisa May Alcott. In 1887, thousands of schoolchildren across the nation sent poet John Greenleaf Whittier greetings on his eightieth birthday; this suggests the high value that the nation attached to its literary culture.

The principal guardians of culture, as of the middle-class home, morality, and refinement more generally, were women. A woman's training began in childhood. No longer serving as an apprentice in mastering household chores, she was expected to spend much of her time reading, keeping a diary, and practicing music. In adulthood, no matter what other gifts she might have, a woman's life was incomplete without culture. She was required, as part of her special obligation in domesticating men and children, to be acquainted with books and able to converse about them intelligently. Women not only comprised the nation's largest reading group, by the 1830s they were also authoring more books than men. Sentimental fiction by such women authors as Harriet Beecher Stowe and Susannah Rowson—books that frequently offered middle-class housewives directions for achieving refinement and changing the behavior of others—poured off the nation's presses. Much to the annoyance of men like Nathaniel Hawthorne, who described them as "scribbling women," these women were the nineteenth-century's best-selling writers. Since they could be paid less than men and since they were regarded as the fitter guardians of young children, women soon held most of the teaching positions in the nation's rapidly expanding school system as well. Though rarely in positions of religious leadership, far more women than men regularly attended church services. Scholar Ann Douglas has summed up these varied trends in the phrase "the feminization of American culture."

THE VALUE AND USES OF CULTURE

The more generous members of the nation's literary and artistic elite dreamed of creating a nation that shared refined manners, a respect for the intellect, and a reverence for the arts. Such a common culture, they believed, would encourage self-control—no mean feat in itself—and serve as a powerful, new social adhesive. In short, the elite transformed culture into an ideology.

Initially, the ideology of culture rose to prominence, not as an answer to social anarchy or individual impulsiveness, but as a means to individual growth. In the antebellum era, amidst the mad scramble of millions of Americans to seize upon the expanding opportunities to acquire wealth, some ministers, orators, and essayists urged the ordinary people to enrich their lives by realizing more fully their moral and intellectual potentials. Instead of a life devoted to moneygrubbing, Emerson envisioned a life in which "the individual declares his independence, takes his life into his own hand, and sets forth in quest of Culture."

After the Civil War, the view of culture as an external force shaping an individual's aspirations and motives became increasingly popular. It was then that Chautauqua, founded in 1874 as a summer retreat for Methodist Sunday-school teachers, eventually brought culture to the nation's most remote towns and cities. It was then that the key institutions of "high" culture, the ones that remain to this day, came into being. Cities built immense central public libraries and colossal municipal museums. Magnates of industry and commerce sponsored symphony orchestras and founded a host of new private universities. Everywhere, from the white middle-class suburbs and the mansions of the rich to the inner city immigrant ghettos and the remote Indian reservations, teachers sought to inculcate their students with the Victorian version of culture. That as late as 1910 over half the high-school students in the United States were taking Latin and more than a quarter of them German suggested the strong persistence of traditional cultural ideals.

Culture had uses other than promoting self-control and a more stable social order. For, above all else, culture, along with refinement more generally, supported class authority. While only the parvenu—the new wealthy magnates of industry and finance—fully embraced the European aristocracy's excesses in consumption and leisure, the possession of culture strengthened the power of the middle class. Culture not only aided the middle class in drawing a firmer boundary between itself and the working class but also its presence or absence could be employed to deny an individual or a group access to power. Not possessing good manners or the ability to converse well, showing bad taste in clothes or ignorance of the arts, could, for example, exclude unskilled working people, recently arrived immigrants, African Americans, and Native Americans from the full range of choices and opportunities that were available to white Protestant middle-class males.

Reformers sought to resolve the contradictions between the ideal of equality and refinement by making everyone cultured, by inviting everyone into the parlor. According to middle-class mythology, even ordinary workers could establish credentials for respectability; they could, if they practiced self-restraint with enough tenacity, purchase their own homes, buy carpets for their floors, and hang lace curtains on their windows. Nothing prevented them from learning good manners, reading great books, and reciting poetry.

No one provided a more forcible confirmation of the possibility of resolving the contradictions between equality and refinement than Abraham Lincoln. "This middle-class country [has] got a middle-class president, at last," exclaimed Emerson in 1865. By the practice of Victorian virtues, Lincoln moved upward—from the spare log cabin of his birth to a home with a white picket fence in Springfield, Illinois, and then finally to occupancy of the White House itself. Lincoln's ascent up the ladder of respectability bore mute testimony to the fact that in America anyone could escape the coils of poverty. Such thinking relieved the middle class of guilt and responsibility for the plight of the poor. For, ultimately, they reasoned, those who failed had only themselves to blame.

MIDDLE-CLASS CIVIC LIFE

As with the residents of today's gated and guarded suburbs, it is tempting to see the nineteenth- and early twentieth-century's middle class in terms of social isolation. And indeed at first the post–Civil War middle class did limit nearly all of its social engagement to churches, fraternal orders, women's clubs, and the promotion of culture. Frequently these activities served mainly the interests of the middle-class members themselves more than the larger society.

Initially hostile to state intervention except to promote economic growth, middle-class Americans for the most part opposed all forms of tax-supported charity. Placing the blame for poverty and unemployment on the less fortunate themselves rather than on the economic system, they admonished the poor to work even harder, to practice refinement with greater alacrity, and to cultivate self-restraint more strenuously. At first, they also distanced themselves from the immigrant city and its complex problems. They fled to their own tight neighborhood enclaves in the suburbs and gave industrial capitalism a free hand in shaping the destiny of the nation's cities. In politics, they limited themselves mostly to an agenda designed to promote cultural unity and conformity. Specifically, these included support for the public school movement, opposition to parochial schools, strict enforcement of the Sabbath, and in particular laws restricting or banishing the sale of alcoholic beverages.

But, by the final decade of the nineteenth century, middle-class Americans increasingly sensed that this was not enough, that to preserve the nation's republican heritage something more needed to be done. One day, or so it seemed to the middle class, the United States had been a nation whose life revolved around farms and small towns and whose communities were ordered by a dense network of localized face-to-face relationships. The next day, Americans awoke to a nation of big cities teeming with immigrants. In these impersonal cities, older social connections were being abraded or even coming apart. One day, America had been a nation of farmers, independent craftsmen, small shops, small retail outlets, small bankers, and independent professional men. "A general equality of condition" prevailed, as one of them said. The next day, Americans awoke to a nation of towering corporate leviathans. A few men had acquired incredible quantities of personal wealth. "A greater number of gigantic fortunes exists [in the United States] than any other country in the world," according to widely read Englishman James Bryce.

Blending mostly but not exclusively Protestant religious fervor with the New England idea of community and a growing faith in scientific expertise, these perceptions ignited a remarkable effort to rebuild what Lydia J. Hanifan, state supervisor of rural schools in West Virginia, described in 1916 as the nation's community life or "social capital." By social capital, Hanifan referred not only to the ties beyond the self that would satisfy personal needs but also to the ties among individuals that would improve "living conditions in the whole community." "The community as a whole will benefit by the cooperation of all its parts," she observed, "while the individual will find in his associations the advantages of the help, the sympathy, and the fellowship of his neighbors." To reconstruct the nation's social capital in the industrial age, the middle class turned primarily to two instruments: voluntary associations and the state.

THE CREATION OF A DENSE NETWORK OF ASSOCIATIONS

While Alexis de Tocqueville noted the popularity of voluntary associations in America as early as the 1830s, the final two decades of the nineteenth and the first decade of the twentieth century witnessed a spectacular growth in civic associations. Everywhere, from the great industrial metropolises to small towns, the number of new fraternal, religious, ethnic, labor, professional, and civic organizations grew faster than the nation's fast-growing population. "From the Red Cross to the NAACP, from the Knights of Columbus to Hadassah, from Boy Scouts to the Rotary club, from the PTA to the Sierra Club, from the Gideon Society to the Audubon Society, from the American Bar Association to the Farm Bureau Federation, from Big Brothers to the League of Women Voters, from the Teamster's Union to the Campfire Girls," observes political scientist Robert D. Putnam, "it is hard to name a major mainline civic institution in American life today that was *not* invented in these few decades."

Not just middle-class men, but also middle-class women, workers, immigrants, and African Americans participated in the movement. Although Free Masonry had much earlier origins, men of all social ranks now joined fraternal orders in record numbers. Fraternal groups not only provided their members with personal ties that aided them in coping with the individualism and anomie of industrial America but also frequently offered them material benefits such as life and health insurance. Immigrants and African Americans formed their own fraternal groups, many of which also extended aid to their less fortunate members and their families. The enthusiasm for voluntary associations helped to pull middle-class women out of the home and into the public arena. "Woman's place is in the Home," wrote suffragist Rheta Childe Dorr in 1910, "but Home is not contained within the four walls of an individual home. Home is the community." By the early twentieth century, women's clubs were deeply involved in public affairs; they were campaigning on behalf of such issues as temperance, protection of child labor legislation, kindergartens, and women's suffrage.

Religious groups played an especially significant role in the massive movement for civic revitalization. While the Salvation Army sought to convert the immigrants and the poor to evangelical Protestantism, thousands of urban middle-class Protestant churches embraced the "social gospel" movement which sought both to strengthen ties within their own congregations and to reach out to the urban underclass. They sponsored and made available their facilities (including frequently newly built gymnasiums) for Sunday schools, concerts, socials, youth groups, benevolent societies, athletic clubs, and scout troops. The Chautauqua movement, founded by Methodist Sunday school teachers in 1874, spread like wildfire. Offering nationwide extension schools, study groups, public lectures, and entertainment, by 1919 one observer estimated that "one out of every eleven persons in the country . . . attended a lyceum or Chautauqua program every year."

Reformers devoted special attention to the problems of urban America and the nation's youth. In less than a decade (1901–10), nearly all of the nationwide youth organizations that would dominate American life in the twentieth century sprang into being—the Boy Scouts and Girl Scouts, Campfire Girls, the 4-H clubs, and dozens of other youth groups. Seeking a surrogate experience for urban children, many of these groups sponsored summer camps in the countryside. By 1910 nearly four hundred settlement houses had been planted in the nation's urban slums. Here young middle-class women and men lived among the poor and sought to bring education, "culture," and "moral uplift" to the urban immigrants. From the ranks of the settlement house workers came scores of twentieth-century social reformers.

Red Cross and Boy Scout Volunteers During World War I. The depth and breadth of middle-class engagement in the nation's civil life may have peaked during World War I. Not only did millions donate their time and energies to the war effort, as this photograph suggests—to pay for the war, the national government also steeply increased the rates of income, capital gains, and inheritance taxes.

THE PROGRESSIVE MOVEMENT

The growth of corporations and vast discrepancies in income between the rich and the poor presented an especially difficult problem to those middle-class Americans seeking to reconstruct the nation's civic life. The corporations, they reasoned, threatened to introduce a new kind of hierarchical order to the United States, one that might be just as dangerous to the republic's survival as the hereditary hierarchies of old. From the Revolutionary era, the middle class had learned the principle that a republic's success depended on a wide distribution of wealth and power among the ordinary citizenry. By the end of the nineteenth century, the nation had undergone a wrenching transformation; by then the richest 10 percent of the population controlled more than 65 percent of the nation's wealth. The giant corporations also challenged middle-class values. In the corporate world, upward mobility seemed to be tied more to the possession of specialized skills, self-presentation, and the ability get along with others than it did to hard work, frugality, and self-control.

Jane Addams Holding an Immigrant Child. In the middle-class effort to rebuild the nation's social capital and sense of community, no single person may have been more influential and indefatigable than Jane Addams. She founded the nation's best-known settlement house—Hull-House in Chicago—and helped to lead a host of national reform movements.

To a substantial degree, the political contests of the Progressive era (approximately 1900–17) revolved around what to do about big corporations and the accumulation of enormous quantities of wealth in the hands of the few. Without sacrificing the increased output of goods and services accompanying the Industrial Revolution, some sought to break up the corporations (the antitrust response), and others to nationalize them (the socialist response). Others argued for letting them alone (the laissez-faire response), while still others sought to regulate the corporations (the regulatory response). In the end, the political system empowered federal and state bureaucracies to alter some of the behaviors of corporations, though as frequently as not the regulators turned out to be the puppets of the very groups that they were supposed to regulate. The progressives also obtained the ratification of the Sixteenth Amendment (1913), which allowed for a graduated federal income tax system, and Congress passed the first federal tax on estates, both measures that potentially could and in fact did limit to some degree the accumulation of great fortunes.

The progressives sought to revitalize the political process as well. To give voters a more direct voice in public decisions, they introduced the secret ballot; adopted the initiative, referendum, and recall (of public officials); set up the first presidential primary elections; and obtained amendments to the Constitution providing for the direct election of senators (1913) and for women's suffrage (1920). Sometimes at odds with the trend toward more participatory democracy was the progressive faith in expertise and what they frequently called "social efficiency." To bring the methods of business enterprise and scientific knowledge to the problems of managing cities, the progressives experimented with the commission, the city manager, and the "strong mayor" forms of city government. To offset the power of immigrants, workers, and blacks—those whom the progressives believed responsible for the dominance of local governments by political machines—they supported city-wide and nonpartisan elections. At all levels of government, the progressives sought to replace political appointees with trained civil servants.

For all their differences, the progressive presidents—Theodore Roosevelt, William Howard Taft, and Woodrow Wilson—shared a belief that the United States should abandon its traditions of isolation in foreign affairs. In the past, while frequently taking an interest in the affairs of the Western Hemisphere, the nation had for the most part remained aloof from Europe. But in the early twentieth century, the progressive presidents embraced the belief that the nation should actively seek to extend its "superior" values and institutions to others. Even earlier, such thinking had provided a rationale for the Spanish-American War and for the annexation of the Philippine Islands. And in 1917 it drew the United States into the Great War (World War I); President Wilson explained that American entrance into the conflict would "make the world safe for democracy." While largely ignoring the European balance of power, Wilson believed that the projection of American ideals and power abroad would prevent future world wars.

In retrospect, it is easy to see the limits of middle-class civic life. Middle-class Americans presumed that they knew what was best for other social groups and for the rest of the world; hence they tried to impose their ideas and values on the working class, immigrants, Native Americans, African Americans, and even foreign nations. Paradoxically, while such measures could strengthen the bonds of community, they could also encourage intolerance, social exclusion, and division. For example, racial segregation increased in the Progressive era, and middle-class progressives provided much of the impetus behind the adoption of the Eighteenth Amendment (which prohibited the manufacture and sale of alcoholic beverages) in 1920 and for immigration exclusion which culminated in the Immigration Act of

1924. Yet for all its limits, the middle class launched an era of remarkable social innovation and civic engagement. Its legacy has continued to shape American history to this day.

CONCLUSION

During the nineteenth and early twentieth centuries, the United States became the world's foremost example of a middle-class society and culture. True, the Victorian age witnessed the rising power of the bourgeoisie, or middle class, everywhere in the Western world, but in Europe aristocracies continued to exercise great cultural power. It was only in America that middle-class ways became so central and so dominant. Indeed, while conveniently ignoring workingmen, Native Americans, and African Americans, it seemed to many observers that the middle class was all there was in America. In constructing its own set of ways, the middle class even emptied other groups of some of their vitality. By appropriating from the working class the value of work, from the aristocracy the value of genteel refinement, and from evangelical Protestants the value of personal morality and high moral purpose, the middle class claimed (and to a substantial extent gained) the cultural and civic leadership of the entire nation.

VIII

THE WAYS OF OTHERS

Nothing worried middle-class Victorians more than passion. "Accustomed to a decorous self-restraint, passion, even trivial passion, was salt on our tongues," recalled Henry Seidel Canby in a highly perceptive memoir of middle-class life in Wilmington, Delaware, in the 1890s. To the Canbys as well as to other middle-class families, it was the absence of self-control that more than anything else distinguished "Us" from "Them." To the white middle class, the new Americans (the immigrants), the working class (who were more often than not also immigrants), the African Americans, and the Native Americans all seemed to have a fundamental character flaw. They all took their pleasures wherever and whenever they could and let tomorrow take care of itself. "They had a better time [than we did]," confessed a palpably envious Canby, "for they let themselves go." Canby, of course, exaggerated. His stereotype revealed as much about his own class as it did about the cultural "outsiders."

Yet the cultural outsiders did share important characteristics. They all greeted the individualistic, bourgeois spirit of the nineteenth century with less enthusiasm than the white middle class did. They saw nothing manifestly superior in the single-minded pursuit of individual gain or in other middle-class Victorian ways. Rather than fully embracing the ways of the dominant culture, immigrants, blacks, Indians, and even many white southerners found in the preservation, invention, and perpetuation of their own distinctive ways a source of identity and of strength. In addition, the ways of the outsiders frequently clashed, not only with those of the dominant northern middle class but also with the ways of one another as well. Indeed, since the early nineteenth century, class, ethnicity, race, religion, and region have been the ultimate sources of many of the nation's most heated cultural conflicts.

15

IMMIGRANT WORKING-CLASS WAYS

During Henry Seidel Canby's boyhood days in Wilmington, Delaware, in the 1890s, the United States was in the midst of two great revolutions, each of which contributed to the growth of a large class of what he and his friends saw as cultural outsiders. First was the Industrial Revolution. In the first half of the nineteenth century, probably two-thirds of the white men in the United States had owned productive property (in particular, farms) or they worked in the shops of small craftsmen. In either case, they were largely free of economic dependencies and of rigorously prescribed rhythms of work. But, as the century wore on, wealth resided less in land and in small shops and more in capital (the money to produce new goods).

Growing numbers of Americans then found themselves employed by large corporations. Such employment meant more economic dependency and a substantial loss of control over one's work experiences. Some workers became salaried professionals and self-employed entrepreneurs, but the vast majority—perhaps two-thirds of all Americans—toiled for *wages* rather than for salaries or profits. This army of wage earners dug the nation's canals, built its railroads, loaded and unloaded its ships and boxcars, and manned its blast furnaces. Millions of immigrants, in particular young Irish women, also toiled as household servants in middle- and upper-class homes.

The second revolution entailed the massive migration of peoples to the United States. In 1820, nearly all of the white people in the nation had origins in England, Northern Ireland, Scotland, and Germany. (African Americans comprised almost 10 percent of the population; the 1820 Census did not attempt to count Native Americans.) Some 95 percent of the population was Protestant. During the next hundred years great waves of immigrants drastically altered the nation's ethnic and religious mix. By 1920, more than half of the white population could trace their origins to places other than England, Scotland, and Northern Ireland. They came mainly from Ireland, Germany, southern and eastern Europe, Canada, and Mexico. By then some 20 percent of the nation's peoples were Catholics and perhaps 2 percent were Jews.

INDUSTRIAL WORK WAYS

While they came mostly from the European countryside, the majority of the new immigrants took up residence in the cities. There, they usually became wage earners—in other words, members of the new industrial working class. "Not every foreigner is a workingman," observed a Protestant minister in the 1890s, "but in the cities, at least, it may almost be said that every workingman is a foreigner." By the first decade of the twentieth century, immigrant men and their male children made up 70 percent of the workforce in fifteen of the nation's nineteen leading industries.

In the factories, the unskilled wage earners encountered an utterly unfamiliar kind of work discipline. In the preindustrial past, daylight hours, the rhythms of the seasons, and ancient customs had dictated the pace and the nature of work. Both on the farms and in the skilled trades, work had often entailed bouts of intense labor mixed with periods of complete idleness. Depending on custom, within the workplace the men might tell stories, sing, gamble, and drink beer. But with the arrival of the Industrial Revolution, employers sought to wipe out the older ways of work. They insisted on a sober and orderly work force. Machines and clocks relentlessly dictated the pace of work. Having lost much of their control over their work experience, factory workers sometimes bitterly complained. They described themselves as "wage slaves."

By their absenteeism from work, by changing jobs with startling frequency, by forming labor unions, and by striking, the wage earners actively resisted the new work discipline. Strikes multiplied from about five hundred per year in the 1880s to more than two thousand in the 1890s. To subdue the strikers, for the first time in American history (except during the Civil War) the state employed massive force against its own citizens. Fears of "the dangerous classes," as the upstart workers were described by the middle-class press, mounted. With the terrors of the Civil War still lurking in their memories, some observers feared that the "labor question" might become the "irrepressible conflict" of their generation.

Yet no civil war between labor and capital ever came. American workers never developed a full-blown "class consciousness." Neither did they ever embrace labor unions or socialism with the same enthusiasm as Europe's industrial workers. Extraordinary ethnic and racial cleavages in America weakened the potential unity of the wage earners. No other society in the world drew so many newcomers from such diverse backgrounds. Old World animosities and differences in language and religion shattered the working class into mutually suspicious groups. In addition, some crafts and skilled workers such as bricklayers, typographers, and toolmakers secured for themselves privileged positions. Referred to as the "aristocracy of labor," these

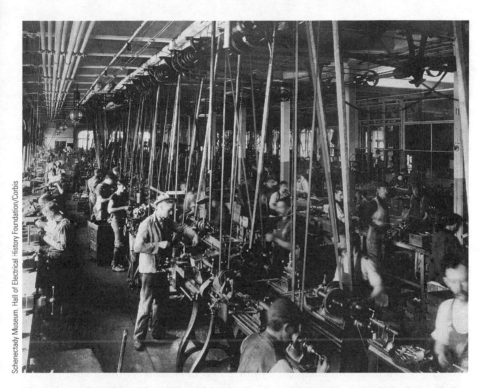

Schenectady Museum. Hall of Electrical History Foundation/Corbis

The Industrial Working Class, 1888. This photo of machinists operating belt-driven lathes in a Lynn, Massachusetts, shop suggests the changing nature of work during the nineteenth century. Small artisan shops increasingly gave way to large manufacturing concerns. Industrialization brought with it a new work discipline. In the new workplaces, such as the one depicted here, employees worked for wages, machines and clocks set the pace of work, and employees rarely knew their employers personally.

workers rarely identified with the unskilled workers at the bottom of the laboring pyramid. Above all, the idea of America as a special land of opportunity and the lure of middle-class respectability worked against the possibility of the working class mounting a full-scale assault on the nation's new industrial order.

Yet, wage-earning immigrants rarely became total converts to the white middle class's ideology of success. In the first place, by equating material success with moral worth, such an ideology implicitly condemned the vast majority of workers to both material and moral failure. Second, the rapid upward mobility of the self-made man, which was so dear to middle-class thinking, was simply beyond the reach of all but a tiny fraction of the working class.

Wage earners tended to define success in more realistic terms. Rather than the fulfillment of individual ambitions, success meant a steady job and ample support of family and kin. In particular, the workers placed the welfare and preservation of family and relatives before that of personal advancement. Literally millions of workers, for instance, sent hard-earned savings back to Europe to enable relatives to pay for their transatlantic voyage to America. Unlike the middle class, blue-collar workers also had large numbers of children. More children meant more family income. Countless sons and daughters of immigrant working-class families passed up opportunities to obtain additional education or skills so they could contribute directly to the family's welfare.

Still, unlike most of their European counterparts, American wage earners could realistically dream of moving up the class ladder even if it were only modestly. By toiling diligently at their jobs and slowly saving a little money, they could imagine one day buying their own homes and perhaps even owning a small business. Although such dreams frequently proved illusory, a majority of the workers eventually did make some improvements in their material lot. They frequently occupied a crowded, insecure borderland between the lower and the middle class.

In addition, within each ethnic working-class group, a sizable minority became successful entrepreneurs. Most started out by providing basic goods and services for their own communities. Exploiting the immigrants' preference for buying goods from their own countrymen, with whom they shared a common language and trust, they opened grocery stores, butcher shops, dry goods stores, and saloons. Some even turned to banking and construction.

Of all ethnic occupations, the best known were those available in politics, entertainment, and crime. The rising number of ethnics became virtually synonymous with the rise of big city political machines and political bosses in the late nineteenth century. Denied opportunities in more respectable occupations, entrepreneurship in crime, show business, and professional sports likewise became ladders of upward mobility for the new Americans. In exchange for "protection," ethnic "mobsters" extorted money from saloon keepers, brothel operators, contractors, and small manufacturers. By the 1920s, during the age when alcohol was legally banned in America, underworld crime escalated into a substantial enterprise. Along with African Americans, immigrants and their descendants also achieved a special prominence as both performers and entrepreneurs in the rapidly growing commercial entertainment industry.

WORKING-CLASS WAYS OF LEISURE

While employers were able to impose a large measure of order on the men, women, and sometimes children in their factories, their hegemony rarely extended to their employees' time away from work. It was outside the workplace—in their churches, neighborhoods, families, clubs, and saloons—that most wage earners succeeded in preserving and creating their own cultures. Within this infrastructure, distinctively working-class rather than middle-class ways predominated.

One of the most important of these ways was leisure. The workers, who as we have seen were increasingly comprised of immigrants and non-Protestants, tended to reject the old-stock middle-class Protestant strictures on recreation. Workers usually placed a higher value on play for its own sake, sensual gratification, spontaneity, and conviviality than on self-control or on recreation as a means of refreshing oneself for more serious duties. Unlike the middle class, many workers, especially bachelors, who comprised a far larger percentage of the population in the nineteenth century than they do today, enthusiastically embraced sports, gambling, and drinking. Outside the parameters of middle-class respectability and frequently illegal, the leisure activities patronized by the working class comprised a kind of Victorian underworld or counterculture.

Prizefighting illustrated the large disparity in views on recreation between the working and the middle class. Illegal almost everywhere, pugilism manifestly mocked Victorian values, especially the cardinal virtue of self-control. The prevailing rules of the ring permitted a battle just short of an unregulated physical brawl. Sensing that their bets were in jeopardy or that their favorite had been treated unfairly, and amply fortified by copious quantities of alcohol, spectators frequently joined the frays. But while the middle class condemned the brutality and disorderliness of the prize ring, workingmen, especially those of Irish origins, held prizefighting and prizefighters in the highest esteem. No one was more admired by workingmen than John L. Sullivan, the heavyweight champion from 1882 to 1892. By his own brute strength, his brawny body, and his swift fists, "the Boston Strong Boy" had conquered all comers in what workingmen considered to be the ultimate metaphor of masculine superiority.

The classes also parted ways over the celebration of holidays. In the first place, immigrants upon their arrival in America were shocked to discover the sheer paucity of official holidays; except for the Fourth of July and Christmas, Protestant America celebrated no national holidays. The calendars of immigrants, on the other hand, literally teemed with holidays. The Greek Orthodox Church alone recognized more than eighty holy days. To add to employer woes, neither Greek Orthodox, Roman Catholic, nor Jewish religious calendars coincided. Immigrants also took off from work (sometimes for several days) to celebrate weddings and funerals. In addition, the immigrant working class typically celebrated holidays (including Sundays) with far more gusto than the middle class. Workers flocked into the streets, the parks, and the saloons (if open), where they carried banners, sang, talked, held parades, played games, and drank alcoholic beverages.

Benjamin G. Rader

Little Mint Saloon on East Third Street, Davenport, Iowa, in about 1900. An important institution of those outside the dominant middle-class culture, saloons fostered spare-time activities that revolved around sharing, public display, and an all-male camaraderie.

Neither prizefighting nor holidays approximated the significance of saloons as centers of alternative ways that were anathema to the dominant culture. To the Protestant middle class, abstinence, or at the least temperance, provided irrefutable proof that one had achieved self-control. To the mostly immigrant working class, on the other hand, drink was a source of nutrition, relaxation, and conviviality. To escape the demanding routines of the workplace, to make and cement friendships, and to preserve ancient customs, workingmen regularly gathered at saloons. That Chicago alone in 1884 had thirty-five hundred saloons, more than existed in all fifteen southern states combined, reflected the special importance of saloons to working-class life.

The saloons fostered an ethic totally at odds with that of middle-class Protestants. Rather than individual moneymaking and the privacy of the home, the saloons encouraged nonmaterial values, sharing, and public display. For example, "treating," a common custom in Ireland and among Irish-American workingmen, required that any man who happened to be in a saloon when acquaintances strolled in must offer them drinks and pay for all the drinks that they consumed. Deeply embedded in working-class lifestyles, such a ritual implied not only a resistance to individual acquisitiveness, but affirmed the reciprocity, solidarity, and equality of all workingmen.

By the time that the United States entered World War I in 1917, leisure had become a less important arena of class conflict. By then the middle class itself had begun a noticeable retreat from its earlier strictures on leisure and even adopted some of the leisure practices of the ethnic working class. In the twentieth century, workers lost some of their communal control over leisure to the recreational entrepreneurs who managed the outdoor amusement parks, the dance pavilions, and especially the movie houses. Yet, according to historian Roy Rosenszweig, the increasing commercialization of working-class leisure fostered a growing solidarity of workers across ethnic lines. For example, commercialized leisure may have encouraged a growing number of intermarriages among Catholics from different ethnic backgrounds.

ROMAN CATHOLICISM AND THE NEW AMERICANS

No aspect of culture was more important to the new Americans than their religion. Nearly all of the immigrants came from countries where Catholicism was the religion of the insiders. In Europe, they could usually take their religious affiliations and identities for granted. But in predominantly Protestant America, Catholics were clearly religious outsiders. Under such circumstances, the Church took on a vastly added importance in the lives of its adherents. The Church's familiar rituals and its authoritarian structure offered the immigrants a source of comfort, certainty, and security.

In time, the Church did even more; it eventually "constructed" what historian Charles R. Morris has described as "a virtual state-within-a-state." This virtual Catholic state within the United States permitted Catholics to "live almost their entire lives within a thick cocoon of Catholic institutions." "I felt that, although I was human and capable of mistakes," explained a young woman, "God and the Catholic community would always keep me safe and free from worry." Catholic institutions shielded countless immigrants from many of the potentially disturbing influences that emanated from the dominant middle-class Protestant culture.

More than to Rome, to early Spanish missions, or to the English Catholic settlers in colonial Maryland, the modern American Catholic Church traces its origins to nineteenth-century Ireland. Shaped by their terribly harsh experiences in Ireland, including the Great Potato Famine and English exploitation, the Irish immigrants brought with them an especially militant and austere form of Catholicism. In America, a series of strong-minded Irish bishops set about rebuilding the Church according to their own understanding of Catholicism. After the Civil War, successive waves of German, Italian, and eastern European immigrants contended with the Irish for hegemony over the American Church, but with only limited success. Until far into the twentieth century, most of the clergy were of Irish descent.

The response of Protestants to the great Catholic "invasion" reinforced and added to the importance of the Church in the lives of countless immigrants.

In the antebellum era, the arrival of great numbers of Irish immigrants sent shock waves through Protestant America. Apart from traditional animosities toward Catholics that originated in the Protestant Reformation, Protestant Americans saw the Catholic Church as antithetical to republicanism. They associated the church with monarchies, hierarchies, and tyrannies. Fed by a spate of "confessions" by former nuns—or more frequently persons claiming to be nuns—who reported that they had been held in sexual bondage by priests, anti-Catholicism turned violent in the 1830s and 1840s. Pitched battles broke out between Catholics and Protestants in Philadelphia, New York, Boston, and more than a dozen smaller cities. The religious war spilled over into politics. The Know-Nothing party of the 1850s, which morphed into the Republican party of the 1850s and 1860s, mobilized electoral opinion against the fast-growing Catholic population. Adding fuel to the religious war was the issue of education. Disturbed that the public schools taught Protestant doctrines and that textbooks even included numerous overt anti-Irish and anti-Catholic statements, Catholics set up separate, church-supported parochial school systems. By the late nineteenth century, parochial schools had become an integral component in the "thick cocoon of Catholic institutions" that perpetuated distinctive Catholic communities in America.

The Church's hierarchy served a similar function. At the top was the Pope, whom Catholics believed was Christ's direct representative on earth. In the realms of spirituality and morality, the Pope was for Catholics nothing less than an absolute monarch. When speaking officially on spiritual matters, the Vatican Council in 1870 ruled that the Pope was infallible. With few exceptions, American Catholics embraced the motto *Roma locuta est; causa finita est* ("Rome has spoken: the case is closed"). Thus Church laws, such as those requiring attendance at Mass on Sundays and on holy days, carried an authority for Catholics that equaled biblical commandments for Protestants. From the Pope, authority flowed downward through an elaborate hierarchy to the local parish priest.

The Church offered dense, richly textured religious experiences to America's newcomers. By insisting that access to the sacred required a set of formal devotional exercises, it bolstered its authority over the spiritual lives of its charges. Without regular confessions of sins to priests, participation in Mass, and the acceptance of penances, salvation was impossible. At the center of Catholic devotion was the Mass. Conducted in an atmosphere of great solemnity and amid the sights, smells, and sounds of burning candles, tinkling bells, fragrant incense, and colorful flowers, the Mass contained all the ingredients of high liturgical drama. Adding to the grandeur of the occasion was the priest, who, dressed in special robes, walked about the altar while praying in Latin, a virtually unknown tongue to the laity.

The importance of ritual to Catholics extended far beyond the celebration of Mass and the other sacraments. A devotion to saints also distinguished the lives of Catholics from Protestants. Parents named their children for saints, and churches, schools, and even baseball teams were named for saints. Because saints were human, they were thought to be more approachable than God; they had the power to mediate between mortals and God. To Catholics, none of the saints were closer to God than Mary, the Mother of Christ. Given Mary's special position within the network of heavenly relatives, Catholics believed that prayers to her were particularly effective. Other popular devotional exercises included the saying of the rosary, the signing of the cross, and the use of holy water.

The parish church, along with the precinct captain's house, the saloon, the funeral home, the fire station, the corner grocery store, and the parochial school—all these were keys to the creation of one of the most remarkable institutions in the American city, the Catholic-ethnic neighborhood. It was to these neighborhoods that the immigrants first flocked; there they encountered familiar sights, sounds, and smells. There the immigrants "create for themselves," observed a visitor, "distinct communities, almost as impervious to American sentiments and influences as are the inhabitants of Dublin or Hamburg. They have their own theaters, recreations, amusements, military and national organizations; to a great extent their own schools, churches, and their own newspapers and periodical literature." Gala processions, scheduled in conjunction with religious holidays, underscored the central place occupied by the parish church in Catholic neighborhoods. "As the procession filed through the streets," historian Jay Dolan has written, "Catholics were marking off their neighborhood, laying claim to it, and telling people that this was their piece of earth."

The building of close-knit Catholic-ethnic neighborhoods was not the only way that the American Catholic Church served as an agency of cultural conservatism. In the late nineteenth and early twentieth centuries, a small but influential group of Catholic leaders, including the archbishop of Baltimore, James Cardinal Gibbons, sought to make the Church more acceptable to mainstream middle-class Victorian America. While by no means departing substantively from Catholic orthodoxy, the reformers placed less stress on devotional supernaturalism and offered mild support to labor unions as well as to social reforms. In what was known as the "Americanist" controversy, the Vatican quickly squelched the incipient liberalization of the American Church. In 1899, Pope Leo XIII issued an encyclical aimed at Cardinal Gibbons that specifically denounced what he called "Americanism."

While Gibbons and his allies insisted that the Pope had condemned a "phantom heresy," the Pope's action in this matter as well as in others effectively intimidated efforts to bring the Church into closer touch with mainstream American culture and with modern intellectual developments. For the

Italian-American Catholics in Chicago Celebrating the Feast of Santa Maria Incoronata Early in the Twentieth Century. Processions such as these helped immigrant Catholics to mark off and stake a claim to their own neighborhoods as well as to public spaces in their new land. The photo also suggests the effectiveness with which the new Americans were able to perpetuate their traditional ways.

next half-century, the intellectual life of Catholic colleges and universities stood in startling contrast to that of Protestant and public-supported institutions. While non-Catholic institutions frequently offered a hearing if not always a warm welcome to the ideas of such seminal thinkers as Charles Darwin, Karl Marx, Albert Einstein, and Sigmund Freud, Catholic schools shut out everything that smacked of what Pope Leo XIII described as "modernism." Instead of including or considering the latest intellectual speculation, their curricula continued to revolve around the classic medieval theology of Thomas Aquinas.

PROTESTANT AND JEWISH NEWCOMERS

Catholicism was, of course, not the only faith of the new Americans. Nearly all of the English, Scots, Scots-Irish, and Scandinavians and well over half of the German immigrants were Protestants. Their Protestantism eased their way into the dominant culture. In terms of numbers, no ethnoreligious group exercised a larger influence on shaping mainstream American culture than the Jews. Unlike most of the adherents of Catholicism and Eastern Orthodoxy, the Jews had always been a minority group in nations dominated by other religions. Rather than from the countryside of Europe, most of the impoverished Jewish immigrants came to the United States from the cities of eastern Europe. Hence, they already had generations of experience in coping with prejudice and with living in urban ghettos. "Their devotion to education," historian Loren Baritz has written, "was virtually religious." In addition to education, a passionate commitment to hard work also contributed to their disproportionate success in their new land.

American Jews eventually divided into three main religious groups: Reform, Conservative, and Orthodox. Founded before the Civil War by Jews from Germany, Reformed Judaism vastly simplified and relaxed the traditional religious observances. Like liberal Protestants, they even allowed women to read from the Torah (the Jewish holy book) and eventually become rabbis. They emphasized the universalism of Hebraic ethics. The Orthodox, whose main support came from the immigrants from Eastern Europe, insisted on a strict adherence to traditional observances; Orthodox worship services, for example, strictly separated men from women. Only men could lead the services. Conservatives stood between the Reform and the Orthodox versions of Judaism. While preserving more of the customary observances than the Reformers, the Conservatives permitted families to worship together. In the early twentieth century, many Jews abandoned formal religious affiliations altogether. By the 1930s fewer than one-third of the Jewish families in America belonged to a temple or a synagogue.

As with Catholics, Jews also experienced discrimination. Christians had long regarded Jews ambivalently; they were viewed as both God's chosen people and responsible for the betrayal of the Messiah. For the alleged latter offense, Christians justified the suffering that Jews experienced through the long course of European and American history. In addition, Jews were the victims of vicious stereotypes; in the popular antisemitic literature of the day they were depicted as aggressive and greedy Shylocks, who controlled the world's financial centers. Discrimination took several forms. Apart from restricting employment opportunities, until well into the twentieth century quotas limited the admission of Jews into colleges and restrictive covenants on the deeds to homes prohibited sales to Jews. Private clubs barred Jewish membership, and in such resorts as Saratoga, Coney Island, and the Catskills, Jews encountered signs reading "No Jews or Dogs Admitted Here." As with Catholics, Jews responded by forming their own ethnic networks. These included the formation of their own private clubs and the purchase of hotels open to Jews in resort towns.

THE ISSUE OF ASSIMILATION RECAPITULATED

Adhering to the ideal of the United States as a special sanctuary for the oppressed and perceiving a need to fill up an empty country, the government between the 1820s and the 1920s left immigration largely unfettered. But the welcoming mat was never universal. As we observed earlier, from the late 1830s to the mid-1850s, an anti-Catholic, anti-Irish movement flourished. It never totally died out. Beginning in the 1870s, Asians were the special target of a second nativist movement. Then in the 1880s, a third nativist movement, one directed at all immigrants, got underway. This movement culminated in the Immigration Act of 1924, which for the next forty years shut the doors to all except a tiny number of immigrants.

The speed and degree to which the immigrants and their descendants assimilated into the dominant culture has occasioned heated debate among scholars. While most immigrants came to the United States hoping to improve their material lot, few of them had any intention of altering their traditional ways. That, to this day, ethnicity and religious affiliation are usually better predictors of whom one will marry, invite to dinner, or vote for than are income or educational level suggests the degree to which the immigrants and their descendants were able to resist complete assimilation. "The Polish children treat their immigrant parents with contempt, . . . speak American slang, are addicted to American popular music, and popular culture, accept fully the American way of piling up money and material goods when possible," sociologist Michael Parenti found in the 1960s. "Yet they keep almost all their social contacts within the confines of the Polish-American community, and have no direct exposure to, and little interest in, middle-class American society."

Nonetheless, in the end, especially as the twentieth century wore on, the vast majority of the immigrants and their descendants became far less discernible as distinctive cultural groups. Such terms as the "steam heat" or the "lace curtain" Irish suggested the upward mobility of Irish Americans and their adoption of at least some aspects of middle-class culture. Other ethnic groups experienced a similar transition. Indeed, by the last quarter of the twentieth century the average income of Catholic and Jewish families exceeded even that of Protestant families.

In addition, the ethnics eventually became citizens, voted, and increasingly thought of themselves as "Americans." In the 1930s they developed a special affection for President Franklin D. Roosevelt and his New Deal, they enthusiastically supported the United States in World War II, they became ardent anticommunists during the Cold War, and in the 1960s they reacted to student radicals with the slogan "America—love it or leave it." Conspicuously exhibiting their patriotism and their adherence to a common set of American ways, they eventually seemed in some respects to be the most archetypical "American" of all social groups.

Scholars have interpreted the relationship between the dominant and outsider cultures in a variety of ways. One is to dismiss the issue of assimilation entirely. Differences in ethnicity and religion were comparatively unimportant, these scholars argue; after all, both the new Americans and the older stock white Americans were products of a common European culture. Another position is to maintain that the immigrants and their offspring *selectively* assimilated the ways of the dominant culture; for example, the new Americans might embrace and participate in the nation's political life while simultaneously retaining in other respects separate ethnic cultures. A third is to emphasize the importance of coercion in assimilation; during World War I, for example, anti-German hysteria made it impossible for German Americans, as historian Gary Gerstle has insisted, to remain "American in politics and German in culture; they had to be American through and through." And perhaps no agency of cultural coercion was more important than the public school; until the 1980s the public schools unrelentingly taught the values of the dominant culture. Finally, scholars have speculated that, in the twentieth century, the powerful forces of the mass media and mass consumption have brought the ways of dominant and outsider cultures closer together. In other words, the nationalization of sights, sounds, and consumption has acted to produce new sets of ways that are shared across ethnic and religious boundaries.

CONCLUSION

Regardless of how assimilation or its absence is to be understood, it is clear that the influence of the new Americans eventually extended far beyond their own ranks. Not only did they provide much of the back-breaking labor during the Industrial Revolution but also soon began to play prominent roles in American politics, in issues of order and disorder in American cities, and in show business. In show business, they, along with African Americans, introduced millions of old-stock, Protestant, middle-class Americans to a set of alternative ways. A familiarity with these ways frequently contributed to a relaxation of the middle class's emphasis on self-control and prepared the groundwork for their adoption of the twentieth century's "modern" ways. Likewise, the new Americans, along with African Americans, helped to foment a rebellion against Victorian art and literature. In the twentieth century, both the blacks and the new Americans became major contributors to the development of the nation's "modern" high culture.

16

AFRICAN AMERICAN, WHITE SOUTHERN, AND NATIVE AMERICAN WAYS

When Henry Seidel Canby composed his memoirs of his boyhood in Wilmington, Delaware, in the 1890s, he easily located the position of African Americans on the nation's social and cultural spectrum. African Americans were on the fringe; they were social and cultural outsiders. Regardless of their educational attainments, wealth, religious persuasion, or place of residence, skin pigmentation automatically excluded them from becoming full-scale participants in the dominant culture. While not mentioned by Canby, had he been asked, he doubtlessly would have also located Native Americans outside of his own social and cultural world.

Locating the position of white southerners posed a more difficult problem for Canby and for others. In some respects white southerners seemed even more Victorian than middle-class Protestant northerners. The South was, after all, "the habitat of the quintessential WASP [white Anglo-Saxon Protestant]," Professor George B. Tindall told the Southern Historical Convention in 1973. "Is it not, in fact," he rhetorically asked, "the biggest single WASP nest this side of the Atlantic?" The great multitude of immigrants who arrived in the nineteenth and early twentieth centuries deliberately bypassed the South. Hence, the southern white population remained overwhelmingly English, Welsh, Scottish, and Scots-Irish in its ethnic origins. Neither did any other region of the country approximate the South's loyalty to and enthusiasm for evangelical Protestantism. Nothing was more central to both white and black southern ways than the "old time religion," a faith based upon a literal reading of the Bible and belief in the experience of a spiritual rebirth (the conversion experience). With respect to ethnicity and religion, then, the white South qualified for full membership in the dominant Victorian culture.

Yet southern ways were not identical with those of the northern middle class. In the South, the ways of traditional hierarchy lingered on with far more force than they did in the North. Despite the enthusiasm and broad claims made on behalf of the achievements of a new, industrial South in the late nineteenth and early twentieth centuries, the full impact of the Industrial Revolution, with its large cities and sprawling middle class, failed to reach the region until the middle decades of the twentieth century. In the South, "there is in substance no middle class," said a Republican Congressman with only slight exaggeration in the 1850s. "Great wealth and hopeless poverty is the settled condition [of the region]." The long-term absence of a substantial middle class precluded the possibility of the South replicating northern ways. So did race. Unlike the North, the South was a manifestly biracial society. "Southern whites cannot walk, talk, sing, conceive of laws or justice, think of sex, love, the family or freedom without responding to the presence of Negroes," explained black novelist Ralph Ellison in 1964.

THE WAYS OF THE NEWLY FREED PEOPLE

The Civil War and Reconstruction (1861–77) seemed to present unprecedented opportunities for radically altering southern ways (see Chapter 12). Initially, President Abraham Lincoln limited Northern war aims to the restoration of the Union. But, as the war dragged on, pressures mounted for broadening the conflict's objectives. One pressure arose from African Americans themselves; during the war they tried to subvert the Confederate cause from within and sought whenever they could to escape slavery and join the Union Army. They also called the attention of northern whites to the war's revolutionary potential. The other pressure arose from northern whites, many of whom eventually came to see the war as a splendid opportunity for remaking the South in the image of the North.

The Radical Republicans, as the northern reformers were dubbed, embraced a set of divergent, but overlapping goals. As products of the antebellum abolitionist crusade, some Radicals wanted to create a far more egalitarian society, one in which skin color would count for nothing. Others cared little or nothing for the fate of blacks but hated the haughty southern white "aristocracy." Despite their differences, the Radicals eventually settled on one principal goal—the extension of equal political and civil rights to African Americans.

Given the racial attitudes of the day, this was no small step. The Thirteenth through the Fifteenth Amendments to the Constitution freed blacks from slavery, made them U.S. citizens, and extended suffrage to black males. The second clause of the Fourteenth Amendment prohibited the individual states from depriving any citizen of his or her rights and privileges without due process of law. This clause eventually served as the text for a far-reaching body of rights, such as the 1954 Supreme Court decision that ended the legal racial segregation of the nation's schools.

But Congress rejected the more extreme proposals of the Radicals. While blacks were in principle to enjoy all of the same rights as white citizens of the United States, in the end the national government was unable or unwilling to establish effective tools for securing this lofty ideal. In particular, the government failed to provide the newly freed people with the economic strength required to realize fully their rights as citizens. There was no large-scale confiscation and redistribution of southern lands, no massive federal financial assistance to the former slaves, nor were there provisions for extended federal protection of the freed people in the former Confederate states. In short, there was nothing comparable to a Marshall Plan (America's economic assistance program for Europe after World War II) for the South. A rumor spread across the South that every former slave family would receive forty acres and a mule, but nothing came of the idea. Even though white southerners had engaged in treason during the war, northerners were reluctant to take away their property (other than their property in slaves). They considered private property to be an inviolable right.

The congressional majority apparently agreed with the self-help philosophy of black leader Frederick Douglass, who in 1862 had said, "Let them [the freed people] alone. Our duty is done better by not hindering than by helping our fellow man." He added that "the best way to help them is just to let them help themselves." Equal legal rights and the right to compete unimpeded in the marketplace—these, the Radicals concluded, were enough aid to the newly freed slaves. With these rights, they thought, the freed people had the same opportunities as ordinary white families in the North. Applying the white middle-class formula of success to the newly freed blacks, they reasoned that by practicing hard work, individual initiative, and frugality the former slaves too could achieve economic self-sufficiency.

Realizing such an idyllic scenario turned out to be far more difficult than the northern Radicals had presumed. Apart from confronting pervasive racial prejudice and discrimination, the propertyless freed people possessed only one economic resource—their labor. Whites owned nearly all of the land, the draft animals, and the tools needed for survival. Despite these handicaps, about one-fifth of the freed families eventually obtained land of their own. But the overwhelming majority of the remainder became sharecroppers, a system that until the middle of the twentieth century came to dominate the southern countryside for both poor whites and blacks. While rarely able to improve their living standards above the subsistence level, by eliminating hated white overseers, detailed white supervision, and gang labor, the black families did enjoy in the sharecropping system more personal autonomy than they had had during slavery.

Blacks quickly seized upon their new opportunities for political participation. While underrepresented as elected officials in terms of their proportion of the total population, during the last half of the nineteenth century more than one thousand former slaves won election to public offices. Eighteen even obtained seats in the United States Congress. On the state level, blacks and their white allies (contemptuously referred to by their opponents as carpet-baggers and scalawags) established public school systems where none had existed before, drew up more humanitarian legal codes, and passed a body of civil rights legislation. However, by the mid-1870s, African American political power began to wane and the black-white coalition began to fall apart. Growing violent opposition by white terrorist organizations such as the Ku Klux Klan and the absence of will by the North to provide continuing support undermined Reconstruction's bold experiment in interracial democracy.

In the meantime, African Americans sought to make the most of their new freedom in other respects. They at once set about distancing themselves as much as they could from older forms of coercion and personal dependency. Insisting that their families should no longer act like slaves, they took new names, moved out of the former slave quarters, and pulled their wives and children out of the fields. Anchored in the ways that had sustained them during slavery, the newly emancipated slaves quickly began rebuilding their own black communities.

At the center of the new communities was the family. Once the war had ended in 1865, separated husbands, wives, parents, and children rushed to seek each other out and to restore severed relationships. Thousands of former slaves reaffirmed their commitments to their families by insisting on official wedding ceremonies. That black parents everywhere enthusiastically embraced opportunities for their children to learn how to read and write reflected an equal dedication to family welfare.

Even more than in the past, religion provided a key pillar of black communities. Everywhere across the South newly freed blacks seceded from white churches and formed their own churches with their own ministers. While sharing with white evangelicals an emphasis on spiritual rebirth, black Methodist and Baptist ministers made Christianity into a religion of liberation. No themes for sermons and Sunday school lessons were more popular than Moses leading his oppressed people out of the land of bondage and of Jesus promising relief from earthly burdens. Congregational participation in worship services included exuberant expressions of religious feelings. Congregations shouted responses to calls by their preachers, clapped their hands, and swayed in unison as they sang moving spirituals.

PRESERVING AND CONSTRUCTING A SOUTHERN CULTURAL IDENTITY

Despite Reconstruction and the efforts of freed blacks to invent and perpetuate new ways, within three decades after the Civil War most blacks and perhaps many whites must have wondered if southern ways had changed very

Billy Graham Center Museum

An African Methodist Episcopal Church in the South. Simple structures, such as this one built in the late nineteenth century, served as churches for the newly freed African American people. Along with families, churches were key institutions in perpetuating a distinctively African American culture.

much. The much vaunted New South, which promised to bring industry, rapid economic growth, and a large middle class to the region, never achieved anything approximating full realization. True, by 1900 the South could boast of significant growth in railroad mileage, iron and steel production, timber and tobacco processing, and textile manufacturing, but still the growth of the South's economy lagged far behind the North's. Indeed, in terms of per capita income, the region fell even further behind the North.

Neither did the destruction of slavery and plantation agriculture bring down the region's hierarchical social order. By controlling a highly disproportionate share of the South's farmlands, the families of the pre–Civil War planters retained most of their traditional economic power. In the meantime, the conditions of the yeoman white farmers deteriorated. Faced with falling cotton prices, some 80 percent of them lost their land in the postwar era.

Aiding and abetting the white South's resistance to cultural change was the invention and perpetuation of powerful myths. One was that of the Old South. In the minds of white southerners, the pre–Civil War plantation South became everything the industrial North was not. Rather than a region of smokestacks, crowded tenements, and screeching machinery, in the imaginations of both northerners and southerners the romanticized Old South evoked images of gallant gentlemen, refined ladies, contented slaves, moonlight, mint juleps, and magnolias. The Old South possessed a way of life that was less material, less hurried, and richer in the possibilities of sensual fulfillment than that of the North.

A second myth was that of the Lost Cause. It told of how brave but vastly outnumbered Confederate soldiers had defended a noble way of life—the Old South—against the rapacious Yankees. Following the leadership of the United Confederate Veterans and the United Daughters of the Confederacy, between about the 1880s and the 1920s, towns across the South erected literally hundreds of monuments with statues of solitary but ever vigilant Confederate soldiers always peering northward. While southern Protestantism was sparse on iconography, the myth of the Lost Cause was another matter. It became in the words of historian Charles Reagan Wilson "a civil religion." The Confederate flag became a special regional icon, which to this day evokes a powerful set of sometimes opposing symbols. White southerners transformed Robert E. Lee, Jefferson Davis, and other wartime heroes into saints and martyrs. For generations, Decoration Day was a special time of regional unity. Decoration Day brought out thousands of people who carried spring flowers to the graves of those who had been killed decades earlier.

Religion also bolstered the South's cultural identity. While northern Protestants were relaxing their insistence on the need for dramatic conversion experiences and on biblical literalism, southern Protestants remained loyal to their evangelical roots. "The South is by a long way the most simply and sincerely religious country that I ever was in," wrote Sir William Archer, an English visitor in 1910. For southerners, he added, "God is very real and personal." Indeed, he was. Religious faith and language extended everywhere; it permeated public discourse, courtship, child rearing, and social relationships. In the twentieth century, the South's striking degree of religiosity led to the region being dubbed America's "Bible Belt."

Likewise, sports and special forms of music promoted southern unity and identity. Having had a long tradition of physical display and aggressive competition, southerners eagerly embraced the rapid growth of organized sports in the post–Civil War era. Baseball came first. By the 1890s, every town of any consequence had one or more teams. The adoption of yet another northern game—football—by southern colleges and universities became an even more effective vehicle for the reassertion of state and regional pride. Teams adopted the colors of the Confederacy; they sought the imprimaturs of legendary figures from the region's past and symbolic regional victories through

Statue of General Robert E. Lee in Richmond, Virginia. In the post–Civil War era, Lee became a specially revered figure among white southerners. As a quintessential representative of such allegedly unique southern traits as honor, bravery, and self-sacrifice, the Civil War hero helped to create and preserve a distinctive southern white identity.

football victories over northern foes. Discontented people from both races helped to make the South what historian Edward L. Ayers has aptly described as "the crucible for the blues, jazz, and country music." Through a complex process of adaptation and invention, a set of young southern musicians, who began to come of age in the 1880s and 1890s, created a distinctive culture of regional music. In time, the influence of this culture would extend throughout the world.

THE NEW RACIAL SETTLEMENT

While the radical phase of Reconstruction essentially closed in the mid-1870s, even as late as the early 1890s, African Americans continued in many places to vote, hold public office, and mingle with whites in public places. But race relations had worsened. Acting on resentments arising from the South's declining rural economy, from black assertiveness, and from stories heard in childhood of the heroism and nobility of their fathers and brothers in the Civil War, a new generation of southern whites escalated the level of rhetoric and violence against blacks.

Between 1892 and 1903, an orgy of violence swept across the South; during these years the lynching of African Americans averaged more than 150 per year. In particular, any behavior interpreted as a sexual overture by black men toward white women brought down the full wrath of white society. White men retaliated not only by killing the offenders but also by torturing (often by burning), mutilating, and dismembering them (which often included castration and cutting off the penis), and displaying their victims in public. Serving as icons of white male supremacy throughout the South and beyond, photographs of the charred and mutilated corpses circulated in the newspapers and on picture postcards. The lynching spectacle dramatized a social hierarchy in which whites and blacks and women and men "knew their places." Perhaps reflecting a white projection of immense sexual power onto blacks, the rituals of lynching may have also reassured white men of their own sense of manhood and honor.

During the same era, law became an important tool for ensuring white supremacy. By passing an ingenious battery of laws requiring voters to pay poll taxes, be literate, interpret state constitutions correctly, and have grandfathers who had been eligible to vote, by 1905 southern white lawmakers effectively denied blacks the right to vote throughout most of the South. Southern white lawmakers also set about legalizing segregation (the physical separation of blacks and whites in public facilities of all kinds), which the U.S. Supreme Court officially sanctioned in *Plessy v. Ferguson* (1896). As long as the facilities provided to each race were equal in quality, the court said, segregation did not violate the equal protection clause of the Fourteenth Amendment. While in fact facilities were rarely equal in quality, expectations of futility, expense, and physical violence frequently dissuaded blacks from contesting the application of the segregation statutes.

The *Plessy* decision reflected the North's acceptance of the South's new racial settlement. By the turn of the century, white northerners no longer resisted the white South's imposition of open segregation, its implicit violations of the Fourteenth and Fifteenth Amendments, or its reign of terror against African Americans. Indeed, the great majority of white northerners shared white southern beliefs in black inferiority. Everywhere in the nation the media and the entertainment industries stereotyped African Americans. The popular theater of the day, for example, featured white men in blackface poking fun at blacks for their alleged laziness, their stupidity, and their physical appearance. Even more ominously, D. W. Griffith in his popular film *Birth of a Nation* (1915) depicted blacks as dangerous savages.

The application of Darwinian ideas to the evolution of races added a supposedly scientific note to the prevailing white racism. Racists argued that peoples with the highest material cultures, namely whites, had succeeded best in the racial "struggle for survival." Such thinking became part of the conventional wisdom of white social scientists and until as late as the 1940s and 1950s supported the treatment of African Americans as second-class citizens. Describing blacks as "children" incapable of appreciating freedom or acting responsibly as free citizens, a group of historians at the turn of the twentieth century offered a "tragic" view of Reconstruction. One of their number, William Dunning, wrote that black suffrage had been a "monstrous" mistake. Soon this view became the standard perspective of school and college history textbooks across the nation. By justifying the northern failure to oppose the blatant subversion of the Fourteenth and Fifteenth Amendments by the white South, the tragic view of Reconstruction helped to freeze the nation's apartheid into place for many generations to come.

Mirroring the new racism, the position of African Americans in the North slipped downward as well. While none of the northern states followed the southern example of disfranchising blacks, both silent and overt segregation and discrimination increased in the North. Antidiscrimination laws adopted by the northern states in the wake of the Civil War went unenforced. Everywhere African Americans were denied opportunities for better jobs and invariably received lower pay than whites. Even as late as 1950, the median family income for blacks was about half that of whites. Excluded by income and color from living where they pleased, most northern and southern urban blacks increasingly squeezed into crowded ghettos.

Despite the odds arrayed against them, urban blacks were able to build some community structures. A sense of community arose in part from sports, the services provided by black professionals, newspapers, small businesses, and, above all, churches. Working-class African Americans frequently sought to express and mark their freedom through parades and fancy dress, exuberant physical displays, and feats of physical exertion.

Based on professions, skills, and businesses that served mainly black customers, as early as the 1880s a tiny but significant African American middle class began to take shape in the major cities of both the South and the North. As with middle-class whites, the black middle class formed fraternal lodges, temperance societies, churches, and business organizations. Middle-class black women's clubs also paralleled white organizations. As with white middle-class Victorian culture, the black middle class strove to promote self-control in themselves and their children. They also saw the home as a refuge from the outside world and sought to distinguish themselves by their refinement and their support of high culture. Yet, no matter how much their ways resembled those of middle-class whites, the two groups were separated by the seemingly unbridgeable chasm of race.

"AN UNSPEAKABLE SADNESS"

No major group, except perhaps African Americans, had a more difficult time in resisting the pressures of the dominant middle class than Native Americans. In 1800, despite nearly three hundred years of almost relentless assaults from European invaders, powerful independent Indian tribes still occupied much of the interior of North America. Each of the Indian nations had its own language, its own customs, its own government, and its own religion. Contrary to modern media images, Native Americans lived mostly in fixed villages where they typically pursued a food-getting cycle of farming, hunting, fishing, gathering, and sometimes raiding.

Over the next century, the situation of Native Americans changed drastically. Many lost their lives. The Indian population plunged from perhaps a million or more people in 1800 to less than a quarter million a century later. The Indians also lost their tribal independence, at least a portion of their culture, and nearly all their lands. By 1900 they had been militarily subdued and pushed off their lands onto tiny, desolate reservations where most of them lived in deplorable poverty.

No simple hypothesis adequately explains this "unspeakable sadness," to employ the moving words that an Indian leader once used to describe what had happened. In theory, the interior of North America could have been set aside as a permanent homeland for the continent's indigenous peoples. There, in principle, the Indians could have carried on much as they had in the past. An indigenous homeland would have also accorded with a generous reading of the Declaration of Independence. The Declaration asserted that all peoples were entitled to the right of self-government. Such a proposal would have won the warm endorsement of the Indians themselves. The Indians repeatedly expressed a willingness and a readiness to live in peaceful coexistence with white Americans.

Unfortunately for the Indians, the idea of a homeland ran afoul of deeply held white convictions. To one large white group, the Indians stood in the way of white men increasing their personal fortunes. Rationalizing their aggrandizement in terms of their self-acclaimed racial superiority, they concluded that the Indians were simply obstacles who should be pushed aside or, if necessary, even killed. To them, the Indians differed little from wild vermin. The prospect of killing Indians appalled another white group, the humanitarians. They dreamed of a day when, by adopting white ways, Indians would be fully integrated into white society.

Yet the humanitarians and the land-hungry whites did *agree* on one key point: The Indians had no legitimate claims to cultures of their own. Equating progress and civilization with individualism and private property, whites found particularly repulsive the Indian practices of tribal (rather than individual) land ownership and the sharing of the fruits of the land among all tribal members. Unless abandoned for white ways, these practices disqualified the Indians for consideration as equals to whites. Whether humanitarians or greedy land seekers, both groups of whites saw Native American societies as anachronistic, as societies destined in the long run to disappear from the face of the earth.

Government Indian policy in the nineteenth century reflected these views. Until 1871, when Congress abolished the practice of making treaties with separate tribes, the government negotiated dozens of treaties—many of them the product of chicanery and corruption—which called for both Indian land cessions and for the establishment of white "civilizing missions" among the tribes. The Indian agents and the missionaries, those whites responsible for the civilizing missions, urged the Indians to renounce their ancestral ways. They visualized the reservations, those lands retained by the Indians, as protected, transitional spaces. Here, the Indians would be granted the time necessary for them to make the transition from "savagery" to "civilization." However, rather than transitional spaces, in time many Indians came to view the reservations as their permanent homelands.

NATIVE AMERICAN RESPONSES

Native Americans devised various strategies for responding to the massive white assaults on their lives, their lands, and their cultures. Sometimes they sank into hopeless despair and resigned themselves to their fate at the hands of the advancing whites. Sometimes they fled. For example, as late as 1877, the legendary Nez Perce Chief Joseph tried to lead his people to safety by a long flight across the Pacific Northwest, into Canada, and finally back into the United States. Throughout much of the nineteenth century, a large portion of the Indian population could, by modern terms, be classified as political refugees.

When unable or unwilling to flee the rapidly advancing white invaders, Indian strategy usually oscillated between resistance and accommodation. The accommodationists cooperated with but were rarely controlled by the whites. They frequently adopted some aspects of white culture. A good example of the accomodationists were the antebellum Cherokees who, even though they adopted many white ways, were forcibly removed from their lands in the Southeast (see Chapter 9). In contrast to the accomodationists, the resisters openly rejected some if not all aspects of white culture. Most Indians probably occupied positions between these two poles or, as the occasion seemed to warrant, shifted from one position to the other.

Resistance to white assaults frequently combined sacred and military power. Military resistance was nothing new. Since the fifteenth century, when the Spaniards first encroached on the native peoples of North America, whites and Indians had been fighting in what historians sometimes describe as the "Four Hundred Years War." In the first phase of this prolonged conflict, the Indians had been able to shrewdly parlay one European power against the other, but, with the rise of the United States, the Indians could no longer count on white allies. The Indians then had to contend alone with a new republic that enjoyed vastly superior numbers and material resources. Armed resistance ended symbolically with the Wounded Knee massacre in 1890.

A group of Indian prophets, extending from Handsome Lake in the eighteenth century to Tenskwatawa and Wovoka in the nineteenth century, supplied the ideological core of the Indian resistance movement. Each of the prophets had apocalyptic visions; in these visions they crossed a boundary that normally separated the temporal and the spiritual worlds. From the world of the spirits they received instructions to carry back to their peoples.

The lessons of the prophets were strikingly similar. Indian woes, they taught, stemmed from a failure of the Indian people to adhere to traditional ways. Dependency on white trade goods, conversion to Christianity, surrendering native lands to alien peoples, and negligence in performing traditional religious rituals—all of these had led to a disastrous loss of sacred power. The restoration of sacred power required a cultural revitalization. Some prophets sought to revitalize their people by blending the old and the new. For example, in 1799 Handsome Lake, an Iroquois prophet, preached a combination of Indian and white ways that included peace, temperance, land retention, and the rituals of Gaiwiio, a new religion that fused Christianity with traditional Iroquois beliefs.

Other prophets urged more radical forms of revitalization and resistance. During the first decade of the nineteenth century, the Shawnee prophet Tenskwatawa exhorted all of the Indian people to renounce alcohol and all other white goods (except guns when used in self-defense) and to return to the old ways of hunting with the bow and the arrow. "You must not dress like the White Man or wear hats like them, . . . and when the weather is not severe, you must go naked excepting the breach cloth. . . ." He condemned intertribal warfare and urged tribal unity.

In 1888, in the wake of Indian military defeat and the virtual demise of the bison, the Paiute prophet Wovoka developed a powerful new religion centered on the Ghost Dance. By conducting proper ceremonies and rituals, Wovoka prophesied that the fallen warriors and the buffalo would return and drive away the whites. While Wovoka's prophesies went unfulfilled, religious revitalization continues to this day to serve as an important means of resisting white assaults on traditional Native American ways.

THE CULMINATION OF THE WHITE ASSAULT

The Dawes Act of 1887, passed during the final military subjugation of the Plains Indians, represented the culmination of nineteenth-century Indian policy. The act allowed for the transfer of 160 acres of former tribal lands to individual Indian families. Private rather than tribal ownership, the humanitarians believed, would awaken in the native peoples desires for personal gain similar to those that preoccupied middle-class whites. The government, with tribal consent, could sell the remaining lands to white settlers. The proceeds from these sales were to be set aside for Indian education and "civilization."

As an alternative to the enormous power of traditional tribal structures and the ancestral ways of the Native Americans, the Dawes Act proposed to create among the Indians a facsimile of middle-class Victorian culture. The Indian families were expected to move out of their tribal villages onto individual farms, to establish male-dominated nuclear families, and to adopt the acquisitive values of white society. By promising the final annihilation of tribal life and by the opening up of new lands for white settlement, the Dawes Act pleased both the white humanitarians and the land-hungry whites.

But the results were less than happy for Native Americans. By the 1930s Indian-owned lands had shrunk from 138 million acres to less than 48 million acres. Left on mostly barren lands unsuited for successful farming and lacking in a plentiful supply of game, shocking numbers of the Indians sank into shattering cycles of dependency, disease, alcoholism, appalling poverty, and early death.

The whites added to Indian miseries by their continuing attacks on tribal customs. In particular, those customs that ran counter to the middle-class white concern with self-control bothered Bureau of Indian Affairs officials. For example, they banned tribal dances and they tried to stop the ingestion of peyote, which was, according to the Reverend G. A. Watermulter (1914), "a habit-forming, physically weakening, will-relaxing, imagination-exciting drug." Acting upon the admonition of Captain Richard Henry Pratt, the founder of the Carlisle Indian boarding school in Pennsylvania, that they should "Kill the Indian in him and save the man," the Bureau established a system of boarding and day schools. By removing Native American children from direct tribal and family influences and teaching them to be ashamed of their traditional cultures, the schools sought to convert the Indian children to white middle-class ways.

Despite staggering white pressures, only a small fraction of the Indian population fully assimilated into the dominant white culture. Neither education in the ways of the whites nor the Dawes Act succeeded in equalizing the conditions of opportunity between Indians and whites. Continuing white

Corbis

New Government Boarding School on the Pine Ridge Indian Reservation in South Dakota, 1891. Notice the juxtaposition of traditional tribal lodgings in the foreground and the new boarding school in the background. Boarding schools, which separated Native American children from their elders and their tribal groups, were designed to convert Indian youths to the middle-class ways of white America.

prejudice and discrimination severely circumscribed Indian opportunities to improve their material lot. The Indians themselves resisted assimilation; few of them found the acquisitive individualism of white culture intrinsically superior to their own. They continued to yearn for a less competitive culture, one in which the earth's bounty was more nearly shared by everyone.

In addition to religion, Native Americans seized on other materials provided by the dominant culture to strengthen their identities and their opposition to white America. The feats of boarding school football teams at Carlisle, Pennsylvania, where Jim Thorpe won renown in the early twentieth century, and at Haskell Institute in Lawrence, Kansas, in the 1920s, where John Levi achieved almost equal renown, provided Indians everywhere with an enormous transfusion of pride and sense of shared "Indianness." Reservations, whose tangled histories in the twentieth century are too complex to render into a few generalizations, also became citadels of cultural conservatism. Beginning early in the twentieth century, Indians from far and wide and regardless of tribal affiliations regularly gathered for powwows. As events specially marked off in time and space and in which Native Americans camped out, visited, ate together, and danced, the intertribal powwows permitted Indians to revisit old and experiment with new identities, and, perhaps more importantly, provided them with a relatively safe setting for the expression of their cultural autonomy and opposition to white rule.

THE WEST OF THE WHITE IMAGINATION

In the meantime, whites shielded themselves from a full recognition of the tragedies and miseries of the Indian people. Rather than seeing Native Americans as they actually were, whites wove about them a romantic shroud of fantasy and nostalgia. The shroud may be summed up in the contradictory concept of the "noble savage." Such a concept allowed whites to assign both positive and negative values to the nation's indigenous peoples.

On the savage side of the dichotomy, dime novels, and then later the movies, radio, television, and finally even history textbooks pointedly avoided telling the true story of a bloody, contested Euro-American invasion of the Americas. According to these representations, it was the Indians—emphatically not the whites—who were the aggressors. In 1883, William "Buffalo Bill" Cody turned the savage version of the relationships between Indians and whites into a successful business formula with his Wild West show. Immensely popular on both sides of the Atlantic, the show featured stereotypical Indians chasing buffalo, performing war dances, and attacking a white settler's cabin. At this juncture of the drama, Bill Cody came to the rescue, saving white "civilization" from "savagery." Such a process of justification for white incursions on Indian lives and properties was so successful that it took a leap of the imagination for most white Americans to realize that only a century or so earlier dozens of independent Indian cultures had existed in the vast interior of North America.

At the same time, many whites found in imagined Indian ways of life an attractive alternative to the ways of modern America. In contrast to the guise and artifice required for navigating life in industrial-urban America with its smokestacks, grime, close quarters, and clocklike work regimens, it seemed to many white Americans that Native Americans lived closer to nature, more simply, and more authentically. So attractive was this imagined alternative that in the twentieth century the leaders of adult-supervised youth movements, such as the Boy Scouts, the Girl Scouts, and the Campfire Girls, made the experience of presumed Indian ways a major part of their programs. Throughout the twentieth century, critics of modernity, especially those in literary and artistic circles, frequently found inspiration in a nostalgic and romanticized version of Indian cultures. During the great cultural upheaval of the 1960s and early 1970s, youthful rebels even went so far as to try to re-create literally in their communes what they believed to be the ways of the "noble savage."

The ennoblement of Indian life was an important constituent of a larger mythology of the American West. The West of the white imagination became a powerful symbol; it evoked, as Henry Nash Smith cogently observed, an idyllic place similar to the Bible's Garden of Eden. There, the poor could escape poverty by obtaining free land and working hard. There, settlers were free of oppressive social hierarchies and governments. There, in short, the individual counted for

American Progress (1872). This allegorical painting by John Gast treats the advance of "civilization" and the retreat of "savagery." The diaphanously clad female figure, a descendant of earlier representations of liberty, wears the Star of Empire as she leads the march of pioneers, enlightenment, and technological progress westward. Notice also that she is stringing telegraph wires that will bind the nation together. Retreating before the tranquility and light (civilization) of the East into the stormy darkness (savagery) of the West are the disappearing Indians and the bison.

everything. In 1893 historian Frederick Jackson Turner offered an influential scholarly defense of this kind of thinking; more than anything else, Turner argued, the frontier had shaped American character. Popular publications and later the movies and television took up the same theme. While such portrayals failed to capture the diversity, complexity, and conflict of the region's history, they offered a powerful reinforcement of the belief that America was a special place in which individuals could pull themselves up solely by their own efforts.

CONCLUSION

During the nineteenth and early twentieth centuries, sharp social and cultural boundaries divided the American people. None was sharper or more difficult to cross than that of race. Religious and ethnic cleavages were almost equally clear. The Irish and the Italians "meant nothing to us," recalled Henry Seidel Canby of his middle-class family in upstate Delaware, "they were only population." Besides, they were Catholics, "which put them still further outside our world." Between Canby's family and the South was yet another dividing line. "To the southward," he said, was "an alien state."

As Canby recognized, each of the outsider or minority groups sought in varying degrees to establish and perpetuate identities of their own. While family, leisure, and work ways frequently served to promote distinctive identities, no institution was more important to the outsiders than their churches. Each of the groups found in their respective religions a reservoir of strength. In addition, simply being outsiders served to bolster distinctive identities; perceptions or experiences of prejudice and discrimination drove countless Native Americans, African Americans, and immigrants to retreat into the security and warmth of their own groups. Finally, the Civil War and Reconstruction and the insecurities arising from the presence of a large black population in their midst encouraged white southerners to cling to and promote a separate regional identity.

IX

THE ORIGINS OF MODERN WAYS

The origins of distinctively modern ways—the ways with which we are familiar today—can be traced back to the era between the 1880s and the 1930s. In this age, evidence of a general retreat from the all-important middle-class concern with self-control was unmistakable. Even earlier (as we observed in the previous two chapters), Native Americans, African Americans, and a fast-growing working class had perpetuated alternative cultures that seemed from the perspective of the middle class to place too little emphasis on restraining the self. Modern ways not only borrowed from the ways of these outsiders but also from a new, more assertive class of the spectacularly rich. The families of the nouveau riche frequently took their behavioral cues from the freer ways of the European aristocracy. Still more distressing to the custodians of traditional middle-class culture was the discovery of discontent within its own ranks. Frequently less evangelical, more impatient with the demands for self-control, and increasingly dissatisfied with the tepidity of their day-to-day existence, a new generation of the middle class hungered for more personal freedom, additional excitement, and greater self-fulfillment.

Expressions of the new hunger took many forms. A rage for competitive athletics, adventurism in foreign affairs, the outdoors, amusement parks, the movies, more energetic music, and dancing—these and other forms of release and excitement swept across the nation. And who could resist the new, mass-produced consumer goods? Great department stores, chain stores, and mail-order houses offered consumers a previously unimaginable cornucopia of consumer delights. Finally, a more liberal Protestantism, new social thought, and daring departures from traditional forms in art and literature—all of these and more reflected growing fissures in the foundations of middle-class culture and morality. By the 1920s signs of the arrival of modern ways were everywhere.

17

CONSUMER CULTURE AND THE QUEST FOR EXCITEMENT

No sign of the coming of modern culture was more important than a shifting emphasis of the nation's economy from production to consumption. In the nineteenth century, the main task of the economy had been the production of more and more goods. Self-control and the middle-class ethos of hard work, frugality, and civic responsibility had been well-suited for a production-oriented society of small entrepreneurs. But in the world of twentieth-century corporate capitalism, mass consumption became equally important to the success of the nation's economy.

Consumption raised to the fore a new dream of the good life. For countless Americans, including the expanded middle class, the new vision supplemented or pushed aside earlier dreams of a Christian City on a Hill, a republic of virtue, a Kingdom of God on Earth, or a nation tied together by a common culture devoted to refinement and a shared respect for great literature and great art. The new vision centered on personal pleasure, comfort, material well-being, buying, and selling and was associated with the cult of the new, with youth, and with money as the measure of all things.

No longer was freedom restricted to the workplace and to the polling booth; for millions it meant the right to buy things. "Every free-born American," said advertising executive Kenneth Goode, has a "right to name his own necessities." Unlike opportunities in the arenas of work and politics, consumer freedom was equally available to women. The "woman of today," declared a Piggly Wiggly supermarket ad, was "free to choose" from a multitude of products. The new culture as Herbert Duce, a merchant, candidly confessed in 1912, "does not say, 'Pray, obey, sacrifice thyself, respect the King, fear thy master.'" Instead, "it whispers, 'Amuse thyself, take care of thyself.'" It was this culture, a culture revolving around consumption, that the peoples the world over came to see as the very essence of American life.

AN ECONOMY OF MASS PRODUCTION

At bottom, the new culture of consumption rested on the economy's capacity to mass-produce goods. In the eighteenth century, nearly every product found in American households was either made in the home or by skilled craftsmen outside the home. The revolution in manufacturing in the nineteenth and twentieth centuries substituted mass-manufactured products for custom-made goods. By the end of the nineteenth century, millions of boys and men dressed in "ready-to-wear" garments rather than clothes made in the home or by high-priced tailors. Similar shifts occurred in the food that people ate and in home furnishings. The necessities of life were not the only mass-manufactured items. The number of pianos sold in the United States, for example, jumped from 32,000 in 1890 to 374,000 in 1904.

No single product epitomized the significance of mass-manufacturing more than the automobile. Initially a luxury item available only to the few or the foolish, by the end of the 1920s the car had become virtually a family necessity. By then, one car existed for each five Americans; with a little crowding, the entire population of the country could have been rolling down the highway at the same time. By introducing an assembly line and other efficiencies in production, Henry Ford slashed the price of his Model T, or Tin Lizzie, as it was affectionately nicknamed by its owners, from $600 in 1912 to $290 by 1924. With the cost equaling only three months of a typical worker's wage, a new Model T was now within the financial reach of millions of ordinary Americans. "Why on earth do you need to study what's changing this country?" a Muncie, Indiana, resident asked the sociologist team of Robert and Helen Lynd in the 1920s. "I can tell you what's happening in just four letters: A-U-T-O." The car opened up new realms of experience to millions whose lives had earlier been restricted to home, neighborhood, and workplace.

The merchandising of mass-manufactured goods underwent a similar revolution. Department stores (so named because they displayed their goods in separate sections or departments) led the way in both the marketing of the nation's industrial largesse and in altering public attitudes toward consumption. In the final decades of the nineteenth century, innovative entrepreneurs such as Marshall Field in Chicago, John Wanamaker in Philadelphia, and Rowland Macy in New York City built department stores into major urban institutions. While department stores sold goods mainly to the middle and upper classes in the big cities, chain stores such as F. W. Woolworth and A & P supplied mass-produced goods to the urban working class and the residents of smaller cities. In the meantime, mail-order houses opened up the horizons of consumption to rural and small town Americans. The encyclopedic catalogs of the Sears & Roebuck company not only offered an amazing array of consumer goods but also educated their readers on up-to-date fashions as well.

Mannequins Displaying the Latest Parisian Fashions. Along with new strategies in advertising, lavish, brilliantly lit department stores, such as Marshall Field's in Chicago, led the way in altering public attitudes toward consumption. Consumption raised to the fore a new dream of what the nation might become. It frequently pushed aside or replaced such earlier visions as a Puritan city on a hill, a republic of virtue, a Kingdom of God on earth, or a common culture built on the cultivation of the beaux arts.

Churches, governments at all levels, and colleges—these and other institutions eventually rallied behind the new order of consumption. In earlier times, independent colleges of commerce had been mainly concerned with how to make rather than how to market goods. But by the turn of the century marketing had become central to the mission of the new business colleges that were rapidly becoming an integral component of the nation's burgeoning university system. While governments during the Progressive era sometimes sought to curb and control the growth of corporate capitalism, in the 1920s the Department of Commerce under the direction of Herbert Hoover freely used federal power to aid corporations in promoting the expansion of the consumer revolution. Except for a tiny minority, church leaders too eventually came to terms with the ethical and spiritual issues raised by consumption. Mostly they sided with America's new, more commercially oriented society.

STRATEGIES OF ENTICEMENT

The marketers of the mass-manufactured goods soon recognized that success required much more than controlling prices and costs. Potential buyers had to be persuaded that they now needed products that they had not earlier realized they needed. "Competitive commerce," wrote the Reverend Walter Rauschenbusch, a critic of the consumer revolution, "spreads things before us and beseeches and persuades us to buy what we do not want. Men try to break down [our] self-restraint . . . and reduce us to the moral habits of savages who gorge today and fast tomorrow."

The main strategy for breaking down self-restraint and enticing buyers to purchase products that they did not previously want was to associate the acquisition and consumption of goods with much more than simply utility or rational needs. The marketers sought to convince potential buyers that the ownership of their goods would bring enhanced personal pleasures, introduce greater excitement into otherwise drab lives, and provide effective therapy for a vast range of personal anxieties.

The history of advertising illustrates the new strategies of enticement. While earlier advertisements had frequently consisted of little more than an announcement in a newspaper of the availability of a product, patent medicine vendors pioneered in the creation of ads designed to grab the attention of their readers with striking visuals and sweeping claims for their products. The new ads pointed away from the presentation of sober information; instead they addressed the nonrational fears and yearnings of potential buyers. For example, an ad in the 1920s for a new Ford depicted a couple with a child walking through a tree-shrouded suburban neighborhood. Gesturing toward the street filled with gleaming Fords, the wife plaintively says to her husband, "EVERYONE OWNS A CAR BUT US." According to the ad, ownership of a new car would "add much to the happiness of your family," "bring more glorious pleasure into your life," and "increase your chances of success."

In order to associate the buying of their goods with excitement, exotic dreams, and the solution of personal problems, retailers transformed the appearance of their stores. Shoppers in the mammoth department stores found not only artfully displayed goods but also stained-glass skylights, spiraling marble staircases, brilliant chandeliers, rich walnut paneling, and plush carpets. The management of visual space on behalf of selling goods reached its apogee in large glass display windows where onlookers could see vivid ensembles of goods drenched in color and light. By 1920 merchants even began to display women's underwear on full-bodied mannequins, an act that would certainly have shocked middle-class sensibilities a decade earlier. No proper Victorian would have been surprised to learn that a character in John Dos Passos's novel *1919* became "terribly agitated" by seeing "girls' underwear in store windows."

Retailers recognized that they could increase the attractiveness of their goods by associating them with fashion. Well before the advent of modern advertising and the modern department store, tasteful consumption had served as a cultural marker of the middle class, but in the new age merchants seized upon the opportunities and anxieties arising from the fluidity of American class boundaries to present their goods as the embodiments of the latest Parisian fashions. By the 1920s department stores staged great fashion pageants, complete with live models, orchestras, and theatrical performances. "Fashion," said a retailer in 1908, "imparts to merchandise a value over and above its intrinsic worth." By purchasing fashionable products, the merchants promised, one could feel special, escape the humdrum of everyday life, and at least temporarily set aside fears of being an outsider.

Strategies of enticement included other kinds of spectacle. In order to publicize the introduction of electric lighting in the commercial districts and to invite people to shop at night, in the 1920s businessmen across the country began organizing dazzling color and light shows. Merchants also seized upon the 1920s mania for public parades. Huge Thanksgiving Day parades sponsored by department stores like Macy's in New York and Hudson's in Detroit ushered in each year's frenzied Christmas retail season. Perhaps nothing was more emblematic of the centrality of consumption to the birth of modern ways than Times Square in downtown New York City. By 1929, the New York City police estimated that every night nearly five hundred thousand people passed in and out of Times Square. Partly they came to patronize the theaters, movie palaces, restaurants, hotels, and retail stores that were clustered there. But they came also to see the bright lights; Times Square was, as one observer put it, "America's Mecca of Light and Color." There, signs— signs that far surpassed the sheer size and intensity of light and color of those in Paris, Berlin, and London—blinked, jumped, and flashed their messages. They all urged Americans to buy, and then to buy some more.

A NEW MIDDLE CLASS

No group participated with more enthusiasm in the new consumer-centered economy than a rapidly expanding middle class. The first or original middle class, which took shape between the 1830s and the 1860s, consisted mainly of shopkeepers, artisans, professional men, successful farmers, and the owners and operators of small factories and retail establishments. Apart from occupation and income, a special moral discipline, one that stemmed mainly from a strong and unquestioning religious faith, distinguished the original middle class from the "dissolute" workingmen from below and the "profligate" rich from above. It had been this class, with its emphasis on evangelical religion, self-control, the family, refinement, and respectability, that had established the supremacy of Victorian culture.

With the rapid growth in corporate capitalism, virtually a new, or second, middle class formed alongside the older class. The new class came mostly from an explosive expansion of the white-collar workforce. Between 1870 and 1930, the number of doctors, lawyers, accountants, architects, engineers, and teachers more than quadrupled while at the same time the number of middle managers, salespeople, and secretaries grew nearly twice as fast as the workforce as a whole. The white-collar working world frequently prized skills in dealing with people as much as entrepreneurial talents or ability to produce goods.

The possession of specialized knowledge also frequently set apart white-collar workers. In the early nineteenth century, the widespread hostility toward hierarchy and privilege, the demands for equality of opportunity, and the pell-mell economic expansion had greatly weakened the traditional entrance requirements into the professions. However, all this began to change at the end of the nineteenth and in the first decades of the twentieth century. To protect their exclusivity, their privileges, and their prestige, each of the professions set up new and far stiffer entry requirements. For instance, the American Medical Association demanded that would-be physicians obtain specialized training and pass a battery of examinations before they could legally practice medicine. Everywhere state and local governments cooperated in the process of making doctors their own professional gatekeepers. Rather than simply mastering the three R's, even teachers of the primary grades eventually had to obtain a college degree and complete a prescribed set of pedagogical courses.

Whether employed as middle managers in corporate bureaucracies, physicians, or educators, the white-collar workers shared an enthusiasm for rationality or what they frequently called "science." Rather than in terms of developing the personal "Character" so important to Victorians (as Robert Wiebe has observed), the new middle class justified itself in terms of acquiring specialized "Knowledge." In the early twentieth century, "scientific management," a movement whose very name evoked the new orientation of the corporate world, swept through the ranks of the middle managers. Rather than as a grand design or an enterprise seeking to discover the ultimate laws of nature, science in their view was nearly always synonymous with a particular method or procedure. Facts became their stock-in-trade; they irrevocably bound themselves to facts about customers, suppliers, markets, trends, timetables, interest rates, and profit margins. Facts in the form of statistics especially intrigued them. The reduction of complex data into numbers, they reasoned, increased the reliability and objectivity of their conclusions.

Their education, their training, and their occupational world—all of these tended to loosen white-collar ties to tradition and to a particular place. While rarely rejecting religion outright, the new class frequently insisted on a less evangelical and more liberal Protestantism. Rather than resting on a national consensus of religiously anchored moral values, the moral values of the new class tended to reflect a conformity with the requirements and expectations of their occupational world.

Away from their workplaces, the new class relaxed the traditional bourgeois emphasis on self-control. Especially in their free time, they were far more likely than the older class to embrace new, more expressive forms of individualism. The new individualism frequently entailed patronizing commercial entertainment, bringing more informality and spontaneity into one's life, and opening one's self up to more intense feelings. Even middle-class housing reflected a noticeable retreat from Victorian formality and restraint. The soaring gothic houses of an earlier era, with their wide verandas, parlors, and hallways, had been built as monuments to individual achievement. But, by the outbreak of World War I, these elaborate structures had given way in popularity to far simpler houses—to bungalow and colonial revival styles—designed mainly for

Nebraska State Historical Society

Bungalow, Lincoln, Nebraska, Built about 1910. The low-slung, one-story or one-and-a-half story bungalows usually featured a generous front porch and a living room but no parlor. Rather than as a statement of the owner's material success or class standing, the house was designed for the comfort of its middle-class occupants. Compare this home with the Victorian mansion on page 192.

family comfort and enjoyment. In the place of formal parlors and grand entrance halls came the living room, a room intended for a more informal style of family life. Its occupants no longer had to sit in bolted-upright positions and dress formally. Advertisers and commercial artists now depicted men, women, and children enjoying themselves in far more physically relaxed ways.

THE QUEST FOR EXCITEMENT

At the turn of the century, middle-class Americans, especially those living in larger cities and those employed in white-collar bureaucracies, began to undo more than their earlier self-imposed constraints on consumption. In the past, suspicion had surrounded those experiences that elicited strong feelings. Too much excitement and the release of feelings might not only jeopardize one's chances for material success, members of the middle class reasoned, but also place in harm's way the nation's entire social order. Thus the middle class expressly condemned drinking, loud talking, extravagant gesturing, wagering, prizefighting, and exhibitions of personal affection.

While concern with self-control remained a central component of middle-class life in the late Victorian age (from the 1880s to World War I), an opposing impulse also began to push its way to the forefront with greater and greater force in all aspects of middle- and upper-class life. Frequently a close ally of the consumer revolution, this second impulse took the form of a widespread quest for more intense experiences. It found outlets or expression in support for commercial leisure and in what Theodore Roosevelt labeled as "the strenuous life." It not only began to effect a revolution in leisure ways but in gender ways as well.

In the past, the middle class had approved only of "rational recreation," those leisure endeavors that remained within the parameters of respectability and that reinvigorated the mind and the body for work and civic duties. Leisure should be confined mostly to the private sphere of the family, to close friends, and to solitary activity. In the security of their homes, middle-class families enjoyed the increasing availability of inexpensive books, newspapers, periodicals, sheet music, pianos, and more exotic foods while avoiding the rowdiness of commercialized public recreation. Consistent with the idea of the home as a moral training ground and as a special emotional refuge, women were expected to be the main providers of middle-class leisure.

Outside the home, middle-class men and women created respectable semi-public or public arenas of spare-time activities. These included fraternal groups for men, church societies for women, and temperance organizations for both sexes. As early as the 1840s, middle-class reformers had also begun to endorse public parks as retreats in which urban residents could escape the ills of the cities and be rejuvenated by the powers of nature. In 1856, New York City employed Frederick Law Olmstead to design Central Park. The rage for city parks then took off. By 1920, nearly every city of any consequence in the nation sported a network of parks.

Slowly in the late nineteenth century and then far more quickly as the twentieth century advanced, middle-class restraints on participation in commercialized leisure also relaxed. Part of the relaxation stemmed from the examples furnished by those from both below and above. Below the middle class, the burgeoning working class (in particular the recent arrivals from Europe) and African Americans exhibited a more physically expressive life than did the middle class. From above, the wealthy, especially the parvenu, likewise flaunted traditional middle-class strictures on feelings and leisure. In their private clubs and summer resorts the wealthy shed lingering suspicions of play-for-play's-sake. The Grafton Country Club of Worcester, Massachusetts, for instance, even adopted as its motto "Each to His Pleasure," a direct rebuke of the middle-class work ethic.

A turning point in the history of middle-class leisure came in the 1880s and 1890s when entrepreneurs of entertainment launched a widespread campaign to woo larger audiences. Since by the standards of the day the presence of substantial numbers of women automatically made an audience respectable, the entertainment entrepreneurs made a special effort to attract middle-class women to their venues. Fortunately for them, such marketing strategies coincided with impulses by growing numbers of women at the turn of the century to free themselves from the more constrictive forms of Victorianism. In particular, dance halls and amusement parks appealed to single working women; at these places, secretaries and other female white-collar workers could experiment with new forms of propriety away from the watchful eyes of their parents.

A series of world fairs or expositions—in Chicago (1893), Atlanta (1895), Nashville (1897), Omaha (1898), Buffalo (1901), and St. Louis (1904)—introduced millions of middle-class women and men to the new world of commercial amusements for the first time. Visitors to these expositions encountered two sharply opposing districts. In one district, the fair's managers featured high culture; they built an ideal, orderly world that included monumental, usually classical, architecture as well as exhibitions of modern science and technology. In the other district, the Midway, entertainment and spectacle ruled supreme. Here, visitors could find garish signs and posters, overdecorated buildings, roller-coaster rides, and stage shows of singers, dancers, comics, and acrobats. To make suspicious visitors feel more comfortable, observed historian David Nasaw, "the concessionaires cloaked their amusements in educational disguise." For example, they billed the performances of gyrating belly dancers as "authentic foreign" dances and women in tights or in skin-tight bathing suits as acrobats or championship swimmers.

Across the country, similar strategies employed by local fairs and traveling circuses helped to break down the middle class's resistance to commercial amusements.

The entrepreneurs of entertainment won a series of smashing victories. By cleansing itself of profanity, smoking, alcohol, and prostitution, vaudeville—while continuing to feature a mix of rowdy singers, jugglers, acrobats, magicians, animal acts, and comics—entered a new age of prosperity and acceptability. "Ladies and Children can [now] safely attend without an escort," claimed Tony Pastor, a former choirboy and a pioneer in courting the patronage of middle-class women who had long been taught to shun the stage and its fruits as the devil's work. "No drink stronger than ice water" would be sold at the shows, boasted Pastor.

While most members of the middle class continued to avoid the traditional saloon (still patronized mainly by the working class), as early as the 1890s in the larger cities restaurant owners began to open cabarets and nightclubs atop hotels and near theater districts. Because dining was the stated function of these establishments, middle-class men and women felt more comfortable about listening to live music, watching professional dancers, or dancing themselves. The cabaret, concluded Lewis Erenberg in his study of New York City nightlife, "relaxed boundaries between the sexes, between audiences and performers, between ethnic groups and Protestants, between black culture and whites." In the 1910s, a dance hall craze swept the country. People danced in new, more provocative ways. The Turkey Trot, the Bunny Hug, the Grizzly Bear, and the more lasting Fox Trot (all animal names suggestive of more sensuality and less self-restraint in dancing) increasingly replaced the more stately waltz. Lavish ballrooms, live music, and usually the absence of alcohol at least partly reassured those middle-class patrons concerned about the abandonment of personal control.

Near the turn of the century, every large city in the country hosted at least one outdoor amusement park, complete with band pavilions, circus acts, and mechanical contrivances such as Ferris wheels, all located in exotic settings. "Coney Island has a code of conduct which is all her own," Guy Carryl explained in 1901. While at amusement parks, patrons felt more comfortable in suspending at least some of their middle-class proprieties. Unlike the gender-segregated leisure of the nineteenth century, the younger members of both sexes and all classes came together at amusement parks where they cavorted, laughed merrily, talked loudly, and embraced one another openly.

A freer spirit also invaded popular music. Until late in the nineteenth century, hymns as well as nostalgic and mournful songs that were frequently drenched in sentimentality and moral uplift characterized popular music. Then, in the so-called Gay Nineties, far more cheerful, energetic, and even sensually suggestive tunes spread through the midways and the burgeoning sheet music industry. The lively marches of John Philip Sousa became a national rage. While roundly condemned by its opponents as black brothel music, the lusty exuberance of ragtime seemed to allow millions of white Americans to imagine that they too could enjoy the freedom from restraints which they attributed to African Americans. Ragtime's "primitive rhythms . . . excite the basic human instincts," concluded a critic of the new music. To the proponents of music as an instrument for promoting self-control and as a source of moral uplift, the arrival of jazz among white audiences in the 1920s was even more startling and dangerous. The emotional release triggered by jazz, according to a critic, led to a "blatant disregard of even the elementary rules of civilization."

In the end, no new form of commercial entertainment equaled the popularity of the movies. While the movies originated in unsavory all-male arcades and cheap working-class nickelodeons, they soon achieved their greatest successes in the huge neoclassical movie palaces of the 1920s. By the end of the decade one

Archive Photos

Midland Beach, Staten Island, 1898. This beach scene suggests a modest retreat from the all-important middle-class concern with self-control. At the beach, as at amusement parks, vaudeville, and later the movies, the sexes and social classes mingled together indiscriminately. In the twentieth century, leisure increasingly became something to be indulged in for its own sake.

hundred million people a week went to the movies, a figure roughly equal to the nation's population. As in the amusement parks, the classes and the sexes (but not usually the races) mixed indiscriminately. Frequently treating movie-goers to a world of lavish homes, fast cars, and equally fast dance steps, films suggested several avenues of escape from Victorian restraints.

Paradoxically, the movies catered to both modern and traditional values. Reeling from criticism of the salacious contents of its films, Hollywood in 1922 set up a censorship office under Will Hays. While Hays permitted sexual sug-gestiveness and innuendo, he carefully monitored which portions of the female anatomy could be exposed on film and insisted that those guilty of promiscuous sex on film be properly punished. In their conclusions, if not in earlier scenes, Hays mandated that the films had to reaffirm traditional values.

THE STRENUOUS LIFE

During the 1890s and in the first three decades of the twentieth century the impulse of the urban, white-collar-centered middle class to relax its empha-sis on decorum and restraint also led in the direction of a more strenuous life. In communing with untamed nature, in more rugged physical activities, and in competitive athletics, growing numbers of Americans saw opportunities not only to enjoy more intense experiences in controlled settings but also to improve their health.

No single person incarnated and popularized the principles of the strenu-ous life more fully than Theodore Roosevelt, the nation's president from 1901 to 1909. Sickly as a youth, Roosevelt took boxing lessons and worked out reg-ularly with dumbbells and horizontal bars for his entire life. In his twenties he left the safety of the East to take up the hazardous life of a cowboy in the Dakotas. With the outbreak of the Spanish-American War in 1898, he orga-nized and led a cavalry unit of cowboys and college students that won national renown for their bravery in Cuba. Preaching to and bullying opponents both at home and abroad, Roosevelt as president enthralled the nation with his vigor. "In life, as in a football game," he once advised the nation's boys, "the principle to follow is: Hit the line hard, don't foul, and don't shirk, but hit the line hard."

Roosevelt's vigor and physicality reflected larger national trends. Musclemen Eugen Sandow and Bernarr MacFadden became national celebri-ties; MacFadden, a friend of Roosevelt's, declared in the first issue of his mag-azine, *Physical Culture* (1899), that "Weakness Is a Crime." In the 1890s a bicycling rage swept across the nation; astride their "wheels," men, women, and children experienced a new sense of physical freedom as they pedaled away from the confines of their homes through the city streets and into the countryside. In the summers, growing numbers of middle-class Americans fled to the seasides and to the mountain resorts. Those seeking more physically demanding vacations hiked, canoed, and camped. Nature lovers embarked on a national campaign to preserve the last of the nation's wildernesses as national parks. Bird-watching became something of a national mania; in a six-year span Boston and New York publishers sold more than seventy thousand books on birds. "A bird on the wing," historian John Higham has speculated, ". . . symbolize[d] for Americans the boundless space they wished to inhabit."

The middle class began to shed much of its suspicions of commercial sports. Earlier, "respectable" people had frequently associated baseball with drinking, gambling, and a loss of self-control, but during the first two decades of the twentieth century the sport "came of age." Gaining acceptability among nearly all social groups, baseball truly became America's "National Game." Even the president of the nation extended his endorsement; in 1910 William Howard Taft established the precedent of the president's opening each season by throwing out the first ball. By then, every city, town, and village of any consequence fielded at least one amateur, semiprofessional, or professional team. The annual World Series (begun in 1903) between the pennant winners of the American and National Leagues became an annual fall rite that furnished an exciting conclusion to regular season play.

The growth in the popularity of college football also reflected the larger quest for excitement. Initially a sport organized and managed by students of upper-class origins, college football "took off" as a commercial spectacle in the 1890s. Locked in circulation wars, the daily newspapers devoted a staggering amount of space to the gridiron wars of the nation's colleges. "Thanksgiving day is no longer a solemn festival to God for mercies given," declared *The New York Herald* in 1893. "It is a holiday granted by the State and the Nation to see a game of football." No sport equaled the capacity of college football in allowing middle-class spectators to express strong emotions within socially acceptable settings.

The development of an ideology of strenuosity accompanied the growth of the commercial sporting spectacles. Earlier, only a small band of "muscular" Christians had had the temerity to suggest that individual and national strength required as much attention to physical fitness as it did to work and to the cultivation of spirituality. But by the 1890s certain members of families of old wealth and a rising corps of experts on the human body were insisting that properly regulated sports and other vigorous forms of physicality were essential to the nation's well-being. "No amount of commercial prosperity can supply the lack of heroic virtues" that were all too prevalent in modern America, Theodore Roosevelt said. To counter the "over-civilized" life, Roosevelt advocated the cultivation of the virtues found in the soldier, the cowboy, and the prizefighter.

The enthusiasm for strenuosity penetrated deeply into the American psyche. It encouraged an admiration for Civil War generals, for medieval knights, for Napoleon, and for foreign adventurism. It shaped the contents of a massive outpouring of boys' literature. Frank Merriwell, the hero of more than two hundred books written by Gilbert Patten, became a shorthand way of describing a boy who not only possessed middle-class Protestant virtues but who could also more than hold his own in physical combat and on the field of play. While downplaying class, ethnic, and racial identities, strenuous activities offered fraternal bonding experiences for men and boys.

The ideology of strenuosity was a core ingredient in a mammoth set of programs designed to manage the spare-time activities of the nation's adolescent boys. In the 1890–1920 era the Young Men's Christian Association, urban churches, public schools, city playground associations, and the Boy Scouts became major sponsors of organized physical activities for boys. Even the more fervent evangelical Protestants, who had once been highly suspicious of sports, became converts to the idea that within controlled settings competitive physical activity could be beneficial to both society and the individual.

CHANGING CONCEPTIONS OF MANLINESS AND FEMININITY

The ideology of strenuosity suggested changing ideas about the proper roles of the sexes. Earlier, *manliness* to the middle class had meant the opposite of childlike; it signified adulthood, maturity, and self-control. But as the opportunities for the overt expressions of manliness in the workplace declined and as male social dominance seemed less secure, manliness, even within middle-class circles, acquired tougher, more assertive qualities. It included the negation of all that was considered soft, feminine, and sentimental. Manly men purged longings for ease and comfort; they welcomed strife, exertion, and physical risks. Near the end of the nineteenth century, daring cowboys, detectives, soldiers, adventurers, and athletes began to replace industrialists, statesmen, clergymen, and literati as manly heroes.

Reflecting in part the formation of an army of female office workers, sales clerks, teachers, and social workers—a development that liberated growing numbers of younger women from the home—the boundaries of acceptable physical freedom for women began to relax. The bicycling craze of the 1890s led the way. An ad for Victor bicycles in 1895 depicted a young woman sitting at a spinning wheel (the woman of the past) and another on her bicycle (the woman of the future). Accompanying the ad was the verse:

> The Spinning Wheels of days gone by
> Give way to Spinning Wheels that fly.
> And damsels fair to lightly tread
> the graceful Victor now, instead.

While critics worried that bicycling might lure young women away from the home and its duties, lead them to remote spots alone with men, where they might be seduced, or stimulate the genitals, resulting in equally unimaginable horrors, cycling not only conjured up images of a more autonomous woman emancipated from Victorian inhibitions but also led to freer forms of female dress. Between about 1895 and World War I, the Gibson Girl (named after the popular drawings of Charles Dana Gibson) became a special heroine of the new urban white-collar class. Witty, sophisticated, and flirtatious, she was at ease on the dance floor, the golf course, the tennis court, or on a bicycle.

Of course there were limits on female physical freedom. Prior to the 1920s, any female activity that smacked too much of manliness or the loss of self-control was roundly condemned. Play for the Gibson Girl required discretion and moderation; for example, a proper woman did not dare place a croquet mallet between her legs to execute a more effective shot or, if playing tennis, smash overheads or run swiftly about the court. Even in the more liberated 1920s, the public admired most those female athletes who retained feminine qualities. While sportswriters dubbed tennis star Helen Wills "Little Miss Poker Face" because she wore a "false, unnatural front . . . like a cold gray veil" when she played, they reassured fans that off the court she was the epitome of femininity—a "gay, sprightly, pleasing young girl who could enjoy herself and be gracious in the process."

Emerging as the nation's foremost commercial entertainment industry from the late 1880s to the end of the 1920s, the theater, which included not only vaudeville, but also musical reviews, comedies, and the so-called legitimate theater, presented the mass public with new models of femininity. While in her performances the enormously popular actress Sara Bernhardt bridged Victorian and modern sensibilities by oscillating between romantic grandeur and unapologetic sexuality, *Salome*, a play that took the nation by storm in the first years of the twentieth century, depicted a woman who in the Dance of the Seven Veils seemed to surrender herself completely to her erotic impulses. But the theater also increasingly offered tamer versions of femininity. In the 1910s and 1920s Broadway invented a fantasy world of alluring but non-threatening women. On stage, as historian Susan Glenn has argued, the chorus girls appeared as obedient sex objects; off the stage, on the other hand, the girls became the symbols of modern womanhood. Paradoxically, they were both the prey and the predator, the exploited and the exploiters, the domesticated pet (the "chick") and the wild animal (the "tigress"). Such contradictory and confusing models of femininity soon became the mainstays of modern womanhood.

A Gibson Girl. While exhibiting impeccable posture, modestly dressed, and in complete control of her bicycle, this
turn-of-the-century cycling Gibson Girl suggests the possibility of a new degree of female autonomy. Astride her
bicycle, the most adventuresome of the Gibson Girls
might ride away from chaperones, family, and at least
some of the middle-class Victorian expectations of women.

North Wind Picture Archives

CONCLUSION

The years between the 1880s and the 1930s constituted something of a water-
shed in the history of American ways. It was in this era that the development
of a new middle class, the growth of large business organizations, the rise of
a mass-manufacturing economy, and new forms of advertising and entertainment encouraged the adoption of values and behaviors conducive to consumption. For growing numbers of Americans, self-control—at least in one's
leisure time—increasingly gave way to greater self-indulgence and a quest
for more excitement. As we shall see in the next chapter, the edifice supporting traditional religious beliefs and the Victorian conception of high culture
weakened. By the 1920s, the nation was in the midst of a new cultural era, one
that for the lack of a better name scholars have labeled as "modern."

18

THE ORIGINS OF THE MODERN
INTELLECTUAL AND ARTISTIC WORLD

At the very moment that middle-class ways commanded their greatest respect and power in American life, they confronted new challenges to their supremacy. As we have seen in the previous chapter, the profusion of new consumer goods and the new opportunities for excitement eroded support for the all-important middle-class value of self-control. But an equally important challenge arose from within the intellectual and artistic world of the late nineteenth and early twentieth centuries. Influential thinkers began to question the bedrock premises of the Victorian belief system. These included the conviction that humans lived in an orderly universe presided over by a benevolent God, belief in a world of absolute truths, and faith in the power of the arts to tame human passions and improve human behavior.

These thinkers contributed to the decline of reliance on religious explanations and a growing respect for the secular authority of science. Even the more religiously inclined frequently acquiesced to or even welcomed scientific explanations of the physical world. They recognized that keeping certain kinds of inquiry free of religious ideas and influences had practical advantages. For example, most religious people at the turn of the century would have viewed with skepticism a claim that a train had jumped the tracks because of God or the Devil. "So in modern America," as historian George Marsden has observed, ". . . scientists and technicians of all sorts, no matter how religious, are expected to check their religious beliefs at the door when they enter the laboratory."

At the end of the Victorian era in the early years of the twentieth century, other spheres of American culture were slipping away from religious influence and control as well. For example, religiously sanctioned marriages in Muncie, Indiana, the sociologist team of Helen and Robert Lynd found, fell from 85 percent in 1890 to 63 percent in 1923. The burgeoning cities were for the most part more secular and less morally strict than rural and small-town America. "Freed from the benevolent restraints of the small town, thousands of young men and women in every great city have received none of the lessons in self-control which even savage tribes imparted to their appetites as well as their emotions," complained social reformer Jane Addams in 1911. Likewise, the giant corporations were more immune to religious influence than were small businesses.

SHAKING THE RELIGIOUS FOUNDATIONS

On the surface, Protestant churches, which had always been at the heart of middle-class ways, never seemed stronger than at the beginning of the twentieth century. Membership, attendance, and revenues were growing at least as fast as the population. In the larger cities, affluent Protestants were building massive gothic churches and promoting a social gospel to ease some of the ravages that the Industrial Revolution had inflicted on the less fortunate. In the early twentieth century, the Protestant churches were at the forefront of the Progressive reform movement. The churches led efforts for civic renewal, cleansing government of corruption, curbing the power of big business, and prohibiting the consumption of alcoholic beverages.

Yet during these same years new ideas directly challenged the very foundations of religious orthodoxy. In the second half of the nineteenth century, "higher criticism," a movement launched earlier by German scholars to subject the Bible to the scrutiny and criticism commonly employed in examining other historical texts, gained momentum in the United States. The higher critics no longer began their inquiries based on the premise that the Bible was supernatural in origin. In 1896, Andrew Dickson White, a founder of Cornell University, described the authority of Scripture as "the tyranny of sacred books imperfectly transcribed, [and] viewed through distorting superstitions." The higher critics saw the Bible as simply a literary text, one composed by ancient Israelites and early Christians to preserve a record of their religious experiences. Furthermore, scholars increasingly considered Christianity as among the world's major religions, but not a religion especially ordained by God.

The theory of evolution presented an equally serious challenge to religious orthodoxy. Whereas the Bible asserted that all species were God's immutable creations, Englishman Charles Darwin in his *Origin of Species* (1859) argued instead that all plants and animals had evolved over eons of time through a process he called "natural selection." Not only did such a theory seem to eliminate the need to call upon a supernatural power to explain the existence of flora and fauna, but also it reduced the elevated position within the universe that humans had long claimed for themselves. Now rather than special creations of God, humans were said to have evolved from lower life forms. In this crucial sense, humans were no different than other plants and animals.

Charles Darwin. The English naturalist Darwin's book *Origin of Species* (1859) challenged not only the Bible's account of the creation of plants and animals but also the idea that humans occupied a special place in that creation. Darwin's theories and the implications flowing from them had (and continue to have) an enormously important influence on American intellectual and religious life.

Contrary to much that has been written on the subject, evolution did *not* become a major subject of popular debate until the 1920s. Before that, many Protestant theologians had reached a compromise with Darwinism. They simply asserted that evolution was God's way of creating and directing natural forces. Interpreting evolution as an engine of material and moral progress also increased its acceptability among Americans. But while these compromises seemingly answered the charges that Darwinism required an abandonment of religious belief, they failed to halt the general trend toward a growing reliance on a worldview grounded in nature and science rather than in the supernatural.

By the 1910s the united front that Protestant churches had presented throughout much of the nineteenth century could no longer be taken for granted. Not only were growing numbers of Roman Catholics and Jews confuting the notion that the United States was a distinctively Protestant nation, but also a major cleavage was beginning to develop within the larger Protestant consensus. Responding to the transformation of the middle class resulting from the massive infusions of new white-collar workers, to the allure of refinement, to the problems of industrialism, and to the challenges presented by Darwinism and higher criticism of the Bible, one group of Protestants—variously labeled as "liberal" or "modern"—retreated from evangelical orthodoxy. Theologically, these Protestants emphasized the ethical rather than the supernatural or miraculous aspects of the biblical narrative.

Not surprisingly, their retreat from orthodoxy provoked a vigorous response. The orthodox, who would become known as "fundamentalists," continued to insist that the Bible was the Word of God and inerrant in all its teachings. In the 1920s, the split between fundamentalist and modernist Protestants widened. It remains to this day an important division within American Protestantism.

SECULARIZATION AND EDUCATION

Since schools were major transmitters of society's values and beliefs, they played a key role in the broader process of secularizing American life. During the public school movement of the antebellum era, the schools had been virtual extensions of the nation's Protestant churches. Teachers not only required students to recite the Protestant version of the Lord's Prayer and to read the King James (Protestant) version of the Bible in the classroom but taught Protestant theological doctrines as well. Seeking to avoid controversy in the face of Catholic protests, the public schools began in the middle decades of the nineteenth century to slowly retreat to a more secular stance. While retaining an emphasis on traditional morality, the later editions of McGuffey's *Eclectic Readers*, the most popular textbook of the day, moderated their religious messages. By the early twentieth century, John Dewey, who was to exercise an incalculable influence on American education for more than a half-century, was even proposing that teachers no longer indoctrinate their charges with fixed truths and absolute moral principles. Instead, Dewey urged teachers to impress on students the tentative, pragmatic nature of all knowledge.

A similar trend occurred in higher education. Prior to the Civil War, ministerial training had been the main purpose of the nation's colleges; nearly all of them had clerics as presidents, required chapel attendance, and taught Protestant theological tenets. Even as late as 1915, it was still "customary in state universities, no less than denominational colleges, to question a candidate for appointment concerning his church connections. Any church connection will do," claimed an article in *The Nation*. Nonetheless, by World War I, religion and religious points of view no longer occupied a central place in the curriculum of most colleges. By then, students could take dozens of courses without hearing any reference whatsoever to religion.

Neither the faculties nor the administrators deliberately set out to secularize the nation's fast-growing system of higher education. Quite the contrary. The educators in the universities, like their pre–Civil War predecessors, sought to impress on the minds of their students the unity of all knowledge. "For them," as historian Julie A. Reuben has argued, "the term *truth* encompassed all 'correct knowledge.'" Whether derived from common sense, science, or religion, all truths were of the same family; they emanated from the same God. Hence, no inherent conflict existed between the truths of science, morality, or religion.

Despite strenuous efforts by turn-of-the-century educators to preserve and promote the unity of all knowledge, their task became increasingly difficult. Darwinism in particular presented a formidable challenge. How could belief in the harmony of truths be sustained when evolution offered an account of the origin of the species completely at odds with scripture? Furthermore, Darwin's theory called into question the contention that the order observed in the universe was proof of God's existence ("the argument from design"). Not only did Darwinism seem to contradict the fundamental premises necessary for belief in the unity of truths, but also it encouraged scientists to reject efforts to adjust their conclusions to fit popular religious or moral beliefs. Indeed, scientists increasingly sought to separate their work from religious and moral dogma. They insisted on a model of science that began with the open questioning of received truths and required the experimental verification of hypotheses.

Neither did the faculties nor the administrators of the universities intend to foment a revolt against the Victorian ideology of culture. Indeed, they continued to urge their students to subordinate material pursuits to the cultivation of the mind and to value the fine arts over the practical arts. Properly trained to appreciate the finer things in life, they envisioned such young men and women evolving into a disinterested, cultivated elite that would take over and ennoble newspaper editorships, political offices, the professions, business firms, and the other seats of power and influence in America. On the campuses themselves, dozens of eloquent professors of English, history, philosophy, and the classics introduced thousands of students to "great" novels, poems, philosophical treatises, and histories.

Yet the proponents of steeping students in the ideology of culture won no smashing victories. Undergraduates typically devoted far more of their energy to their social lives than to Shakespeare or Goethe. Rather than entering college to become connoisseurs of high culture, the students came mostly to obtain degrees that would enhance their prospects for acceptance into high society or allow them to enter occupations that qualified them for admission into the upper ranks of the new white-collar class. At best, students majoring in engineering, agriculture, or business took only a few courses in the arts and the humanities.

SHAKING THE INTELLECTUAL FOUNDATIONS

New ideas in philosophy and the social sciences also inflicted damage on the intellectual foundations of Victorian culture. Social scientists increasingly sought to understand the "laws" or "principles" that governed society without resorting to supernatural authority or assumptions that a superintending pur- pose (for example, God's) guided the universe. Influenced by Darwinism, they sometimes reached startling conclusions. For example, William Graham Sumner, a minister turned Yale professor, once declared that "man had no more right to life than a rattlesnake; he has no more right to liberty than any wild beast; his right to pursue happiness is nothing but a license to maintain the struggle for existence. . . ." Others, such as Lester Ward, sought to soften the implications for humans of a world devoid of ultimate purpose. Since (unlike other animals) humans had minds capable of invention and control, Ward rea- soned, they could to some degree escape the rigors of the struggle for existence.

Perhaps no two intellectuals were more responsible for preparing the way for modernism in America than William James and John Dewey. A product of a New England literary family, early in his career James rejected the typi- cal Victorian dichotomy between humans and animals. He became a convert to the Darwinian premise that humans existed on a continuum with other animals. As with the brains of other animals, the human brain was simply a biological organ that had evolved capacities for selecting and employing perceptions that were useful for the species' survival.

While the human mind could formulate abstract concepts based upon these perceptions, these concepts were necessarily selective and distortions of "truth" or the reality presumed to exist outside the senses. "No theory is absolutely a transcript of reality," wrote James. To conclude that truths were proximate or relative was, to say the least, unsettling to many of James's con- temporaries. But, to James himself and those influenced by him, it opened up an infinitely exciting new way of looking at the world. Ultimately, it com- pletely annihilated the possibility of assuming that such Victorian conceptual polarities as human/animal, man/woman, and civilized/savage had a "real" existence apart from how humans thought about them.

Dewey, who described ideas as instruments to be tried out in the real world, had a similar outlook. Without predetermining the ultimate shape of society, Dewey proposed to employ the methods of science to reach judg- ments about whether human institutions and traditional practices improved the odds for survival and/or enhanced the quality of life. If alternatives (including some variant of socialism) proved superior by these twin tests, then society should consider their adoption. A broadened meaning of democracy followed from Dewey's reasoning. Rather than consisting only of the principles of individual liberty and equality of opportunity, Dewey argued that democracy should also include the principle of "fraternity" or "community." Only through a rich communal life, Dewey said, could individuals fully realize their potentialities and obtain their fullest personal satisfactions.

Although by no means fully recognized at the time, "the culture of inquiry" that Dewey and James among others were helping to create contributed to growing fissures in the very footings of Victorian culture. In history, Frederick Jackson Turner ascribed American democracy to the existence of a

John Dewey Presenting the American Woman's Association Award to Margaret Sanger, 1932. Both Dewey and Sanger were extraordinarily important figures in undermining Victorian culture and ushering in modern America. Dewey, a philosopher, educator, and reformer, proposed the abandonment of earlier certainties and a startlingly new way for humans to cope with the world (frequently summed up in the term *pragmatism*), while Sanger virtually founded the twentieth-century birth-control movement and abetted the growing popularity of a "modern" sexual ideology.

frontier (a naturalistic explanation) and Charles A. Beard argued that the nation's founders, when drawing up the Constitution, were guided as much by their personal as by the public interest. Oliver Wendell Holmes, Jr., and Roscoe Pound concluded that law arose not from eternal verities but from day-to-day human experience. And Thorstein Veblen insisted that modern institutions, such as marriage, were simply survivals from earlier historical eras (and hence frequently archaic) rather than the products of immutable natural laws or institutions ordained by God.

SHAKING THE LITERARY AND ARTISTIC FOUNDATIONS

New developments in literature and the arts also foreshadowed the arrival of modern ways. In the latter half of the nineteenth century, a group of writers, magazine editors, book publishers, Protestant ministers, art gallery directors, and college professors constituted the guardians of the Victorian or genteel conception of culture. Led by New Englanders, they saw the best in literature and the fine arts, and refined tastes and good manners as major pillars of morality and as sources of noble ideals. A shared culture, they believed, could serve as a powerful social adhesive. It could help to tie together an otherwise divided people.

As powerful as these guardians of culture were, their ideology of culture had never held complete sway over American life. Neither vaudeville, minstrel shows, dime novels, nor comic books ever met their moral or esthetic standards. From the standpoint of genteel culture, the popular cultural forms too often placed considerations of entertainment and amusement before the value of edification. In addition, several of the nation's distinguished writers bridled at the arrogance and pretentiousness of the New England literati and their followers. "I have never tried . . . to help cultivate the cultivated classes," sneered Mark Twain, the Missouri-born novelist and humorist. With "the word Culture," added poet Walt Whitman, "we find ourselves abruptly in close quarters with the enemy."

Without breaking completely with the prevailing conventions of their age, first European and then American novelists and poets in the 1880–1920 era began exploring new subject matter that frequently shocked Victorian sensibilities. One region of exploration was the depths of the mind that lay below and frequently hidden from rational thought. For example, in a moving short story, "The Yellow Wallpaper," Charlotte Perkins Gilman described the mental breakdown of a Victorian woman imprisoned in the domestic sphere. Novelists also began to explore the underside of Victorian life—the world of crime, prostitution, brutality, depravity, and poverty. Sometimes labeled as literary naturalists and frequently influenced by Darwinism, these writers told stories of people whose lives were governed by natural forces beyond their control. The premise of such stories ran counter to the Victorian faith in the capacities of humans to determine their own destinies.

A similar trend occurred in the visual arts. At the turn of the century a group of New York painters, known as the Ashcan School, breached the Victorian dichotomy between "life" and "art" and departed from Victorian subject matter by depicting gritty street scenes and the vibrancy of working-class life. "A child of the slums will make a better painting than a drawing room lady gone over by a beauty salon," exclaimed George Luks, one of the Ashcan painters. Even more shocking to Victorian sensibilities were the paintings exhibited at the Armory Show in New York City in 1913. There, Americans saw for the first time European avant-garde or abstract paintings, paintings that made no pretenses of representing likenesses to objects that could be seen with the eyes or captured on camera. Neither did the "modern" painters accept the Victorian notion that art should be morally uplifting or inspiring; instead, they frequently endorsed as a rationale for their work the aphorism "art for art's sake."

In the years immediately preceding World War I the Armory Show was just one indication of the beginnings of a far larger literary and artistic uprising. Another was the development of Greenwich Village in New York City as the gathering place for a group of young men and women who openly flaunted their rejection of middle-class ways. They adopted experimental, bohemian lifestyles. The women bobbed their hair and smoked and drank in public, women and men lived openly together outside of marriage, and whites fraternized with blacks and Jews with gentiles. The Village not only became the center of avant-garde painting, music, literature, and drama but also served as the major entrepôt for the latest European ideas.

Several currents of thought influenced these "modernist" rebels. As we have seen, Darwinism unleashed a profound rethinking of the nature of mind, religion, and morality. Many of the young rebels owed large debts to such American thinkers as James, Dewey, and Veblen. In the immediate prewar years, radicalism, especially that of the homegrown Industrial Workers of the World, inspired the Greenwich Village rebels. They also seized upon such daring European writers as Karl Marx, Friederich Nietzsche, Oscar Wilde, George Bernard Shaw, and Henrik Ibsen and such painters as Paul Cézanne and Vincent van Gogh.

Above all, Sigmund Freud, the Viennese doctor who invented psycho analysis, provided them with ammunition for casting aside the strictures of middle-class ways. Unlike the Victorians who viewed the mind as a conscious, rational, lightening-quick, almost error-free, calculating machine, Freud emphasized the unconscious, that portion of the mind often inaccessible to

Indianapolis Museum of Art/The Bridgeman Art Library

Red Kimono on the Roof (1912). In this painting John Sloan depicts in unsentimental terms an ordinary woman hanging up laundry on the roof of a tenement house. Perhaps he painted it looking down from the window of his studio. In any case, with their realistic paintings of life in New York City's Lower East Side, Sloan and other so-called Ashcan painters helped to foment the "modernist" artistic rebellion in early twentieth-century America.

conscious comprehension or control. Within the unconscious (the id) dwelled powerful primitive instincts. Of these, the sexual drive was by far the most potent. These desires or drives, said Freud, were locked in a never-ending struggle with the conscious (the ego), which determined what a person could do, and the moral values (the superego), which prescribed what a person should do. Although Freud offered no easy resolution of the warring impulses within the psyche, his popularizers frequently suggested or implied that the freeing of instinctual drives (especially the sexual) could result in greater individual happiness.

World War I (1914–18) hastened the arrival of the modern literary and artistic rebellion. The war irreparably damaged the Victorian faith in moral progress and in the unity of Euro-American culture. "The plunge of civilization into the abyss of blood and horror," wrote aging novelist Henry James, "so gives away the whole long age during which we have supposed the world to be gradually bettering and [the] meaning is too tragic for words." Stripping life and death of dignity and eroding confidence, the war encouraged the young intellectuals to turn inward, to the self rather than to society, for inspiration and fulfillment. With the war, "the bohemian tendency triumphed in the Village," Malcolm Cowley later wrote, "and talk about revolution gave way to talk about psychoanalysis."

The rebellion reached a kind of fruition in the 1920s. Not since the 1840s and 1850s had the nation witnessed such a flowering of literary and artistic works, many of which were destined to become classics. They included the poetry of T. S. Eliot and Ezra Pound; novels by F. Scott Fitzgerald, Ernest Hemingway, Willa Cather, and William Faulkner; and the paintings of Edward Hopper, Charles Sheeler, and Georgia O'Keefe. Frank Lloyd Wright led an idiosyncratic but ultimately modernist movement in architecture. And finally there was jazz, America's most original contribution to the world's music.

The rebels universally attacked what they usually called puritanism, by which they meant Victorian America rather than the historical Puritanism about which they knew little. Puritanism, as Charles A. Beard wrote, became an epithet for "anything that interfere[d] with the new freedom, free verse, psychoanalysis, or even the double entendre." It had overvalued respectability, propriety, and material things while restricting the pursuit of pleasure and choking off creativity. Prizing novelty and originality, the rebels valued art for its own sake and its capacity to provide personal liberation from conventions rather than for its capacity to instruct or provide moral uplift. The rebels frequently turned upside down or merged the polarities that were so precious to the Victorians. They gloried in the presumed innocence of childhood, in the primitive, and in the impulsive.

In the end, the rebellion nearly destroyed the Victorian ideology of culture. No longer did England, the slavish admirers of English high culture, nor the northeastern white Protestant intellectuals exercise such a commanding influence over the nation's high culture. The center of the nation's intellectual life shifted from Boston and its environs to New York City and to Chicago. Several of the most prominent of the young writers and artists became expatriates; they fled the country for the friendlier confines of the Left Bank in Paris. Freer of racial, ethnic, and gender prejudice than most Americans, the rebels experimented with greater sexual equality and praised the artistic works of the black Harlem Renaissance. Even before World War I, Jewish intellectuals began to achieve a special prominence. In the 1930s, the diaspora of Jews from fascist Europe added to the heterogeneous and cosmopolitan character of the nation's literary and artistic leadership.

Not only did the rebels consciously break with earlier standards of art and literature, but also they experienced a profound alienation from the mainstream of American society. Victorian intellectuals had shared the major assumptions of their age and had believed that they had a large responsibility in instructing and uplifting the masses. Although several of the most creative intellectuals had long been critical of mass tastes (consider for example Henry David Thoreau), the intensity of their estrangement had never been as great as that experienced by the artists and literati of the 1920s. Their rebellion fostered a widening chasm between the artistic and literary community on the one side and society on the other.

CONCLUSION

Not only did changes wrought in American consumer and leisure ways at the turn of the twentieth century herald the beginnings of modern ways, but so did new developments in American thought. Higher criticism of the Bible and the theory of evolution challenged a worldview based on belief in an all-powerful, superintending God. Social scientists sought to develop theories of social behavior without reference to God, and philosophers William James and John Dewey propounded the view that the "truth" available to humans was relative and proximate rather than absolute. Equally important challenges to Victorian convictions came from literature and the arts. By the 1920s, an influential set of literary and artistic rebels rejected the view that the main purpose of the arts was to provide inspiration and moral uplift. Eroding if not shattering the foundations of the middle-class world view, the new ideas were setting the stage for the appearance of a radically new cultural paradigm.

THE COMING OF AGE OF MODERN WAYS

No one knows for certain when the term *modern* was first used to describe a set of ways associated with the twentieth century. Perhaps English novelist Virginia Woolf was responsible. At least nearly all subsequent writers on modern ways seem to feel obligated to quote her statement that "on or about December 1910, human character changed." Or perhaps it was Nebraska-reared novelist Willa Cather, who wrote, "The world broke in two in 1922 or thereabouts." While scholars quarrel about an exact date for the arrival of modern ways, they have increasingly come to agree that sometime early in the twentieth century there was a profound shift in sensibility. In its vanguard stood a group of rebellious artists and intellectuals. These rebels embarked on a remarkable explosion of creativity—in painting, music, and sculpture, in architecture, in the novel, and in poetry.

But the intelligentsia was not the only group to engage in new modes of thinking, seeing, hearing, and behaving. Eventually modern ways would come to encompass much of American life in the twentieth century. The adherents of modern ways counted more on expertise than on personal character, more on the accumulation of information than on folk wisdom, more on moral relativism than absolute notions of right and wrong, and more on a secular-scientific outlook than on a religiously orthodox worldview. Above all else, they placed less emphasis on self-control and more on self-fulfillment than their nineteenth-century predecessors.

Yet, while few Americans were willing to deny themselves all of the pleasures and the advantages offered by modern ways, many—indeed perhaps most—continued to build their lives around traditional ways. Even those who embraced modern ways most fully and enthusiastically frequently experienced agonizing doubts. In their personal if not in their public lives, they tried the difficult if not impossible task of accommodating the older with the newer ways.

19

MODERN WAYS IN TIMES OF PROSPERITY AND DEPRESSION

"A vast dissolution of ancient habits"—this was how columnist Walter Lippmann characterized the modern ways of the 1920s. While Lippmann surely exaggerated, the decade has struck observers then and since as a pivotal one in the history of American culture. It was in the 1920s that the trends we observed in the previous two chapters—the growing ethnic and religious pluralism of the United States, the development of a mass-consumption economy, the quest for greater excitement, and the increasing secularization of American life—all came into sharper focus. In that "decade of prosperity," millions of Americans joined in an unprecedented orgy of individual consumption. In the same decade, many Americans seemed to seize every opportunity they could to "have fun"; novelist F. Scott Fitzgerald called it "the jazz age," a label that conjured up images of primitive rhythms, of "flaming youth," and of unrestrained sexual behavior. In the 1920s, many Americans continued to retreat from a religiously based life. The "irreligion in the modern world [is] radical to a degree for which there is, I think, no counterpart," concluded Lippmann in 1929.

Responding to the Great Depression of the 1930s pulled Americans in opposing directions. In one direction, there was the powerful appeal of the past. It seemed to many that recovery from the economic disaster could be achieved only by renouncing the excesses of the 1920s. Americans must return to the virtues of yesteryear—to the self-control and hard work that had served them so well in the nineteenth century. In another direction, there was the allure of the future. The Great Depression, proponents of this view said, had discredited the idea that the economy could be left on its own. The state must in the future play a far greater role in guiding the nation's destiny.

THE CITY AS THE HOME OF MODERN WAYS

Modern ways enjoyed their greatest support in the cities. Not only did the majority of the American people now live in cities for the first time in the nation's history, but also city residents began to insist that the urban style of life was superior to that of the small town and the countryside. Life in the city, claimed its enthusiasts, was far more exciting, glamorous, fulfilling, and receptive to new ideas than in the countryside. To the delight of his big-city audiences in the 1920s, essayist H. L. Mencken characterized rural Americans as the "anthropoid rabble" who were determined to shield themselves "from whatever knowledge violated their superstitions."

The city also furnished the home for most of the nation's ethnic and religious minorities. In the 1920s, these "outsiders" began to articulate more boldly defenses of their own ways. To the advocates of the "new pluralism," one could be a loyal American without abandoning his or her ethnic or religious distinctiveness. A march on Washington by one hundred thousand Catholic men on September 21, 1924, vividly suggested the possibilities of the new pluralism. As representatives of the Catholic Holy Name Society, the men carried both papal banners *and* tiny U.S. flags. When they were addressed by Boston's William Cardinal O'Connell, who "flung the challenge to those who would question the loyalty of Catholics to America," the "entire assemblage . . . rose to its feet spontaneously and cheered so enthusiastically that it temporarily halted the address. . . ."

Such exhibitions of loyalty to the nation hardly implied an enthusiasm for complete cultural assimilation. If anything, ethnic and racial minorities stepped up their efforts to preserve their ways from the influence of the dominant culture; they sought to strengthen their kinship networks, their churches, and their voluntary associations. To a substantial degree, as historian Lizabeth Cohen has shown, ethnic stores, mutual-aid societies, and banks succeeded in resisting chain stores and other nationalizing institutions.

Even intercollegiate football rallied Catholics around their shared religious identity. Beginning in the 1920s Catholics everywhere, regardless of ethnic origins and even those who had never gone to college (dubbed by sportswriters as the "subway alumni" if they were from the cities or as the "coalfield alums" if they were from the Catholic communities in western Pennsylvania or eastern Ohio), became rabid fans of Notre Dame football. "The custom began in primary and secondary parochial schools, each Friday in the fall, to have students pray for a Notre Dame victory the next day," recalled Mary Jo Weaver, a professor of religion at Indiana University. "It was an important part of our 'Holy War' against the Protestant majority in America."

Supplemented by the arrival from the southern countryside of two million blacks in the 1910s and another million in the 1920s, the visibility of African Americans in the northern cities increased. In 1917 and in 1919, the presence of more blacks, competition for jobs, pressures on housing and public services, and racial prejudices spawned bloody race riots in more than a half-dozen northern cities, giving the lie to any thoughts that the cities were uniquely free of racism. In the 1920s, the Harlem Renaissance, a great outpouring of black literature, painting, and music, called national and even international attention to the nation's submerged black population. "Negro life is seizing its first chances for group expression and self-determination," asserted Alain Locke in an anthology revealingly entitled *The New Negro* (1926). The black role in popular entertainment, though as often as not confirming white stereotypes of African Americans, became more conspicuous than ever before. Those white Americans seeking freedom from Victorian constraints often found in the black jazz of Louis Armstrong and Duke Ellington and in the blues songs of Bessie Smith sources of personal liberation.

The northern urban experience encouraged a stronger racial consciousness and more aggressive efforts by blacks to assert rights. Rather than divert their energies into futile opposition to racial segregation and disfranchisement, Booker T. Washington had told blacks in the era preceding World War I that they should develop the skills and the self-discipline that would secure their self-respect and prove their economic worth to potential employers. But, in the same era, W. E. B. DuBois countered Washington by arguing that African Americans should insist on the restoration of their civil and political rights. Taking a similar position was the National Association for the Advancement of Colored People (NAACP), an organization cofounded by DuBois in 1910 that experienced rapid growth in membership among urban blacks in the 1920s. Receiving far more attention in the media of the 1920s was Marcus Garvey's Back to Africa movement. With a half-million followers, Garvey's movement promised racial glory in an Empire of Africa and sought to instill among the urban black poor a sense of racial pride and courage.

Representatives of minorities were not the only advocates of a new cultural pluralism. During the World War I era and afterwards, the artistic and literary rebels also welcomed ethnic and racial diversity; they conspicuously rejected both the value of a single, unitary culture as well as the Victorian ideology of culture. In place of the ideal of a single culture, Randolph Bourne argued as early as 1916 that the United States ought to adopt as its goal a cosmopolitan "federation of cultures." A member of the Greenwich Village circle, John Collier, who would later be appointed Commissioner of Indian Affairs by President Franklin D. Roosevelt, saw in the collectivism of Navajo Indian culture a healthy antidote to white individualism.

Even more "responsible for demolishing Victorian certainties about culture," contends historian Lewis Perry, were the anthropologists. Beginning with their teacher, Franz Boas, Margaret Mead in *Coming of Age in Samoa* (1928) and Ruth Benedict in *Patterns of Culture* (1934) introduced literally thousands of readers to the decidedly modern value of cultural pluralism. Mead even audaciously suggested that the adolescent girls in allegedly primitive cultures suffered from fewer anxieties than they did in the more repressive industrial cultures of Western societies.

THE "NEW" WOMAN AS A SYMBOL OF MODERN WAYS

Nothing was more central to the modern spirit of the 1920s than the arrival of the much-ballyhooed "new" woman. Well before the 1920s, urban middle- and upper-class women had begun to bump up against the perimeters of their "separate sphere." The bicycling craze, the Gibson Girl, and freer forms of dance all suggested an expanding realm of physical freedom for women. By 1920 women were attending coeducational high schools and colleges in record numbers, young women were pouring into the job market as secre- taries and sales clerks, and a few more women were entering the professions (especially teaching) than formerly. In 1920, with the ratification of the Nineteenth Amendment, women finally realized the long-deferred dream of nationwide suffrage.

But there was far more involved in the idea of the new woman than sports, education, jobs, and the right to vote. No longer a clone of her mother, according to a *Chicago Tribune* advertisement of the 1920s, the new woman relaxed self-imposed restraints. "Today's woman gets what she wants," flatly declared the ad. Fashionable consumption was important to the new woman's sense of personal well-being. She bought "glassware in sapphire blue or glowing amber," read the ad, and "soap to match her bathroom's color scheme." She was a more erotic creature than her mother. In dress, she replaced "voluminous petticoats" with "slim sheaths of silk." Rather than buying particular goods to establish her family's middle-class identity, she sought through consumption to refashion her own identity. Creative engage- ment with consumption could aid her in projecting images of youthful exu- berance, sex appeal, and urban sophistication, all of which, as historian Pamela Grundy has observed, "encouraged young women to judge them- selves largely through the reactions they produced on others, especially 'popularity' and attractiveness to men."

As the *Tribune* ad hinted, it was the young, unmarried, urban, middle-class woman, the flapper, who became the ultimate and perhaps most enduring symbol of the Jazz Age. In just about every respect imaginable, the flapper flaunted her rejection of the Victorian code of proper female behavior. Rather than behave as a model of propriety and self-restraint, the flapper talked freely, laughed gaily, gestured extravagantly, and, in the eyes of her Victorian predecessors, dressed immodestly. Blithely, she smoked and drank illegal alcoholic beverages. Indeed, she sometimes drank enough that it visibly affected her behavior. She bobbed her hair, flattened her breasts, threw away her corsets and petticoats, and shortened her skirts. Rather than pinching her cheeks to make them rosier, as her mother had done, she painted her cheeks with rouge—not so much to enhance her sexual appeal but to make another

Underwood & Underwood/Corbis

Flappers. Precariously but confidently dancing atop a skyscraper in the 1920s, these flappers openly defy the Victorian ways of their mothers. Representatives of the "modern" woman, the flappers took chances, used makeup, wore short skirts, and publicly exhibited their feelings.

gesture of defiance against older ways. The flappers also relaxed the traditional constraints on courtship. "None of the Victorian mothers—and most of the mothers were Victorian," wrote novelist F. Scott Fitzgerald, "had any idea of how casually their daughters were accustomed to being kissed."

The flapper danced with abandon. No longer did young people in the big cities dance the stately waltz at arm's length to the romantic notes of the violin. Instead, they now danced cheek-to-cheek in "a syncopated embrace" to the "barbaric" notes of the saxophone. There were, of course, pockets of resistance, even on college campuses. In 1921, the *Daily Nebraskan* described its campus as safely immunized against the "Eastern dances" and reported that University of Nebraska students had rallied behind "simple dress" as a means of returning the nation to "normalcy."

The flapper was not alone in helping to usher in modern sexuality. In the late Victorian age (1880s to World War I), some doctors, health reformers, and middle-class couples had already begun to dissolve the ages-old associations of sexual intercourse with sin and reproduction. By the turn of the century, according to historian Kathy Peiss, it was not unusual for working-class girls in the larger cities to exchange sexual favors for "treats" from men. In the meantime, influenced by Sigmund Freud, Havelock Ellis, and Ellen Key, the literary and artistic rebels in Greenwich Village and elsewhere advocated and practiced freer forms of sexuality. The sexual radicals insisted that women, like men, possessed erotic capacities and that sexual gratification was essential to emotional health. The career of Margaret Sanger, the leading exponent of birth control, illustrated the growing acceptance of a more liberated and positive sexual ideology. Before World War I, Sanger had been something of a social pariah; she had been arrested and jailed for distributing birth control information. After the war, she became a heroine of modern Americans. She published birth control manuals, gave public lectures on birth control, and opened family planning clinics.

The mass media and the advertising industry contributed even more to the creation of modern sexual ideology. The glamorous woman with undisguised sex appeal became a favorite trope of advertisers. For example, a 1924 Palmolive soap ad depicted a scantily clad woman in an exotic setting and promised the "beauty secret of Cleopatra hidden in every cake." A bumper crop of new magazines offered readers who had never heard of Freud or the libido stories with such alluring titles as "Indolent Kisses," "Confessions of a Chorus Girl," and "What I Told My Daughter the Night Before Her Marriage." The movies were equally provocative. Clara Bow became the "It" girl of the 1920s, and movie ads promised kisses "where heart, soul and sense in concert move, and the blood is lava, and the pulse is ablaze."

The prevalence of sexual suggestiveness and the growing acceptance of a positive sexual ideology fed the impression then and since that the 1920s experienced a "sexual revolution." When compared with the middle-class sex ways of the nineteenth century, perhaps there was a revolution. The prevalence of intercourse, particularly between married couples in the urban white-collar class, may have increased. And, according to the studies of Alfred Kinsey, middle-class women born after 1900 were more likely to engage in premarital intercourse than those born in the nineteenth century.

Yet there were clearly limits on the sexual revolution of the 1920s. Although the widely publicized form of sexual play known as "petting" shocked contemporaries, Paula Fass has found that petting entailed conventions of physical intimacy that usually fell short of intercourse. While modern women were expected to be sexually alluring, almost no one endorsed promiscuity. Modern women were supposed to arouse male desire but not to initiate sexual relations. Any woman transgressing these boundaries jeopardized her reputation. For other Americans, particularly those living in the countryside, in small towns, and in the ethnic enclaves of the larger cities, sexual behavior may have changed little if at all in the twenties.

"What Sex Brings to the Race," a Poster of the American Social Hygiene Association, 1922. Part of a campaign to prevent the spread of venereal disease, this poster represents a step away from the restrictiveness of the middle-class Victorian ideology of sexuality. While not endorsing sex as a pleasure to be enjoyed for its own sake, the poster does suggest that when sexuality is channeled into marriage and reproduction it can bring enormous benefits to the lives of both sexes.

Both the new woman and the acceptance of a modern sexual ideology may be interpreted as victories of male over traditionally middle-class female values. The popular media and the advertisers encouraged women to engage in such stereotypically boyish and manly acts as smoking, drinking, betting, freer forms of dance and music, prankishness, and other traditionally antifeminine and antibourgeois behaviors. For example, advertising pioneer Edward Bernays sold cigarettes to women as "torches of freedom." (He noted at the same time that smoking cigarettes stimulated the erogenous zone of the lips.) A similar trend toward more boylike or manlike behavior by women was evident in literature and the arts. In short, the "new" or "modern" woman aided and abetted what Ann Douglas has described as the "masculinization" of American culture.

These new, more expressive forms of individualism may also have contained largely hidden costs for women, for they seemed to unleash earlier restraints that men had imposed on themselves in their relationships with women. Ultimately, men may have felt even freer than in the past to mistreat women both emotionally and physically.

Built into the adventurous autonomy of the modern woman was a new set of expectations. Instead of a complete release from the "tyrannies" of the home, the modern wife and mother was told that she needed to do even more. To feed her family properly, she should have a scientific knowledge of calories, vitamins, and food groups. To promote her husband's career, she should become a skilled hostess. No longer was moral training of children enough. Children should be happy. To rear happy children, the mother should acquire a knowledge of modern psychology. For guidance in performing her enlarged range of duties, the modern housewife was expected to turn away from the folk wisdom handed down by family, friends, or ministers. Instead, in a characteristically modern admonition, she was advised to look to outside expertise.

In particular, no modern woman could escape the commandment that she remain forever youthful. Hence, the arrival of the modern woman coincided with the growth of the modern cosmetics industry and the proliferation of beauty parlors. Perpetual youthfulness required slimness. Thus, dieting became a major preoccupation of the modern woman. In the face of the new cultural requirements of womanhood, older feminist causes slid into the background. In 1921, for example, feminists unveiled the Equal Rights Amendment, a proposed constitutional amendment that called for the end of sexual discrimination. But it was never adopted. That same year, Atlantic City, New Jersey, crowned the first Miss America. Miss America was soon to become a powerful symbol of the coercion imposed on women by the modern beauty culture.

WAYS AT WAR

Not surprisingly, the widespread outburst of shockingly new behaviors in the 1920s provoked a cultural war, a war whose issues continue to reverberate into our own times. According to observers then and since, the opposition to modern ways came primarily from the countryside and from small towns. Peoples from these places tended to see themselves as under siege by the big city's ethnic and religious pluralism, its commercial amusements, and its moral relativism. They yearned for the restoration of a golden past of middle-class families and communities. In these idealized communities, independent farmers, public-spirited businessmen, and industrious workingmen lived side by side in complete harmony. Everyone practiced self-control and agreed that religion provided the ultimate source of moral authority.

Yet the opposition to modern ways did not come exclusively from nonurban areas. Regardless of where they lived, the majority of Americans probably found some or most of the modern values and behaviors to one degree or another objectionable. While urban Catholic ethnics usually disagreed sharply with Protestant traditionalists regarding prohibition and the desirability of pluralism, they too objected to the new woman and to modern sexual ideology. The older middle class of small businessmen, locally oriented professionals, prosperous farmers, and skilled working people also approached the expressive individualism of modern culture with caution. Unlike the new urban white-collar class, these traditionalists more often than not continued to find their identities and their values in the familiar ways handed down from the past and in their families, their churches, and in their local communities or neighborhoods rather than in their occupations or in what was currently fashionable. As the older middle class sensed that it was losing cultural authority to the newer white-collar, urban-centered middle class, it became more defensive and suspicious.

Above all else, traditionalists and modernists divided on the ultimate source of moral authority. For moral direction, both Protestant and Catholic traditionalists relied upon revealed religion—for Protestants, the Bible, and for Catholics, the institutional church. On the other hand, modernists were just as likely, or perhaps more likely, to look elsewhere. They turned to scientific and professional expertise, to the cultures of their workplaces, to the opinions of others, and to media models for guidance on how they should behave.

While traditionalists were never in full agreement on how to respond to the modernist challenges, they launched two major counteroffensives. One took aim at the modern notion of a pluralistic order that recognized the intrinsic value of minority cultures. This counteroffensive had direct origins in the anxieties spawned by World War I. "Once lead this people into war," President Woodrow Wilson had warned before America's entry into the conflict, "and they'll forget there ever was such a thing as tolerance." Wilson's prediction proved to be chillingly accurate. Everywhere, the war fanned the flames of cultural conformity. Acutely aware of the absence of enthusiasm on the part of many Americans for entering the war in the first place as well as of the ties that bound American ethnic groups to their homelands in Europe, national, state, and local governments as well as private groups launched a massive propaganda campaign on behalf of the war effort.

Ironically, ethnic Germans, the immigrant group frequently praised as the most assimilable before the war, now became the special targets of nativist bigotry. Regardless of protests to the contrary, German Americans found themselves treated as enemy agents. Cloaking themselves in wartime patriotism, opponents of radicalism likewise employed both legal and extralegal weapons against the Industrial Workers of the World and the Socialist party. Wartime anxieties and the Russian Revolution of 1917 contributed to a nationwide "Red Scare" in 1919.

Fears that ethnic and religious pluralism and alien ideologies jeopardized the nation's cultural homogeneity continued after the war. Under the battle cry of restoring "one-hundred percent Americanism" and frequently under the umbrella of their local churches and/or the revived Ku Klux Klan, the more militant of the traditionalist Protestants made Catholics, Jews, African Americans, and foreigners their special targets. They resurrected ages-old charges of an international Jewish conspiracy to take over the world, exposed "papal plots" against traditional liberties, tried to close parochial schools, and sought to reduce Catholic and Jewish influence in politics. They led the campaign to obtain the passage of the Immigration Act of 1924, an act that not only brought a halt to massive immigration to America but also blatantly discriminated against Asians and immigrants from southern and eastern Europe. However, to attribute anti-Jewish, anti-Catholic, and antiblack attitudes only to the more extreme traditionalists of the 1920s would be a serious mistake. When non-Protestants tried to enter the nation's elite colleges, clubs, and boardrooms, they frequently encountered there, too, unscalable ethnoreligious barriers—but in these instances the barriers were usually disguised as character tests or as merit systems.

The noisy, organized, and sometimes violent campaigns against non-Protestants and blacks echoed aspects of the European fascist movements. Both movements, as George Mowry has observed, idealized a preindustrial world, were intensely nationalistic, insisted on racial purity, attacked minorities, and condemned modern ways (especially the personal behavior of those living in the large cities). But the revived Ku Klux Klan, the major organizational form of America's variant of fascism, was never as successful as the fascist movements in Germany or Italy. In the United States, Klan supporters confronted a stronger tradition of respect for individual liberties and for political accommodation than in Italy or Germany. And, unlike the European fascist movements, the Klan won little support among intellectuals or those employed in managerial bureaucracies. But, even as the Klan faded in the late 1920s, large numbers of Americans continued to blame non-Protestants and modern ways for what they considered America's fall from a golden age.

Traditionalist or fundamentalist Protestants aimed a second major counteroffensive at modern science and modern Protestantism. While World War I had temporarily brought Protestants together, once the conflict ended, the smoldering divisions of the prewar era resurfaced. In the 1920s the trend within urban white-collar congregations toward modernism or liberalism gained momentum. Pastors of these congregations downgraded the importance of a religious conversion experience and theological orthodoxy; they preached more soothing sermons that accommodated religion with biblical criticism, Darwinism, and modern ways more generally. Rather than emphasizing salvation or personal sin, these ministers were more likely to stress amiable human relationships, personal fulfillment, and greater tolerance of non-Protestants.

The highly publicized Scopes trial in Dayton, Tennessee, in 1925 brought the conflict between modernist and fundamentalist Protestants to a dramatic climax. Consistent with their belief in the inerrancy of the Bible, fundamentalists had obtained the passage of several state laws banning the teaching of "atheistic" evolution in the public schools. Supported by the American Civil Liberties Union, John T. Scopes, a high school biology teacher, challenged the constitutionality of Tennessee's statute. The subsequent trial attracted the attention of the entire world. William Jennings Bryan, thrice the Democratic presidential nominee and the nation's leading crusader against evolution, joined the prosecution. Bryan was not completely amiss when he charged that a "scientific soviet is attempting to dictate what shall be taught in our schools and, in so doing, is attempting to mold the religion of the nation." Clarence Darrow, a famous trial lawyer and a publicly confessed agnostic, joined the defense team. Darrow mercilessly ridiculed Bryan's "fool ideas" about the Bible. The court found Scopes guilty, though his sentence was later reversed on a technicality.

Contrary to impressions cultivated by the urban press and subsequently by historians, the Scopes trial did *not* signal a defeat or the end of traditional ways. Despite the negative conclusions of the big-city press, it is quite likely that a majority of the American people continued after the trial to oppose the teaching of evolution in the public schools. Neither did the modernists rout the traditionalists politically in the 1920s. The traditionalists won nearly all of the decade's political frays, including the election of three presidents and, more important in symbolic terms, succeeded in retaining the prohibition of alcoholic beverages as the law of the land.

LOOKING BACKWARD
AND FORWARD IN THE GREAT DEPRESSION

Like a mighty earthquake, the Great Depression of the 1930s rocked the nation to its very foundations. At the bottom of the Depression in 1933, nearly a quarter of the labor force was out of work. For those who did have jobs, their wages plunged downward. In the major cities, hungry women and men lined up in front of soup kitchens; thousands more lived in shanty towns known as "Hoovervilles," a derisive reference to President Herbert Hoover. Confronted with an uncertain future, the birth rate fell to the lowest point in the nation's history and the marriage rate dropped 20 percent. Only in the early 1940s, in the midst of World War II, did the nation finally recover the prosperity that it had enjoyed in the 1920s.

The exigencies of the Great Depression quickly pushed aside or into the background the major cultural conflicts of the 1920s. In the immediate wake of the stock market crash of 1929, large numbers of Americans believed that they had gone too far, that they were now paying the price for their free spending, their frivolity, and their pursuit of personal pleasure. Skirt lengths dropped to well below the knees and, along with the price of common stocks, public support for modern architecture, music, painting, and literature plummeted.

Amidst the confusion and the futility of the present, many Americans resurrected visions of a more purposeful and coherent past. The reconstructed colonial village of Williamsburg, Virginia, opened in 1935, served well this longing for an idyllic past. Cleansed of nearly all evidence of squalor and slavery, Colonial Williamsburg, according to its sponsors, depicted the "moral and spiritual values" that were of "lasting importance to all men everywhere." Baseball's Hall of Fame and Museum, opened in Cooperstown, New York, in 1938, evoked a similar nostalgia for a simpler, supposedly superior past. "Turning back to the past when men presumably did things right," to quote historian Francis O'Connor, was the favorite theme of more than twenty-five hundred murals produced through the relief efforts of the Federal Arts Project in the 1930s. Historical novels were in vogue; no novel of the depression decade approximated the popularity of Margaret Mitchell's *Gone with the Wind* (1936), an epic that recalled the glory of the Old South. Americans responded warmly to majestic biographies. Their favorite subject for biography was Abraham Lincoln, the president who had guided the nation through an earlier crisis.

In their enthusiasm for "streamlining," a popular industrial design concept in the 1930s, other Americans seemed to be looking forward to the possibilities of technology and science as means of escaping the Great Depression. Inspired by the airplane and the imagery of flight, industrial designers assaulted sharp corners and abrupt protrusions in favor of extended lines and fluid curves. To create feelings of aerodynamic smoothness, they employed such newer materials as aluminum, chrome, and plastics. Finding its most compelling form in the bullet-shaped railroad locomotive, which was introduced with great fanfare in the 1930s, designers applied the concept of streamlining to nearly everything. Perhaps the smooth-formed aluminum diner served as the most enduring symbol of the streamlining fad. Within the home, streamlined products found their way into kitchens and bathrooms.

A reconciliation of the old and the new may be detected in Walt Disney's tremendously popular cartoon *The Three Little Pigs*, which first appeared in 1933. On its surface, the cartoon seemed to be simply an endorsement of such old-fashioned virtues as hard work and self-constraint. In the cartoon, as well as in the folktale versions of the story, two of the three porkers quickly assemble a fragile house of straw and sticks so that they may "play around all day." Righteously asserting that "work and play don't mix," the third porker laboriously built himself a sturdy house of brick and stone. In the folktale version, the arrival of the wolf spells disaster for the pigs who had neglected the practice of old-fashioned virtues. But in Disney's cartoon, the third pig elects to save his fun-loving cohorts from the jaws of the wolf (read Depression) by inviting them to stay at his house. We also learn that the third pig, despite his admonitions on behalf of the virtues of hard work, is ultimately no enemy of play. He owns a piano and, presumably to the mounting annoyance of the wolf, plays it with great gusto. At the end of the story, to a honky-tonk pianistic rendition, the three little pigs sing merrily together "Who's Afraid of the Big Bad Wolf?" Echoing Franklin D. Roosevelt's plea in his inaugural address in 1933 that the "only thing we have to fear is fear itself," the song became an instant hit. As Terry Cooney has observed, Disney's cartoon offered at least a tentative resolution of the conflict between traditional work and modern leisure. It may also be understood as endorsing the idea of mutual sharing in a time of crisis.

Even before the advent of the Great Depression, popular culture began a process of revising the traditional formula for success. As if unconsciously recognizing that success had to be won increasingly in the bureaucratic maze of corporations or through salesmanship, the need for heroes who leaped to fame and fortune outside the world of ordinary work seemed to grow more pronounced. No longer were the heroes lone businessmen, statesmen, or philanthropists but the stars of sports, the movies, and popular music. From the movies in the 1920s came Rudolph Valentino, Clara Bow, Charlie Chaplin, and Douglas Fairbanks, and from the world of sports came Babe Ruth, Jack Dempsey, and Red Grange. These heroes from the world of entertainment rather than production assisted the public in compensating for feelings of individual powerlessness, concern for the erosion of Victorian values, and gnawing doubts about the efficacy of the traditional formulas for achieving individual success.

No hero of the day equaled the capacity of Babe Ruth in projecting multiple images of the quick, decisive problem solver, the quintessential consumer, and the embodiment of the American success dream. Ruth was dramatic proof that men could still rise from lowly beginnings to fame and fortune. The simple, direct solutions represented in Ruth's mighty home run blasts reassured and inspired millions of Americans who were frustrated by the absence of potency that they felt in their jobs and in their personal relationships. At the same time, Ruth's ethnicity and religion (of German and Catholic origins) and his hedonistic lifestyle were powerful symbols of modern ways.

Contrary to what might have been expected, the Great Depression produced few instances of a complete renunciation of the older ideas of success and opportunity. Rather than disavowals, popular magazines of the day as well as ordinary citizens (including the jobless) were more likely to reassert with renewed vigor their faith in America as a special land of opportunity. Indeed, rather than seeing widespread joblessness as a failure of the economic system, many if not most of those out of work saw their unemployment as evidence of personal moral failure. They frequently refused to accept relief.

Nonetheless, the most popular success manual of the decade, one that continues to sell widely to this day, Dale Carnegie's *How to Win Friends and Influence People* (1936) indicated by its very title that those striving for success needed to develop character traits beyond the older formula of industry, thrift, dependability, and self-control. To Carnegie, the key to success lay not so much in the cultivation of traits that were conducive to ever greater productivity but in the management of the impressions that one made on others. To be successful, the ambitious should avoid conflict, develop good manners, and, above all else, strive to make others feel important. The cultivation of a hollow or false sense of self as suggested by Carnegie became the subject for Arthur Miller's tragic drama, *Death of a Salesman* (1949).

INDIVIDUALISM (OR LIBERALISM) REFORMULATED

While reaffirmations of the old were commonplace in the 1930s, the exigencies of the Great Depression virtually forced Americans to reexamine their adherence to individualism (sometimes also described as liberalism or classical liberalism). From the struggle against monarchal and hierarchical authority during the Revolutionary era and from the opening of the doors of opportunity for ordinary white men in the nineteenth century, individualism had emerged as a powerful if not carefully articulated American ideology. To its proponents, the rights and interests of the individual came ultimately before those of the society or the community. They tended to see the state (and not the economic system, for example) as the individual's primary oppressor. Individuals and society prospered most, the proponents of acquisitive (but not necessarily expressive) individualism said, when the economic laws of supply and demand were allowed to operate free of state control. This laissez-faire (hands-off by the state) policy ensured that individuals got what they deserved, for economic success or failure was the individual's responsibility, and his or hers alone.

During the Great Depression, the most comprehensive indictment of acquisitive individualism came not from Franklin D. Roosevelt's New Deal but from the left—from Marxism, socialism, communism, and variants thereof. Confidently predicting that capitalism was on the verge of collapse, leftists renounced traditional or, more precisely, acquisitive individualism (leftists were far less likely to criticize the expressive individualism found in a modern or bohemian lifestyle). Many of them looked to the newly founded communist state of the Soviet Union. The USSR offered a concrete model of a possible alternative to American individualism. With the Great Depression, the apparent Soviet success with a centrally planned society stood in stark contrast to the helplessness of the western capitalistic nations. While the United States permitted the "anarchy" of the marketplace to determine its destiny, the Soviet Union appeared to harness its economy to the satisfaction of the needs of all. The USSR's militant antifascism added to its appeal.

The influence of the left extended well beyond its critique of acquisitive individualism. Before many leftists suffered a profound disillusionment with Stalinism in the late 1930s, some hundred thousand men and women joined the American Communist party or cooperated with it in an effort not only to defend the USSR as the world's first "worker's state" but also to organize industrial workers into labor unions and to do battle with racial injustice. In particular, artists and writers, acting in concert with the Popular Front, a broad alliance of leftist groups between 1935 and 1939, rediscovered the ordinary people. In dozens of novels, museum exhibitions, murals, Hollywood films, and theater productions, they celebrated the virtues and the strengths of "the common man." Their subject matter and style became known as socialist (or sometimes Marxist) realism.

Many, perhaps most, intellectuals did not go so far as the communists in repudiating individualism. Especially influential among the meliorists was philosopher John Dewey. In *Liberalism and Social Action* (1935), Dewey indicted both acquisitive individualism and Franklin D. Roosevelt's New Deal. Dewey called for a "renascent liberalism." The older liberalism in which society rested upon individual contracts and a maximum degree of freedom to pursue personal economic gain was no longer adequate, Dewey wrote. Industrialization, the formation of giant corporations, and more particularly the Depression required a new liberalism committed to bold social experimentation. Rather than starting from the preset dogma represented in either socialism or capitalism, Dewey said that the vision and the authority for such experimentation should flow from the bottom up (democratically) and be guided by the principles of systematic scientific inquiry.

In the end, the more ad hoc, piecemeal measures of the New Deal received far more public support than did the more radical departures from individualism suggested by Dewey or by the Communist party. Without a guiding social philosophy or a comprehensive vision of an alternative to individualism, Roosevelt invoked traditional values while supporting a wide-ranging set of new initiatives by the state. In sum, these initiatives are frequently described as "welfare capitalism" or the "welfare state." FDR also transformed the meaning of the word "liberalism." With Roosevelt, liberalism no longer meant a hands-off role for government but instead an activist state that provided at the least a minimal safety net for all its citizens. As early as 1934, FDR juxtaposed his idea of "liberty" as the "greater security for the average man" against the older idea of the freedom of contract which he said served "the privileged few." To be truly free, FDR said, each citizen must have a modicum of economic security.

The New Deal's redefinition of liberalism established the expectation that in the future the national government would not hesitate to use some of its powers to counter the worst aspects of economic depressions. Borrowing from the theory of English economist John Maynard Keynes, future (but not New Deal) policymakers sought to maintain high levels of employment through the use of government taxing and spending powers. Otherwise, Keynesian principles left most of the economic decision making in private hands. In this sense, Keynesian economics accorded with traditional American individualism.

Consistent with the principle that a roughly equal distribution of wealth was vital to the health of a republic, the New Deal also sought to do something about what FDR called the "unjust concentration of wealth and economic power" in the hands of the few. The Revenue Act of 1935 (called the "Wealth Tax Act") threatened, according to its critics, to "soak the rich," but in fact loopholes resulted in a bill that only moderately raised taxes on high incomes and inheritances. New revenue measures during World War II and the early Cold War that imposed heavier taxes on the upper income brackets and on estates contributed more than the 1935 act to a minor redistribution of wealth in America. Between the 1940s and the 1980s, the portion of the nation's total wealth owned by the top 10 percent dropped slightly—to about 65 percent.

The New Deal's limited and tentative expansion of the state's role in American life was not the only significant departure from traditional individualism during the Depression. In the past, workers and employers alike had frequently perceived the collectivism of labor unions to be at odds with individualism. But in the 1930s the effects of the Depression and support by FDR's New Deal led millions of workers to join labor unions. Comprised of skilled workers, the older American Federation of Labor had for the most part ignored workers in the mass-production industries, but the Congress of Industrial Organizations (CIO), founded in 1935, spread the message that the "political liberty for which our forefathers fought" had been "made meaningless by economic inequality" and "industrial despotism." "Can you really be free if [your rights in the workplace] are not recognized and respected?" queried one union newspaper. Acting collectively, the unions sought in effect to redefine individualism so that it included the right to a living wage, to greater economic equality, to some control over the conditions of work, and to greater job security. With their successes in unionizing the nation's major industries, labor unions not only became a far more important force in the lives of the working class but also exercised (until the 1980s) far more power than in the past in the nation's economic and political life.

Of course not all Americans embraced either the CIO's or the New Deal's reformulation of individualism into what was increasingly called "liberalism." Opponents, who were now usually labeled as "conservatives," harked back to the earlier, more restricted meaning of individualism. Rallying around the slogan "freedom of enterprise," they insisted that the formation of unions and the New Deal's welfare state restricted economic freedom. The growing dependency on the state, former president Herbert Hoover said, was turning Americans into "lazy parasites." Conservatives frequently saw the retreat from laissez-faire as a slippery slope, one that could ultimately lead to a totalitarian state. Austrian economist Frederich A. Hayek, in a surprise best-seller entitled *The Road to Serfdom* (1944), even equated FDR's New Deal with Hitler's Germany and Stalin's Soviet Union. In the postwar era, such an equation—as exaggerated as it surely was—became virtually a truism for the opponents of the New Deal's version of liberalism.

CONCLUSION

Nothing affected the history of American ways in the years between World War I and World War II as much as the performance of the economy. The booming prosperity of the 1920s permitted and encouraged cultural experimentation. For ever larger numbers of Americans, it was now possible for them to enjoy a dazzling array of new consumer goods and experience the excitement offered by commercial leisure. The promise of jobs and growing incomes encouraged a new assertiveness among ethnics, African Americans, and women. But the outburst of shockingly new behaviors in the 1920s, especially among Americans in the cities, provoked a full-scale counterattack. Traditionalists everywhere viewed with alarm the city's ethnic and racial pluralism, the arrival of the new woman, and the growing popularity of expressive forms of individualism. In response, they supported prohibition, immigration restriction, and laws prohibiting the teaching of evolution in the public schools.

While pushing aside or into the background the cultural war of the previous decade, the Great Depression of the 1930s in effect placed on trial some of the deepest commitments of the American people. Could the problem of massive unemployment and underemployment be met simply by the practice of such individual virtues as self-denial and hard work? Did the economic system itself, one in which the market governed nearly every decision, require replacement or at the least an overhaul? In responding to these questions, Americans were pulled in opposing directions, both to a reaffirmation of traditional values and a willingness to embark on new paths. Out of this confusing mix came a reformulation of traditional individualism. Frequently called "liberalism" then and since, the new conception of individualism insisted that for society to function humanely some restraints had to be placed on the marketplace by the state and that the state must provide at least a minimal social safety net for all its citizens.

20

"THE AMERICAN WAY OF LIFE"

Few if any events impinged on American ways more deeply or broadly than World War II and the early Cold War (from the 1940s through the 1950s). World War II brought with it economic recovery, and, while many Americans worried about the return of a depression, the economy continued to bound forward with a few minor setbacks until the 1970s. With the explosion of nuclear bombs over Japan in 1945, the "antibiotic revolution," and the development of the marvelous new medium of television, American scientific and technological know-how once again astonished the world. As in the past, Americans moved and then moved again—from the countryside to the cities, from the inner cities to the suburbs, and from the "rust belt" (the Northeast) to the Sunbelt (the South and Southwest). In the meantime, threats, both real and perceived, from abroad provided a justification for the United States to take on a permanent (even a dominant) role in world affairs. To fight both hot and cold wars, the size and scope of the national government expanded far beyond anything previously imaginable.

In complex ways not easily understood, these events came together to encourage an ideology that called for the homogenization of American culture. In all aspects of the culture, it seemed, the urge was to unite, to include, to blend, in short, to create a single, unitary "American way of life." Once the ingredients of this way of life had been formulated and agreed upon, they were juxtaposed against the nation's ideological enemies: first the Axis Powers in World War II and then the Russian and Chinese communists during the Cold War. But the ideology of an American way of life became far more than simply a rhetorical weapon to be employed against foreign foes. It soon evolved into an ideal standard by which countless Americans measured themselves.

"FREEDOM"

During both World War II and the Cold War, the elusive but highly evocative word *freedom* became the centerpiece of the American-way-of-life ideology. This was mainly because both the Axis Powers in World War II and Soviet

---

Communism were seen as totalitarian, that is, nations in which the state ultimately left no room for individual freedom. In 1941, in the face of the threatening Axis Powers, President Franklin D. Roosevelt announced the Four Freedoms—freedom of speech, freedom of worship, freedom from want, and freedom from fear. The Four Freedoms became the nation's rallying cry for fighting World War II. But it was left to a popular illustrator, Norman Rockwell, to flesh out and relate the Four Freedoms to the American way of life.

For the cover of the *Saturday Evening Post* in 1943, Rockwell translated FDR's Four Freedoms into terms that vividly conveyed the distinctive ideological posture of the United States. In the first panel, representing freedom of speech, Rockwell depicted a workingman speaking at a town meeting. In the second panel, which represented freedom of worship, he pictured members of distinctive religious groups worshiping peacefully together. These two panels not only served as statements of traditional American freedoms but also indicated the value placed on inclusiveness and presumably tolerance

OURS...to fight for

Freedom of Speech   *Freedom of Worship*

Freedom from Want   *Freedom from Fear*

The Norman Rockwell Museum

Four Freedoms. This popular Office of War Information poster, which was reproduced from Norman Rockwell's painting *The Four Freedoms,* sought to juxtapose American ideals with those of the Axis Powers of Germany and Japan.

of peoples of diverse class, ethnic, and religious backgrounds. (African Americans, however, were conspicuously absent from all four panels.)

While freedom of religion and of speech certainly predated the Great Depression, the other two panels representing freedom from want and the freedom from fear were essentially new freedoms. Implicitly, if not explicitly, they had been among the primary objectives of the New Deal. In the freedom from want panel, Rockwell presented a family enjoying a sumptuous Thanksgiving dinner. It suggested that all Americans could unite behind the promise of consumption and material abundance. In the freedom from fear panel, Rockwell drew a mother and father standing over a sleeping child. It not only reflected the need for personal security but suggested that the nuclear family was the bedrock of the American way of life.

When contrasted with Nazi Germany's blatant racism, the establishment of the Four Freedoms as the essence of the American way of life encouraged the nation to embrace the modern value of social inclusiveness. In sharp contrast to the Nazis, who endorsed Aryan superiority, Americans now officially claimed to stand for the enjoyment of freedom by all racial, ethnic, and religious groups. With the offspring of pre–World War I immigrants now filling the ranks of the nation's military units, many Americans saw a shared belief in pluralism as a great unifying force. Writing for the Office of War Information, novelist Pearl Buck put it succinctly: "persons of many lands can live together . . . and if they believe in freedom they can become a united people." Wartime movies typically featured an assortment of ethnics as well as "old American" types. Throughout both World War II and the Cold War, the popularity of inclusiveness in government propaganda and the popular media made many ethnics, Catholics, and Jews, in the words of historian Eric Foner, "feel fully American for the first time."

While elevating freedom and tolerance to a new prominence encouraged the acceptance of ethnic and religious minorities, their consequences were far more problematic for racial minorities. During the war, government propaganda and war films depicted the Japanese as bestial and subhuman rats, dogs, snakes, and gorillas. Even after learning about the horrors of the Holocaust, eight out of ten Americans believed that the Japanese were more "cruel at heart" than the Germans. Apart from Japanese Americans themselves, almost no one protested the most blatant violation of freedom since slavery—the forced relocation and incarceration of Japanese Americans during World War II.

The glaring discrepancy between the rhetorical enthusiasm for freedom on the one hand and racial discrimination on the other was not lost upon African Americans. In the face of Nazi racism and threats of a march on Washington by blacks, FDR in 1941 issued an executive order banning discrimination in hiring based on "race, color, or national origins" by the national government or its contractors. But severe labor shortages in World War II did far more to expand work opportunities for blacks than the poorly enforced executive order. During the war, black newspapers also launched the "Double V" campaign for victory over fascism abroad and racism at home. Despite the second-class citizenship of blacks, the wartime proliferation of official and unofficial propaganda on behalf of tolerance and social inclusiveness portended the possibility of a better future for African Americans.

Neither was the ideal of an American way of life free of ambiguity for women. During World War II, millions of women flocked into factories to fill industrial jobs vacated by men. The celebrated emblem of the female factory worker was Rosie the Riveter. But few Americans seemed to think that Rosie's work might emancipate her from traditional female roles. Instead, Rosie was, according to the popular view of the day, making temporary sacrifices on behalf of the war effort so that she could one day become a full-time house-wife with "a little house of [her] own, and a husband to meet every night at the door."

Neither did all Americans agree with Roosevelt's and Rockwell's rendition of the Four Freedoms or, at least, Rockwell's interpretation of them. Even during World War II, conservatives observed that freedom from want implied a dependence on government, indeed, a backhanded endorsement of the New Deal. By implication, the conservatives suggested that the freedom to starve might be a more accurate statement of traditional American principles. Any creed seeking to sum up the American way of life, they insisted, should include "freedom of enterprise." In their campaign on behalf of making "free enterprise" the centerpiece of the American way of life, the conservatives achieved striking successes. Not only did freedom of enterprise frequently supercede or envelop the other Four Freedoms in the post–World War II ideological confrontations with the Soviet Union; it also became a powerful rhetorical weapon in the conservative postwar defense of the status quo.

ANTICOMMUNISM

In the post–World War II era, anticommunism joined "freedom" as an integral component of the American-way-of-life ideology. In 1947, President Harry S. Truman announced what became known as the policy of containment when he asserted that in the future the United States would support "freedom-loving peoples" everywhere against threats from international communism. Soon American policymakers and the media conceptualized the Cold War as a conflict between the free and the enslaved worlds. Apart from the debasement of the language entailed in classifying Franco's Spain and dozens of other tyrannical regimes as part of the "free world," this simplistic bipolar conception of the world encouraged Americans to confuse the rising power of revolutionary nationalism with a monolithic communism directed from within the walls of the Kremlin. In other words, in the postwar era Americans tended to see the Soviet Union behind every social upheaval in Asia, Africa, and Latin America.

Even art became a weapon in the Cold War. Unlike the USSR, which insisted on a socialist realism in its arts, Americans, according to the popular media, championed complete artistic freedom. Abstract expressionism, a postwar style of painting in New York City, satisfied perfectly the need for positioning the United States vis-à-vis the USSR. Swirling and splattering paint on giant canvasses in unrecognizable forms, the paintings of Jackson Pollock seemed the complete antithesis of socialist realism paintings. The abstract expressionists demonstrated, in the words of one cold warrior, the virtues of "freedom of expression" in an "open and free society." Cooperating publicly with the United States Information Agency and clandestinely with the Central Intelligence Agency, the Museum of Modern Art in New York City displayed abstract expressionist paintings at art shows around the world.

The anticommunist crusade was not restricted to foreign policy. Setbacks in the Cold War and sensational revelations of spying by public officials encouraged the belief that any person, organization, or idea that could be linked in any way with communism was an enemy of the American way of life. In the late 1940s and in the 1950s, such a linkage touched off a nationwide anticommunist witch hunt, a mass hysteria that frequently made a mockery of the nation's much-vaunted freedoms. As one historian has noted, "a pervasive kind of democracy was practiced: all accusations, no matter from whom, were taken seriously."

Elbowing his way to the front of the crusade was the junior senator from Wisconsin, Joseph McCarthy. McCarthy capitalized on a multiplicity of fears and anxieties: anger of ethnics from Eastern Europe arising from the Soviet domination of their homelands, fears that the American government was "riddled" with communists or communist sympathizers, and anxieties arising from the triumphs of modern ways. Traditionalist-oriented Americans frequently identified communism with secularism (more specifically atheism), greater sexual freedom, social novelty, and intellectualism. To the more extreme of the traditionalists, modern ways and communism were virtually one and the same.

The anticommunist crusade narrowed sharply the range of political and social discourse. It helped to bring to a screeching halt proposals to extend New Deal programs. Invoking the specter of "socialized medicine" and hinting at its similarities to the Soviet system of medicine, the American Medical Association successfully blocked Truman's proposal for a national health insurance plan. And campaigns to identify the Democratic party with communism helped to elect a popular World War II general, Dwight D. Eisenhower, as president in 1952. Eisenhower considered FDR's New Deal and Truman's Fair Deal as examples of "creeping socialism." The anticommunist crusade limited the range of choices by labor unions and social organizations. Either they had to come to terms with the anticommunist movement or face extermination. Both the CIO and the NAACP renounced all former associations with the American Communist party and expelled leaders and members considered too far to the political left.

The anticommunist crusade deeply affected the nation's intellectual life. Some artists and intellectuals stood firm; before congressional committees, they refused to name former associates in communist or other left-wing organizations. Such individuals paid a heavy price. Apart from jail sentences for contempt of Congress, they frequently found themselves occupationally blackballed.

Others who had been Marxists or had been on the far left of the political spectrum during the 1930s openly repudiated their former allegiances. They took a hard stand against both communism and the Soviet Union. Some turned their backs on politics altogether while others called for the extension of New Deal social reforms. Of those who remained socially and politically engaged, their thought frequently took a decidedly conservative turn. With knowledge of the Holocaust, the horrors of the Allied bombings of civilian populations in World War II, and the savagery of Soviet purges looming in the background, they rediscovered the human propensity for evil and the importance of power. Joining an informal group dubbed by philosopher Morton White as the "atheists for Niebuhr," many of them endorsed theologian Reinhold Niebuhr's dim view of human nature.

The title of a much-discussed Daniel Bell essay, "The End of Ideology" (1960), captured much of the postwar intellectual mood. No longer committed to ideas or prescriptions that called for social revolution, the intellectuals accepted America's basic institutions and an economy that included a mixture of private enterprise and government involvement. Social problems remained, they agreed, but their solution required technical, piecemeal adjustments rather than wholesale changes. "Functionalism" became the theoretical rage of the day. Rather than focusing on what society should be, functionalists gave attention to how existing relationships "functioned" or worked to preserve the status quo. Sometimes labeled as the "consensus" school, historians of this period downplayed the significance of ideology and conflict in American history. They contributed to the homogenization of the larger culture by attributing conflict in the past as well as the present to psychic inadequacies rather than to region, ideology, ethnicity, race, religion, or social class. For example, the abolitionists, the populists, and the contemporary "far rightists" were said to have had "paranoid personalities."

Even the long-standing adversarial relationship between the modern artists and the general public relaxed. Not only did authorities employ abstract expressionist paintings as a weapon against the Soviet Union in the Cold War, but also by the 1950s the avant-garde literature and arts of the early twentieth century now found general acceptance in university curricula and lecterns. The former avant-garde no longer gave "offense," wrote critic Leslie Fiedler, except to "a diminishing minority of ever more comical bigots." Public acceptance of modernism, several writers concluded, signaled the arrival of a new age of artistic sensibility that some described as "postmodernism." (However, a renewed outbreak of adversarial relationships and "wild" experimentation in the 1960s suggested that such a conclusion may have been premature.)

Public-school history texts uncritically proclaimed the wonders of the American way of life. "Inside their covers," Frances FitzGerald concludes on the basis of her study of postwar history texts, "America was perfect: the greatest nation in the world, the embodiment of democracy, freedom, and technological progress." Unlike earlier texts that had taken account of change and conflict in American history, the postwar texts extolled a seamless American past of stability and tranquility. They particularly praised the "free enterprise system," though, perhaps fearing that such an activity might imply to students the existence of an alternative system, they rarely made much of an effort to delineate its characteristics. The state legislature of Texas not only required that all writers of school texts sign a loyalty oath but also passed a resolution urging that the "American history courses in the public schools emphasize in the textbooks our glowing and throbbing history of hearts and souls inspired by wonderful American principles and traditions."

Even sports served as an arena for exhibiting the merits of the American way of life. Beginning in World War II, movies, magazines, and newspapers began to flood the country with athletic narratives that reached far beyond the standard fare of outstanding physical feats and formulaic virtue. They depicted athletes whose lives intersected with parents, spouses, teammates, churches, community, and country. In tales of how second-generation immigrants were transformed into Americans, movies such as *Knute Rockne-All American* (released in 1940, starring Ronald Reagan, and about the famed Notre Dame football coach) and *Pride of the Yankees* (Lou Gehrig's biography released in 1942) preached social inclusiveness. According to Cold War rhetoric, American victories over the Soviet Union in international sports competition demonstrated the superiority of U.S. institutions and virtues. Sports were likewise vital to the nation's internal health: "Our Olympic team and athletes play a significant role in preserving our way of life," concluded President John F. Kennedy in 1961.

RELIGION

Religion became yet another way of distinguishing the United States from the USSR. To the surprise of many secular-oriented scholars, the postwar era witnessed a widespread turn toward religion. Church membership jumped from 50 to nearly 70 percent and weekly attendance at religious services nearly doubled between 1940 and 1958. Public opinion polls revealed a degree of religious orthodoxy in the United States that was far higher than anywhere else in the industrial world. For example, nineteen out of twenty Americans believed in the existence of God and three out of four believed in life after death. Growing religious tolerance accompanied the renewal of religiosity. As did World War II, the Cold War encouraged Protestants to accept Jews and Catholics as full-scale participants in the American way of life.

Billy Graham, who started his revivalist career under the auspices of Protestant fundamentalism, became an icon of both the nation's renewed religiosity and the anticommunist crusade. In revivals that took him all over America and throughout the world, the charismatic and popular Graham warned repeatedly against the spread of "atheistic" communism. He equated anticommunism with religious devotion. In 1952, Congress permitted Graham to hold the first ever formal religious service on the Capitol steps. The nation's presidents found it politically obligatory to invite Graham to the White House. There he met and prayed with a succession of presidents from Harry S. Truman to George W. Bush.

Rather than discouraging religiosity, modernity, particularly the growth of suburbs, seemed to encourage the postwar resurgence of religion. "For every trip to the mall," argues religious historian Jon Butler, "suburban families easily made two, three, or even five or more trips to suburban congregations. . . . " The suburban churches and synagogues not only offered suburbanites spiritual succor and potential sources of identity, but, in the tradition of the earlier social gospel movement, they also provided organized youth groups, choirs, kindergarten classes, nursery school classes, counseling groups, and gyms for exercise. As suggested by these services, postwar churches and synagogues tapped into the modern therapeutic impulse; they implied or explicitly argued that belief and piety could relieve personal problems, increase happiness, and enhance one's prospects for material success. In 1955, Billy Graham transformed even Jesus into an apostle of contentment with his *The Secret of Happiness: Jesus' Teaching on Happiness as Expressed in the Beatitudes*. But no book of this genre was more influential than Norman Vincent Peale's blockbuster, *The Power of Positive Thinking* (1952), which sold (and continues to this day to sell) millions of copies. Peale emphasized the power of religious commitment to effect change in one's personal life, including not insignificantly the achievement of individual material success.

But, while conceding the utility of religion as a means of coping with contemporary life, there were reasons to question the depth of the postwar religious revival. For example, less than half of those who claimed to be practicing Christians could name a single one of the four Gospels. Instead of requiring belief in a set of traditional or orthodox principles, more and more Americans seemed, in the words of religious historian Martin Marty, to have "faith in faith itself." Faith and patriotism frequently blended. The Soviet Union was an avowed atheist state; the Americans were a religious people. Religion is a "good thing," said President Dwight Eisenhower. "Our government makes no sense, unless it is founded in a deeply felt religious faith—*and I don't care what it is.*" Postwar political leaders quickly enacted such thinking into law. In 1954, Congress added "under God" to the hitherto secular Pledge of Allegiance and declared in 1956 "In God We Trust" as the nation's official motto.

Yet at the same time that there was a flowering of religious "piety along the Potomac" and elsewhere, American faith in expertise and secular ways of thinking continued unabated. Indeed, public respect for scientists, social scientists, engineers, doctors, and the other professions soared to new heights. Even in the most sensitive areas of their personal lives, Americans increasingly turned to experts. While Americans had long valued education, in the postwar era more and more of them associated education with material progress, personal advancement, and success or failure in the Cold War. By providing for living allowances and tuition payments to veterans, the GI Bill of Rights Act (1944), along with the expansion of scholarships and loans, triggered a revolution in higher education. For the first time in American history, literally millions of men and women from lower-middle-class families obtained college degrees and thereby obtained the means of joining or firming up their membership in the nation's middle class.

CONSUMPTION AND LIFE IN THE SUBURBS

Americans in the postwar era saw consumption and suburban living as the most important components of their way of life. No incident in the postwar era made this point more dramatically or concretely than the famed "kitchen debate" between Vice President Richard M. Nixon and Soviet Premier Nikita Khrushchev in 1959. Before flying to the Moscow trade exhibit, Nixon had been urged by a former ambassador to the USSR to emphasize how American values differed from the Soviets: "We are idealists; they are materialists," he said. But Nixon ignored the ex-ambassador's advice. In the kitchen exhibit of a suburban ranch-style house—allegedly a house that could be owned by the average American steelworker—Nixon responded to each of Khrushchev's claims for the superiority of the Soviet system *not* by reminding the premier of America's commitment to democracy, freedom, or philanthropy but by pointing to the vast array of wonderful consumer goods that he claimed were available to the typical American family. As *Time* magazine observed, the entire nation applauded Nixon's logic in equating life in the suburbs and consumer abundance with the American way of life.

By 1959, a large range of facts supported the importance of suburbia to American life. While there was nothing new about suburbs, in the postwar era soaring automobile sales, growing family incomes, subdividers with a knack for mass-producing houses, the construction of miles and miles of multilane freeways, and federal subsidies to new homeowners transformed cornfields and cow pastures into acres and acres of suburbs. "Most of the people that I worked with [during World War II] lived in rented houses and close to slum conditions," explained Robert Montgomery, a factory worker in Elyria, Ohio. "By the fifties almost everybody in that kind of social world expected that they would live in a suburban house—one that they owned themselves. The war integrated into the mainstream a whole chunk of society that had been living on the edge."

Looking back, it is clear that the fifties were something of a golden age for the nation's skilled workers. With an abundance of well-paying jobs, subsidies for education provided by the GI Bill, the security offered by powerful labor unions, and a government-sponsored safety net, many working-class families joined the middle class. Not all urbanites, however, had the financial wherewithal or the right skin color to join the middle class or move to the suburbs. Blacks, Hispanics, and the impoverished remained behind—in the rapidly decaying inner cities.

With the emergence of the suburb as the chief site for fulfilling the American way of life, pressures mounted for women to quit industrial workplaces and retreat to the home. Symptomatic of the pressure was Marynia Farnham and Ferdinand Lunberg's best-seller, *Modern Woman: The Lost Sex* (1947). Women who preferred to work outside the home, the psychologist-sociologist team wrote, were "neurotically disturbed" and afflicted with the much-dreaded "penis envy." Those women who did continue working outside the home—and in fact some 40 percent remained in the workforce—now toiled for the most part in low-paid clerical, sales, and service jobs. Frequently employed part-time, they no longer worked so much to escape poverty or to pursue a career as to ensure the existence of their family's middle-class suburban lifestyle.

According to the suburban dream, the father was the family breadwinner while the mother devoted her life to children, husband, and home. Ironically, it was in the suburbs of the 1950s, and not the Victorian age of the 1890s, that the United States came the closest to realizing on a massive scale the

The Stay-at-Home Mother. Dad is nowhere in sight in this Johnson & Johnson ad that appeared in a 1947 issue of *Life*. Perhaps unconsciously, the ad suggested a downside to motherhood in the postwar era. Historian Susan Douglas has suggested that the ad may have terrorized mothers into "concentrating all their energies on baby sputum and talcum powder."

"Whoa, Mom! Can't you take it?"

Johnson's Baby Oil
Johnson's Baby Powder

Johnson & Johnson

middle-class ideals of domesticity and a "separate sphere" for women. Inevitably, the luxury of having women stay at home became a weapon in the Cold War. Unlike the Soviet Union, where mothers toiled away from home while their children were being taught to become "good little comrades" at state-run child-care centers, American mothers, by staying home, ensured that the nation would remain forever the "land of the free." The stay-at-home mother was one of those things "that separates us from the Communist world," concluded James O'Connell, undersecretary of labor in the Kennedy Administration.

Life in the suburbs contained a mixture of the traditional and the modern. The reaffirmation of the virtues of domesticity, the renewal of religiosity, and the clear-cut separation of gender roles harked back to the Victorian era. Marriage returned to favor. To the utter surprise of demographers, who had associated a falling fertility rate with the Industrial Revolution, Americans began having babies again. According to a 1953 poll, nearly three-fourths of the American people believed that an ideal family consisted of three or more children. They did not quite reach that lofty goal—the average increased from two to three—but the "baby boom" was in full swing. It ended only when the birth control pill became publicly available in 1960.

Ralph Crane/Time & Life Pictures/Getty Images

Diaper Service Delivery Trucks. This photograph vividly conveys two profoundly important social developments of the 1940s and 1950s—the rapid building of suburbs and a sharp increase in the nation's birth rate. Notice that the yards are teeming with children and in this newly built suburb the predominance of ranch-style housing.

After women had taken on man-sized jobs and more "masculine" ways of dressing and behaving during World War II, the popular media and the fashion industry set out after the war to "refeminize" the American woman. The "New Look," in the words of French fashion designer Christian Dior, emphasized "full feminine busts, and willowy waists above enormous spreading skirts." The "current ideal," explained no less an authority than *Good Housekeeping* magazine, was "firm, full, cone-shaped breasts, standing up and out without visible means of support." However understood in other respects, the obsession with breast size in the postwar era seemed to reflect an impulse to draw a firmer boundary between cultural conceptions of femininity and masculinity. In this respect, it echoed the Victorian age.

On the other hand, the daily lives of suburban families reflected less patriarchal dominance, frugality, and self-restraint than in earlier times. Even women's roles were less constricted than is commonly perceived. Popular periodicals of the day, as Joanne Meyerowitz has shown, frequently celebrated the feats of women in both the domestic and the public realm. Modern marriage, popular singer Pat Boone crooned in 1958, was a "fifty-fifty deal." In the modern suburban family, at least according to the popular media, husbands/fathers no longer ruled with an iron fist; indeed, like Dagwood Bumstead in a popular comic strip revealingly entitled *Life with Blondie,* husbands were often depicted as rather good-natured but bumbling incompetents. Also contrary to popular interpretations of the 1950s, both wives and husbands expected to enjoy marital sexual pleasures. Neither did middle-class families any longer deny themselves consumer delights. As never before, they bought cars, home appliances, carpets, barbecue grills, television sets, and dozens of other consumer items. No longer did women monopolize family buying. Youth too, especially teenagers, joined the consumer binge.

Consumption's importance extended to family celebrations. While consumption had long been tied to the life-cycle rituals and the major holidays of middle- and upper-class families, the postwar era saw these families staging ever more elaborate and expensive weddings, birthdays, Christmases (or Passovers), Thanksgivings, and Easters. No family celebration grew in consumer extravagance as much as weddings. Wedding consultants, guidebooks, bridal magazines, florists, and photographers became obligatory for such occasions. Unlike in the past, the wedding experts usually recommended the purchase of manufactured rather than hand-made wedding gowns and marriage gifts. For millions wedding receptions became larger and ever more elegant; the number of attendants, ring bearers, and flower girls more than doubled in the postwar years. Advertisers tied happy marriages to consumption. Splurging on weddings, they said, signaled the couple's seriousness and commitment to one another.

Like the English gentry of the eighteenth century, each suburban family had its own rural estate (albeit miniaturized), complete with a private yard, shrubs, a tiny garden, and an unattached single-family dwelling. Rooted in architectural features pioneered by Frank Lloyd Wright at the turn of the century, the suburban house of choice was the one-story ranch and split-level styles. With its picture window, built-in conveniences, open interiors, air-conditioning, central heating, and outdoor patios, the ranch-style house presumably allowed families to re-create anywhere in the nation the relaxed, fun-loving lifestyle popularly associated with sunny southern California. As with other aspects of postwar life, the ranch and split-level style houses helped to level out regional differences and leave in their wake a national suburban culture.

Leisure activities increasingly shifted from public places to the privacy of the home. In the first half of the century, city dwellers had patronized a burgeoning commercial entertainment industry, but by 1960 the movies, sports venues, big dance bands, and amusement parks had witnessed a free fall in public support. Do-it-yourself projects, home repairs, conquering the crabgrass frontier, and watching television occupied much of the suburbanite's spare time. "No man who owns his own home and lot can be a Communist," observed William J. Levitt, one of the mass-builders of suburban housing. "He has too much to do." For many, the home was a self-sufficient recreation center, or a "family playpen," to use anthropologist Margaret Mead's apt phrase. The enjoyment of children and "family togetherness," according to the popular media of the day, became virtually a moral obligation.

Television reinforced the homogenization of the culture. At first, in its early days following World War II, the new medium had offered glimpses into the nation's social and cultural heterogeneity; a series of working-class situation comedies presented families in inner-city neighborhoods and explored value conflicts that revolved around class, ethnicity, gender, and consumer spending. But in the 1950s, television programming bleached out differences. Introduced in 1953, a family sitcom, *Father Knows Best*, exemplified the shift toward a world of suburban uniformity. Insulated completely from ethnic, racial, and class conflict, the Anderson family lived an idyllic existence in a large house; the father was a benevolent despot, the mother always perfectly coiffured, and the children never given to outright rebellion.

Everything about suburban living seemed to encourage conformity. With their lives no longer anchored in small towns, rural communities, or big-city ethnic enclaves, and with the husband's job tied increasingly to the impressions that he made on others, suburban families actively sought approval from their peers. The "inner-directed" personality of the nineteenth century had given way, according to sociologist David Riesman in 1950, to an "other-directed" personality. Suburbanites not only bought similar cars and houses but also watched the same programs on television, shared similar opinions on social issues, and behaved the same. They dressed alike: blue jeans became the teenager's uniform of choice while women began wearing slacks or shorts. No group served as more compelling examples of Riesman's other-directed personality than suburban teenagers. Radio's archetype of the other-directed teenager was Henry Aldrich, who made it his "chief endeavor [in life] to find out what are the mores [of his peers] and to obey them."

CONCLUSION

In the decades between World War I (1914–18) and the turbulent 1960s, modern ways "came of age." Intellectually, the dichotomies that were so precious and so central to the conception of the world held by Victorian Americans collapsed. To modern Americans, such categories as "good" and "bad," "civilized" and "savage," "right" and "wrong," "godly" and "ungodly," and "animal" and "human" were no longer set in concrete. To them such terms seemed far less certain and more ambiguous than they had to earlier generations. To modern Americans, values were never fixed; they were always in flux. Whereas middle-class Victorians had sought to suppress volcanic passions, modern Americans tried to get in touch with and explore their feelings. They were far more likely than their ancestors to embrace and savor all varieties of raw experience. Hence, they frequently elevated the values of consumption, leisure, spontaneity, and immediate gratification above those of production, hard work, frugality, and self-control.

Yet modern ways never achieved a complete triumph. Far from it. The majority of Americans had some reservations about the drift of the nation away from traditional values and behaviors. Indeed, in the 1920s, traditionalists and modernist engaged in a full-scale cultural war, with the traditionalists enjoying some striking successes in curtailing modern ways. Confronted with the crisis of the Great Depression, modern Americans themselves were torn between visions of the future and impulses that led them back to the ways of the past. Confronted with powerful ideological enemies during World War II and the Cold War, Americans sought to define and conform to an American way of life that consisted of a combination of both the modern and the traditional. What few Americans could foresee in the 1950s were the seething changes bubbling below the surface. In the next decade, these exploded into a great cultural paroxysm.

THE CULMINATING MOMENT
OF MODERN WAYS

During the tumultuous 1960s and early 1970s, pent-up modernist impulses—some of which had been restrained since the 1920s—again surged onto the national scene. Employing sit-ins and marching in the streets, African Americans and their supporters demanded the fulfillment of the promises implicit in cultural pluralism. Hippies, as the most advanced agents of a youthful rebellion were known, openly flaunted all forms of authority. All artistic and literary barriers came tumbling down. Annihilating the ages-old dichotomy between art and life, the Living Theater, in its *Paradise Now*, invited the audience to come on stage, take off their clothes, and join the cast in sexual merrymaking. Millions of girls went from singing "I Want to Be Bobby's Girl" to chanting "I Am Woman (Hear Me Roar)." In a banner headline on its cover, *Time* magazine even posed the ominous question "Is God Dead?" All of this and more added up to a culminating moment in the history of modern ways.

But the "long sixties" (the 1960s and early 1970s) were more than this. The rebellion's participants built upon and sometimes carried to logical conclusions ideas and dreams grounded in the distant past. On behalf of African-American civil rights, for example, Martin Luther King, Jr., in his "I Have a Dream" speech delivered at the Lincoln Memorial for the March on Washington in 1963, explicitly brought together the nation's evangelical religious and republican political heritages. Recalling the revolutionary implications of the Declaration of Independence, he said, "We hold these truths to be self-evident that all men are created equal." From the revivalist Christian tradition, he thundered, "I have a dream that . . . 'the glory of the Lord shall be revealed, all flesh shall see it together.'" And, while many of the cultural rebels of the day renounced religious orthodoxy altogether, the cultural rebellion of the long sixties frequently reminded scholars of the Second Awakening, nineteenth-century romanticism, and the outburst of social reform in antebellum America. Just as their nineteenth-century predecessors had done, the new generation of protesters condemned the "false" gods of technology, science, materialism, and self-interested nationalism. They sought to simplify and rebuild society on a foundation of love rather than war. And similarly to earlier romantics, the rebels sought liberation from restraints on the self ("do your own thing"), put their faith in intuition, and pursued self-fulfillment ("getting good vibes").

A convergence of circumstances set the stage for the momentous upheavals of the long sixties. One was a declining concern with internal subversion. Few Americans objected when the U.S. Senate censured Senator Joseph McCarthy in 1954 or when in the late fifties the U.S. Supreme Court began to strike down the Cold War's legal restrictions on "subversive" speech and associations. Even more corrosive to restraints on modern ways was economic abundance. As it had not done since the 1920s, the economy's performance opened up to millions (not only in the United States but throughout the industrial world) previously unimaginable vistas of greater self-fulfillment. It made possible an exceptionally large, affluent youth culture, and it encouraged rising expectations among the less privileged. In short, general prosperity underwrote the innovation and daring of the long sixties while minimizing its risks.

21

THE RIGHTS REVOLUTION

Of its many complex and frequently opposing departures from the past, nothing was more central to the cultural tumult of the long sixties than the rights revolution. Prior to the sixties, rights had consisted of a finite body of entitlements enjoyed mainly by white men. But, beginning in the fifties with the civil rights movement and continuing into the sixties and long thereafter, the promises implicit in the nation's political and religious heritage joined with the modernist urge for individual fulfillment in encouraging one aggrieved group after another—African Americans, women, Native Americans, Hispanics, gays, welfare recipients, the handicapped, the elderly, and even consumers (among others)—to press forward claims for equality, relief from discrimination, and additional opportunities. Not only did these groups obtain greater recognition and a growing body of legal protections, but the rights revolution also brought with it far-reaching rearrangements in American race, ethnic, and family relationships.

AFRICAN AMERICANS
AND THE RIGHTS REVOLUTION

No cause was more central to the rights revolution than that of African Americans. The black civil rights movement not only swept aside a long-established system of *legal* segregation and discrimination, but also it affirmed in a spectacular fashion the modernist values of tolerance and pluralism. Sensitizing and heightening consciousness of repression, it also furnished a model for the organized movements of other discontented groups.

By the end of World War II, not much had changed since the turn of the twentieth century in the nation's system of race relations. While white Americans had gotten to know something of African Americans through jazz and the blues in the 1920s and 1930s, so-called race music could be heard only on a few radio stations. Through the 1950s, the limited number of televised images of blacks came from such age-old stereotypes as Jack Benny's butler, Rochester, and in particular the characters in the Amos and Andy show. As had been the case in 1900, law everywhere in the South still mandated the physical separation of blacks and whites in nearly all public situations. Segregation ranged from baseball parks and telephone booths to buses and classrooms. Neither could most African Americans vote in the South. And everywhere in the nation, housing segregation, either legal or de facto, was the rule. As late as 1960, of the fifty-two thousand people living in the model suburb of Levittown, Long Island, not one was known to be black. Job discrimination also existed everywhere. No matter where they lived in America, African Americans at mid-twentieth century could daily feel the awful sting and humiliation of being seen and treated as inferior human beings.

In retrospect, the precipitants of a massive assault on the nation's traditional ways of race are clear. They include the "Double V" campaign—victory over the Axis Powers abroad and victory over racism at home—sponsored by black newspapers during World War II. They include the massive migration of African Americans from the southern countryside to the cities. The new urban dwellers helped to make possible the important symbolic breakthrough of the integration of major league baseball by Jackie Robinson in 1947, and they became a major component of the Democratic party coalition sympathetic to black rights. The precipitants of the civil rights revolt include the rise of new African states and the demand for ethnic and racial inclusiveness during and after World War II. They include a decided shift in educated white opinion. By the 1940s few white intellectuals any longer subscribed to theories of racial inferiority. In principle if not always in practice, modernist whites endorsed the ideal of success based on talents rather than skin color. A poll taken in 1956 revealed that 75 percent of white college graduates outside the South favored the racial integration of the schools.

Initiatives for the postwar assault on traditional racism came from several quarters. One was from the urban-centered NAACP (National Association for the Advancement of Colored People). Responding to a suit brought by the NAACP, in 1954 a unanimous U.S. Supreme Court reversed its *Plessy v. Ferguson* decision of 1896. In *Brown v. Board of Education,* the court ruled that school segregation violated the equal protection of the law guaranteed to each citizen by the Fourteenth Amendment. Reflecting a characteristically modernist mindset, the court cited in support of its ruling a body of social science research. According to the findings of scholars, African-American children suffered irreparable psychological damage from the experience of school segregation. Hence, separate schools prevented African Americans from fully realizing their individual potentialities. Americans with modern values (including many in the urban South) applauded the *Brown* decision while traditionalists everywhere saw it as jeopardizing the American way of life.

Another major initiative for change came *not* from northern modernists, but from African American ministers and women living in the urban South. They found a leader in Martin Luther King, Jr., an eloquent young black minister. A product of both southern black Christianity and a northern modernist education, King brilliantly blended the old with the new. He repeatedly called upon an ages-old trope of black Christianity, the story of a divinely inspired Moses leading the children of Israel out of Egyptian bondage and into the promised land of Canaan. Echoing the abolitionists of the antebellum era and Mahatma Ghandi's nonviolent resistance to British rule in India in the 1940s, King called on higher law. Whenever man-made law, such as segregation statutes, contradicted higher law, he wrote in his "Letter from Birmingham Jail" (1963), then it should be resisted by nonviolent means.

He drew upon the existentialist theology of Martin Buber. Segregation, King argued, diminished human individuality. By substituting an "I-it" relationship for an "I-thou" relationship between peoples, segregation allowed whites to perceive of and to treat blacks as things or objects rather than as human beings. By taking the movement into the streets, the new medium of television aided King's cause. On nightly television news shows, King's peaceful resistance and moderation stood in sharp contrast to the violence of local police, the inflammatory rhetoric of segregation's supporters, and the partiality of southern courts.

Comprised of blacks and whites, civil rights demonstrations reached a massive crescendo in the summer of 1963. During one week in June, police arrested more than fifteen thousand demonstrators in 186 cities. Demanding both an expansion of freedom and more jobs for blacks, that summer a quarter of a million people (including a substantial white minority) marched on Washington. There, on the steps of the Lincoln Memorial, Martin Luther King, Jr., announced his "dream that one day . . . the sons of former slaves and the sons of former slave-owners will be able to sit together at the table of brotherhood."

One vital ingredient was still missing from the movement. This was political leadership. Lyndon Johnson, a Texan who became president by virtue of Kennedy's assassination in 1963, filled that vacuum. The Civil Rights Act of 1964 and the Voting Rights Act of 1965, both utterly unthinkable at the beginning of the decade, struck heavy blows at the legal bases of segregation. The 1964 act outlawed discrimination against both blacks *and* women in public places and prohibited discrimination in employment for most businesses. Perhaps as important as the act itself in promoting racial and gender equality was its enforcement. Beginning with the administration of Lyndon Johnson and fully institutionalized in the Richard M. Nixon administration, "affirmative action" required businesses, universities, and other institutions receiving federal dollars to take positive steps to ensure equal opportunities for nonwhites and women.

A far less noticed but an almost equally striking example of the startling advances of modern pluralism was the Immigration Act of 1965. The new act

Hulton-Deutsch/Corbis

Martin Luther King, Jr., at the March on Washington in 1963. Such a massive demonstration on behalf of civil rights and jobs for African Americans would hardly have been conceivable a decade earlier. Other groups seeking liberation from traditional constraints drew upon the civil rights movement for inspiration and tactics.

ended the national quota system that had long stigmatized southern and eastern Europeans as well as Asians. When combined, the new immigration law, the civil rights acts, and affirmative action represented gigantic steps in realizing more fully the egalitarian principle found in Thomas Jefferson's assertion in 1776 that "all men are created equal."

Lyndon Johnson not only presided over these momentous triumphs of egalitarian principle but also contributed to the rights revolution in other ways. Building upon the ideas of freedom from want and freedom from fear that FDR had enunciated in his famed Four Freedoms speech in 1941, Johnson implicitly urged the impoverished and the elderly, among others, to see economic and medical security as a right or an entitlement. It was no longer enough, said Johnson in 1965, to think of equality of opportunity only in terms of eliminating discrimination that barred upward mobility. In "the next and more profound stage of the battle for civil rights . . . we seek . . . not just equality as a right and a theory, but equality as a fact and as a result." In an effort to move the country in that direction, the national government enacted the largest domestic agenda since the New Deal. It included a "war on poverty" program, medicare, medicaid, and increased federal expenditures on education.

In the meantime, the civil rights movement had polarized the nation. From the outset, traditionalist opponents had believed that racial differences were embedded in biology, the Bible, and custom; hence, they thought that it was sheer folly for humans to think they could or should alter existing racial relationships. Throughout the South massive resistance greeted the *Brown* decision, and the peaceful marches, sit-ins, and mass arrests that King and his followers had used so successfully earlier in the South utterly failed to dismantle the North's black ghettos nor close the wide economic gap separating blacks from other Americans. A year before his death by an assassin's bullet in 1968, an incredulous King said he had never "seen as much hatred" as he encountered when he tried to integrate the white ethnic enclaves of Chicago. He confessed that open housing and equal employment opportunities for blacks remained "a distant dream."

A series of violent uprisings in northern ghettos during the late 1960s indicated that many African Americans had given up on King's strategy of nonviolence. Triggered by actions of the predominately white police force, which many ghetto residents saw as an occupying army, the Watts Riot in Los Angeles came only days after President Johnson signed the Voting Rights Act of 1965. An estimated 50,000 persons participated in the "rebellion"; the rioters assaulted police and firefighters, looted white-owned businesses, and burned buildings. Before order was restored by police and the National Guard, some thirty-five people were killed, nine hundred were injured, and $30 million worth of property was destroyed. By the summer of 1967, riots had broken out in most of the big-city ghettos across the country. A special commission appointed by President Johnson to study the urban rioting reported in 1968 that the violence was due to "segregation and poverty." "Our nation is moving toward two societies, one black, one white—separate but unequal," it concluded.

Against this backdrop, growing numbers of blacks gave up not only on King's advocacy of passive resistance but also on his modernist goal of racial integration and inclusiveness. Drawing on the nationalist tradition of Marcus Garvey, Malcolm X, a leader of the Nation of Islam, rejected alliances with sympathetic whites or federal assistance; he insisted that blacks must rely on their own resources. The slogan "Black Power" struck an especially responsive chord among young black activists. While never winning many victories or ever carefully articulated, the Black Power movement encouraged racial separatism. A similar separatist impulse would lead Native Americans, Chicanos, and third-generation ethnics to retreat from modern pluralism's inclusionist goal.

Meanwhile, African Americans did win some significant victories during the late 1960s and the 1970s. With the vigorous enforcement of the Voting Rights Act of 1965, blacks began voting in record numbers; they dramatically increased their representation in Congress, state houses, and town halls across the nation. Despite stout resistance by whites in the South and in some parts of the North, the Supreme Court vigorously enforced school desegregation

Watching an Urban Riot. In this poignant, undated photo, a National Guard soldier and a young African American watch an urban riot. The outbreak of violence in the big-city ghettos of the North indicated that many blacks in the ghettos had given up on Martin Luther King, Jr.'s dream of racial inclusion and integration.

and initially approved the busing of school children when necessary to achieve integration. The court also sanctioned "affirmative action" programs that were designed to achieve equality by reserving opportunities for minorities in education and in the job market. Nonetheless, while millions of African Americans moved into the middle class, millions of others remained far behind the national average in all indicators of equality with whites. At the end of the 1970s, race remained the nation's most salient and persistent social division.

WOMEN AND THE RIGHTS REVOLUTION

As with African Americans, women at the beginning of the long sixties also lived with major obstacles to their self-fulfillment. These included their intimate relations with men, where they frequently experienced a world of constrained choices and belittling remarks. Married women could not borrow money in their own name, and, as a legal concept, sexual harassment did not exist. Having taken jobs outside the home so that they and their families could enjoy more of the fruits of the consumer society, many women found their hands simultaneously full of shopping lists, stenographic pads, dinner dishes, and diaper pails. At work, they usually held lower-paying jobs and found upward job mobility blocked. No laws required men and women to receive equal pay for exactly the same jobs. Graduate and professional schools imposed official or unofficial quotas that limited women's admissions to 10 percent or less of their totals.

There were other underlying precipitants of the women's rights movement or what is sometimes called "second wave feminism." The number of female college students doubled in the 1960s, creating a vastly larger pool of those who were more likely to become discontented with the gender status quo. The downward plunge of the birthrate in the 1960s left more women with more years of their lives free of child-care responsibilities. Finally, in the 1960s the divorce rate, which had been creeping upward throughout the twentieth century, suddenly shot upward. The upshot of all of this was that the typical woman's life included work, marriage, child-rearing, a span of her life free of child-care, and, if divorced, supporting and bringing up children alone—a far cry from the fifties' ideal of domesticity.

The arrival of a new set of female icons anticipated and contributed to the revival of feminism. A hint surfaced in 1961 that neither the cheerful housewives of television sitcoms nor the blank-faced, big-breasted, blue-eyed blondes of Hollywood would any longer suffice as models of womanhood. To many women, Jacqueline Kennedy, the new president's wife, seemed to keep in perfect suspension an older femininity and a new, more modern womanhood. Slim, stylish, rich, a dutiful wife, a mother, and formerly a career woman, she read voraciously, spoke French fluently, and loved horseback riding. Even the heroines of sixties' television sitcoms changed; on *Bewitched, I Dream of Jeannie,* and *The Flying Nun,* the female leads all possessed magical powers. Suggestive of yet another impulse toward greater female freedom and empowerment was the popularity of a revolutionary style of dancing. Bursting on the scene in 1960, "The Twist," a hit by Chubby Checker, featured teenagers dancing without touching or the man leading.

Yet neither Jackie Kennedy, magical women, nor dancing apart were free of traditional feminine stereotypes. They sent women mixed, even schizoid, messages. Nothing illustrated this point more forcefully or grotesquely than the go-go girl dancing in a cage. Autonomous as she danced alone, the go-go girl was literally trapped in a cage. She could be considered simply as an "object" before the voyeuristic gaze of her mostly male audience.

In 1963, into the popular culture's confusing cross-currents, came a bombshell—Betty Friedan's *The Feminine Mystique.* Friedan stood the idealized postwar American way of life on its head. Just four years after Richard

Nixon had made the suburban home, with its stay-at-home mother and its abundance of consumer goods, the emblem of the American way of life, Friedan described it as nothing less than "a comfortable concentration camp." Rather than being "gaily content in a world of bedroom, kitchen, sex, babies and home," wrote Friedan, the camp's inmates (the suburban house-wives) felt "empty" and "incomplete." Despite more than a hundred years of agitation for equal access to opportunities, she continued, "our culture does not permit women to accept or gratify their basic need to grow and fulfill their potentialities as human beings." Those who sought careers, according to Friedan, were deemed neurotic and unwomanly. Influenced by Freidan's book, almost overnight—or so it seemed—women seeking career opportu-nities won a series of smashing victories.

Yet new federal mandates expanding opportunities for women in the job market arising from the civil rights laws and affirmative action failed to alter other forms of gender tyranny. Traditional stereotypes continued to pervade the popular media and, while an accompanying sexual revolution freed women of some of the double standard's restraints, it simultaneously seemed to reinforce the prevailing notion of women as objects for the sexual pleasure of men. Influenced by participation in the civil rights and the antiwar move-ments, where pleas for gender equality were usually ignored by the male leadership, a new, more radical feminism burst onto the national scene in 1968. At the Miss America beauty pageant (the only television show that Richard Nixon let his daughters stay up late at night to watch), protestors sought to call attention to how the culture placed a higher value on the way a woman looks than on her achievements by filling a "freedom trash can" with bras, girdles, hairpins, and false eyelashes.

The momentum for the organized phase of the revived feminist movement reached high tide in the 1970s. Membership in the National Organization of Women, founded in 1966 by Betty Friedan, multiplied rapidly, and hundreds of thousands of women joined "consciousness-raising groups" where they discussed with other women job discrimination and relationships with their boyfriends and husbands. Frustrated by feelings of entrapment in traditional housewife roles and angry over unfair divisions of household labor, many confronted their husbands or partners. They demanded new arrangements. Initially viewed as a radical idea (or even as a communist-inspired one in the 1950s), feminists succeeded in expanding the number of child-care centers. In 1973, the U.S. Supreme Court decided that women could legally terminate pregnancies within the first three months after conception.

Spurred on by affirmative action, employment opportunities for women, especially in the professions, increased sharply. Symbolic of feminist suc-cesses was the sudden proliferation of women in sports and eventually in the armed forces, arenas long considered special bastions of "masculinity" and

Bettmann/Corbis

Women Demonstrating on Behalf of the Equal Rights Amendment, Washington, D.C., 1970. While the Equal Rights Amendment fell short of ratification, perhaps no change in American ways during the last half of the twentieth century was more profound than that revolving around the expectations, roles, and behaviors of women.

"manliness." Within five years after the passage of Title IX of the Educational Amendments Act of 1972, nearly every high school and college in the country rushed to form varsity programs for women. In startling contrast with the 1950s, by the mid-1970s the revived feminist movement had opened up a far larger world of choices and opportunities for women.

   As with the civil rights movement of African Americans, the feminist movement provoked a traditionalist counterattack. Led by Phyllis Schlafly, the traditionalists insisted that the Supreme Court's abortion decision in 1973 and the proposed Equal Rights Amendment (which stated that "equality of rights shall not be denied or abridged . . . on account of sex") represented radical departures from roles assigned by God to wives and mothers. The amendment would encourage lesbianism, Schlafly claimed. Schlafly's affirmation of ages-old gender roles received a warm response not only from traditionalist men but also from many religiously orthodox women as well as from working-class women and homemakers, many of whom shared few of the values and experiences of the middle- and upper-class leadership of the feminist movement. Three states short of ratification, the Equal Rights Amendment (ERA) died quietly in 1982.

Yet, while gender discrimination continued and the organized feminist movement never recovered, the gains on behalf of women during the long sixties were by no means lost. Even had the ERA been passed, observed Jane Mansbridge, its effect would have been mostly symbolic; by then nearly all sex-differentiated laws that would have been changed by the amendment had already been wiped out. Indeed, of all the rights movements, none succeeded in obtaining more enduring results than the feminist uprising of the long sixties.

THE SUPREME COURT
AND THE RIGHTS REVOLUTION

From an unexpected and historically conservative branch of the national government came yet another major contributor to the rights revolution. In a series of landmark decisions, the "Warren Court," so named for its chief justice, Earl Warren, who served from 1953 to 1969, vastly expanded the constitutional protections of individual rights. Apart from the 1954 school desegregation decision, in the late 1950s the court began to strike down the Cold War strictures on freedom of speech. Reflecting the nation's growing religious pluralism and in effect disestablishing Protestantism as the nation's unofficial religion, in the 1960s, the court extended the rights of religious minorities by prohibiting prayer and Bible readings in the public schools. Defending the rights of the less privileged and the powerless, the court required that the state provide indigent defendants in felony cases with attorneys at public expense and that the police advise suspects of their constitutional rights as well as the right to have counsel present during questioning. Dismantling a long-standing system of state and local censorship, the court extended constitutional protections to all sexually explicit materials that had any "literary or scientific, or artistic value."

Not only did the court provide an immense transfusion of additional substance into traditional civil liberties, but also it created or invented essentially new rights that would have far-reaching consequences for the history of American ways. One was the right to privacy. "The right to be let alone is the beginning of all freedom," wrote Supreme Court Justice William O. Douglas. Conceding in effect that the decade's sexual revolution could not be reversed, the court extended access to birth control not only to married couples but also eventually to unmarried adults and to minors. Although Earl Warren was no longer on the bench, these decisions led directly to *Roe v. Wade* (1973), which gave women the constitutional right to terminate a pregnancy. Furthermore, a bundle of court rulings and legislative actions essentially redefined the family as a collection of sovereign individuals rather than as a single unit headed by a husband/father. Consequently, within the domestic sphere, women (and to a growing extent children as well) experienced a vastly expanded set of legal protections.

CONCLUSION

The rights revolution of the long sixties represented giant steps toward the fulfillment of promises implicit in the nation's religious and revolutionary republican heritage as well as in the modern values of cultural pluralism and toleration. Once again, as they had done earlier in American history, African Americans and women seized on the Declaration of Independence's assertion that "all men are created equal" to claim for themselves the same rights and privileges previously enjoyed only by white men. In addition, modernists' assaults on dichotomies that had posited race, sex, and other categories as intrinsic or fundamental to the nature of the universe prepared the way for the wider acceptance of African Americans, women, and other minorities as equals. Important to the early civil rights movement in particular were religious ideas and leaders; both black and white ministers, priests, and rabbis were at the forefront of demands for greater racial equality and inclusion. Yet, simultaneously, opponents of change in the nation's social relationships also employed religious ideas; in defending traditional racial and gender ways, they frequently cited the authority of the Bible.

Rather than subsiding during the final decades of the twentieth century, issues revolving around rights continued to occupy a central place in the national colloquy. More and more Americans demanded the removal of all obstacles to their individual fulfillment. Native Americans, gays, and lesbians, for example, sought guarantees of a life free of violence and discrimination. The Disabilities Act of 1990 expanded the possibilities for the handicapped to realize fuller lives. Children, the mentally ill, and the imprisoned also claimed as rights opportunities for greater self-gratification and contentment. In the name of rights, claims were even made on behalf of endangered species and unborn fetuses. In addition, "rights" became a favorite rhetorical weapon in the campaigns for clean air, safe water, and healthy foods.

22

INDIVIDUALISM UNLEASHED

As with other modernist impulses, an extraordinary series of crises—the Great Depression, World War II, and the early Cold War—had served to set back or to contain the more expressive forms of individualism. But, alongside and frequently interacting with the revolution for rights during the long sixties was a remarkably widespread tendency to unleash restraints on individual intuitions and feelings. Pushing the earlier twentieth-century revolt against Victorian self-control to its outer limits, the cultural rebels of the day (most of whom were youth), embraced aphorisms such as "If it feels good, do it," "Let it all hang out," and "Do your own thing." True, there was a pull in the sixties toward the creation of smaller, more intimate, face-to-face communities, but in the end this urge gave way to a far more powerful appetite for self-fulfillment and self-expression. Nearly all of the decade's cultural rebels believed that each individual possessed a unique inner core or self, one that could be released only by rejecting artificiality and external authority.

CONCERN FOR THE FATE OF THE INDIVIDUAL

Well before the 1960s, even in the midst of the enthusiasm for the idealized, fifties way of life, there was evidence in the culture of a growing concern for the fate of the individual. Artists, intellectuals, and even those employed in the world of white-collar bureaucracies began to ask with increasing frequency, "In a society of giant bureaucracies, mass media, and suburban conformity, where is there room for the individual?" Despite the creation in the sixties and afterward of a culture that seemed far more attuned to the unrestrained individual, Americans continued long afterward to voice this and related questions.

The answers proffered by social critics in the 1940s and 1950s to the place of the individual in contemporary society were far from reassuring. More than a few saw authentic individuality swamped in a flood of consumer goods. "People no longer have opinions," complained one writer, "they have refrigerators. Instead of illusions, we have television." Others worried about the effects of the media on individualism. According to a brilliant group of refugees from

Nazi Germany, the mass media left modern societies dangerously susceptible to totalitarianism. The media "automatized reactions and . . . weaken[ed] forces of individual resistance," charged Theodor Adorno. Another critic, Dwight Macdonald, sarcastically described American middle-class suburban literary and artistic pretensions, because of their banality and conformity with media-provided mediocrity, as "midcult." Even fifties suburbanites themselves worried about the effects of movies, comic books, advertising, television, and rock-and-roll music on the nation's youth.

Still others complained about the sacrifice of individuality required for achieving personal success in a world of institutional behemoths. Sociologist David Riesman in *The Lonely Crowd* (1950) set the tone for a large body of social criticism in the fifties when he juxtaposed the "inner-directed man" of the nineteenth century against the "outer-directed man" of the twentieth century. *The Man in the Gray Flannel Suit* (Sloan Wilson), *The Organization Man* (William Whyte), and *White Collar Class* (C. Wright Mills)—the very titles of these popular books evoked similar images of a stifling conformity to outside pressures. To describe those whose lives were caught up in the labyrinth of organizational leviathans, beginning in the 1950s the term "rat race" became something of a cliché in newspaper stories and in everyday conversations.

Fiction and movies too reflected a concern for the individual. While fiction in the Great Depression had characteristically emphasized society and social problems, that of the forties and fifties focused on the self. Some of the most popular novels and movies championed the defiant individual. Such individuals overcame insuperable dangers by resorting exclusively to their own internal resources. "I do not recognize anyone's right to one minute of my time," announced the contumacious hero of Ayn Rand's best-selling novel, *The Fountainhead* (1943). The public responded with equal fervor to less selfish Western heroes whom they encountered in countless postwar movies and later in television shows. Acting alone and against overwhelming odds, the Western heroes invariably restored justice and order in a cleansing rite of violence. Mickey Spillane's private detective, Mike Hammer, offered yet another formulation of the defiant individual. While frequently breaking society's rules, Hammer single-handedly dispatched drug dealers, mobsters, and communists.

Other depictions of the individual were far less sanguine. Ultimately no personal choice nor inner resource made any difference, according to the novelists of World War II; one soldier was just as likely as the next to fall victim to a stray bullet. The most compelling examples of this kind of fiction came from writers outside the mainstream culture. Unlike the Western hero, individuals in the South, according to a group of regional writers, found themselves shackled in an invisible prison from the past while Jewish writers explored the anguishing inner turmoil faced by the offspring of immigrants in contemporary America. In his powerful novel, *Invisible Man* (1952), Ralph Ellison cried out against the loss of individuality and the depersonalization suffered by African Americans in white society.

Yet none of these writers anticipated or influenced the rebellious cultural styles of the sixties as much as the "beats." Echoing Walt Whitman, whom they admired, the beats renounced suburban conformity and consumerism. "Robot apartments! invisible suburbs! skeleton treasures! blind capitals! demonic industries!" shouted Allen Ginsberg in his poem *Howl* (1955). While conspicuously rejecting acquisitive individualism, they warmly embraced all of the expressive forms of individualism. Hence, they experimented with drugs, celebrated uninhibited sexuality, took to the open road, and, believing that African Americans were less culturally repressed than whites, incorporated into their argot such words from black ghetto culture as "dig," "hip," "man," "split," and "cool." Not only in the sixties but also long afterwards the beats continued to serve one generation after another with heroic prototypes of cultural rebellion.

Allen Ginsberg/Corbis

A Group of Beats Outside the City Lights Bookstore, San Francisco, California, 1956. From left to right are Bob Donlin, Neal Cassady, Allen Ginsberg, Robert LaVinge, and Lawrence Ferlinghetti. In their rejection of suburban America's conformity, the beats not only helped to usher in the cultural tumult of the long 1960s but also became enduring icons of late twentieth- and early twenty-first-century rebel cultures.

THE YOUTH CULTURE

The development of a new, more powerful, and ultimately more autonomous youth culture in the post–World War II era also foreshadowed the expressive individualism of the turbulent sixties. In the postwar era, the return of prosperity, the sheer number of youth who were becoming teenagers, and the mass media all contributed to the shaping of the new youth culture. Seeking to make life for their children easier and happier than their lives had been, parents with modern values tended to relinquish authority and influence over their children's lives to others. As in the past, modernist parents turned to outside experts. No authority for child rearing was more influential than Dr. Benjamin Spock. In his *Baby and Child Care* (1946), a book second in sales in the postwar era only to the Bible, Spock told parents to "be flexible and adjust to the baby's needs and happiness." Spock urged less old-fashioned discipline and more indulgence. "Don't be afraid to love him [your child] and enjoy him. Every baby needs to be smiled at, talked to, played with, fondled—gently and lovingly— just as much as he needs vitamins and calories."

From the mid-fifties onward, the new media of television probably exceeded the influence of advice from experts in shaping the lives of youth. The baby boomers—as the exploding population born in the 1940s and 1950s came to be known—literally grew up with television. Both the media and advertising moguls knew that if they were to succeed in the fast-growing youth market they had to produce movies, television shows, songs, and commercials that spoke to a new generation of teenagers. The attention lavished upon teenagers by advertisers and the media encouraged the young to feel a special sense of entitlement and generational power. Having frequently left behind extended families and older forms of community and having abandoned moral absolutes or perhaps any standards at all, suburban parents were left in a vulnerable position. No longer did they have at their disposal the same resources as their parents had had in shielding their children against the influences of peer groups, the media, or the advertisers.

While for the most part youth values and behaviors conformed to those of the adult world—after all, they were said to be "the silent generation"— there were in retrospect manifest signs in the postwar era of a potential youth rebellion. In the late 1940s a nationwide debate erupted over the "problem of juvenile delinquency," though in fact there was no significant increase in youth criminality. In the next decade, "hot-rodding," rock-and-roll music, "going steady," peculiar hair styles (long and greasy), tight pants, and a special teenage argot aroused fears that growing numbers of middle-class suburban teenagers were adopting the cultural values of the black ghetto, of juvenile delinquents, and/or of the urban working class.

The entertainment industry contributed to a growing youth-centered challenge to authority. Youth reveled in Walt Disney's comic character *Bugs Bunny* (introduced in 1938), a principled rebel who lived by his wits. While staring down the barrel of a gun, Bugs uttered the classic hipster phrase: "Eh, what's up doc?" *Mad* magazine, widely read by youth in the 1950s, even more directly and mercilessly lampooned authority. Millions of youth identified with the magazine's silly looking, gap-toothed icon, Alfred E. Neuman, who sought to assuage readers' fears by exclaiming "What—Me Worry?" Hollywood also quickly discovered the rebellious youth. Films such as *The Wild One, Rebel Without A Cause*, and *The Blackboard Jungle* and young stars such as Marlon Brando and James Dean offered sympathetic portrayals of teenagers allegedly trapped in an alienating world of suburban, middle-class adults.

But nothing disturbed suburban parents, ministers, and educators more than the arrival in the mid-1950s of rock-and-roll music. Adapted from black rhythm and blues, rock and roll's heavy beat and frenetic energy were far more expressive than the decade's mainstream music. At the center of the revolution in teenage music swaggered Elvis Presley. Exuding raw sexual power by suggestively swaying his hips, Presley shocked white middle-class adults. The more parents condemned Presley and other rock stars, the more their teenage children seemed to love them. By the end of the fifties, nothing separated the generations more sharply than their respective musical tastes.

THE YOUTH REVOLT

Rather than emerging from the opposing cultural styles of the adults and their offspring, however, the youth revolt got its initial impetus primarily from visions of a more humane society. For a brief but significant moment, John F. Kennedy, the newly elected president in 1960, stimulated the as yet vague urge for change. Unlike his fatherly predecessor, Dwight D. Eisenhower, the youthful president, novelist Norman Mailer predicted, would shake up suburbia with its "spirit of the supermarket, [its] homogeneous extension of stainless surfaces and psychoanalyzed people, packaged commodities and ranch houses." The expectation of change arose in part from Kennedy's image; his and his family's stunning good looks and their sheer vigor suggested change. "All at once you had something exciting," one young political campaign worker explained. Expectation of change partly arose from Kennedy's bold rhetoric. In contrast to the allegedly purposeless drift of the 1950s, he called for a renewal of national purpose. "Ask not what your country can do for you—ask what you can do for your country," he challenged in his inaugural address. While timid in conceptualization and in execution,

Kennedy's brief presidency (he was assassinated in 1963) helped to trigger the long decade's great cultural paroxysms.

In the meantime, a tiny group of radical college students began to formulate a more explicit alternative vision of what America might become. It incorporated neither the dreams of traditional socialists nor the piecemeal measures of post–World War II liberal reformers. Indeed, the Democratic party, they said, was implicated in and an integral component of the oppressive "establishment." In its Port Huron Statement, adopted by the Students for a Democratic Society in 1962, the "New Left" saw the main problem of contemporary life in terms of *alienation* rather than class conflict. In place of the alienating ways of fifties' suburbia, the New Left proposed a restoration of craft modes of work, the construction of small face-to-face communities, and participatory democracy in all aspects of group life. Influenced by such thinking, inspired by the civil rights movement, and increasingly opposed to American involvement in Vietnam, in 1964 large numbers of students protested the University of California at Berkeley's strictures on speech and assemblage. As the United States' troop commitments in Vietnam ballooned after 1964, protests spread like wildfire.

In 1968, the climactic year of the student uprising, more than two hundred major demonstrations involving more than forty thousand students rocked the nation. In dorms and crash pads, walls that had once been adorned with Beatles posters were now sporting Viet Cong flags and portraits of Ho Chi Minh, the leader of North Vietnam, and Che Guevera, the Cuban revolutionary. In utter astonishment, a writer for *Fortune* magazine warned that "these youngsters are acting out a revolution—not a protest, and not a rebellion, but an honest-to-God revolution." The protests took on worldwide dimensions. In every major city in the noncommunist industrial world during 1968, students demonstrated and marched in the streets.

The long sixties witnessed a rekindling of interest in ideology. Intellectuals reexamined sympathetically the ideas of Karl Marx, more often his early writings which were concerned with alienation than his later work which emphasized class conflict. Several sought to incorporate one or another form of expressive individualism into their visions. Passionately convinced that humanity possessed immense reservoirs of untapped spiritual and emotional powers, they explored the potentialities of drugs, Eastern mysticism, and the release of behavioral restraints. Even one of the more dispassionate spokespersons of the cultural rebellion, Herbert Marcuse, argued that human unhappiness arose mostly from repression by industrial capitalism of the fundamental human drives for sensual fulfillment.

The uprising extended far beyond politics. Though the civil rights and antiwar movements were crucial catalysts to the long sixties counterculture, many of the rebels had no or little interest in social causes. While some youth remained clean-shaven and immaculately dressed as they campaigned for the election of antiwar candidate Senator Eugene McCarthy for the presidency in 1968, others embraced a lifestyle that in gesture if not in substance conspicuously repudiated the ways of their parents. Labeled as "hippies," they let their hair grow long, donned bizarre clothing, and took mind-bending drugs. Disgusted with all forms of artifice, they insisted on the importance of absolute candor in all personal and social relationships. Frequently rejecting the competitive and acquisitive individualism that they attributed to their parents, they established little worlds of their own in New York's East Village, San Francisco's Haight-Asbury district, and in some two thousand communes across the nation.

Drugs, music, and sex emerged as the rebellion's most powerful symbols. Illegal hallucinogens had long been associated with literary and artistic rebels and with "hip" African Americans, but among the rebellious young, marijuana, more commonly called "pot," replaced tobacco and alcohol as the drug of choice. The youth supported two kinds of music: folk ballads and rock and roll. The folk songs frequently protested racism, pollution of the environment, the bomb, and the Vietnam War. While initially neatly groomed and nonthreateningly boyish, the Beatles, an enormously popular English rock group, soon grew straggly beards and donned bright clothing; they became promoters of drugs ("I'd love to turn you on") and sex ("Why

Vince Streano/Corbis

Hippies in a Park, New Orleans, 1971. No group in the late twentieth century reflected the key impulse of expressive individualism more dramatically than the hippies. Notice the hippies' free-flowing body movements and loose-fitting clothes. In addition, notice that, to the rebellious youth, hair and clothing no longer serve as unambiguous signs of gender differences.

don't we do it in the road") while rejecting revolution ("You know, it's going to be alright"). The cultural side of the youth revolt exploded into an ecstatic and orgiastic climax in 1969 when some four hundred thousand youth gathered at the Woodstock festival in upstate New York. Heralding the festival as the dawn of a new age of love and peace (the Age of Aquarius), for three days and nights the youth reveled in drugs, sex, and rock music.

While the expressive individualism of the rebellious youth pressed well beyond the mainstream culture, it was fundamentally an extension of the modern values and behaviors of their parents. Scholars studying the youth revolt quickly discovered that its participants came almost exclusively from modern families, that is, suburban families who were better educated than the average, who were better-off financially than most Americans, and whose fathers worked in management or in the professions. Rather than complete opposition, the differences between children and parents were largely ones of degree. In child rearing, their parents had been guided by the gentle admonitions of Benjamin Spock; in rearing their own children the rebellious young planned to be even more permissive than their parents had been. Neither were parents and their offspring totally at odds over divorce, open sexuality, marijuana use, and relaxed lifestyles. Rather than standing in complete opposition to their parents, the youth carried the values and behaviors of their parents to their ultimate and sometimes absurd conclusions. Both modern parents and their offspring called for greater self-fulfillment.

THE SEXUAL REVOLUTION

Nothing more concretely illustrated the unleashing of expressive forms of individualism in the long sixties than the sexual revolution. As early as the 1920s modernist Americans had begun to embrace a positive sexual ideology. When confined to heterosexuality and marriage, modernists had seen sexual intercourse as essential to emotional health, an important source of mutual pleasure, and a valuable means of psychic self-expression. Apparently, however, the actual sexual behavior of many Americans extended far beyond the marital bed. According to surveys of middle-class sexual behavior published by Alfred Kinsey in 1948 and in 1953, 90 percent of the males and 50 percent of the females had engaged in premarital coitus, half of the men and a quarter of the women had had extramarital sex, and more than a third of the men had participated in adult homosexual activity. Given the weakening or dissolution of traditional sources of moral authority, anthropologist Margaret Mead warned that Kinsey's findings might themselves serve as standards of sexual conduct.

Yet, despite Mead's worries, Kinsey's studies ushered in no immediate or drastic changes in the nation's sex ways. Until the 1960s, formal censorship or self-imposed restraints governed the sexual contents of much of the popular media. As late as 1953, the movie industry denied its seal of approval to *The Moon Is Blue* because the film's dialogue included the words *seduction* and *virgin*. Novels of the 1940s and 1950s continued to employ euphemisms for sexual acts. The infamous "double standard" remained largely intact. While high school and college males could gain status within their peer groups for their sexual exploits, their female counterparts did not enjoy the same freedom. Females continued to be told that "nice girls don't."

But then, as the 1950s gave way to the 1960s, the walls that had kept sexuality within certain bounds seemed suddenly to give way. Behind the collapse was the staggering fact that 46 million baby boomers (of 150 million total population) entered their teens in the early 1960s. At the same time, the courts began to relax the standards for censorship (a turning point came when the judiciary permitted the sale of D. H. Lawrence's long-suppressed novel, *Lady Chatterly's Lover*, in 1959), the Federal Drug Administration approved the distribution of the birth control pill (in 1960), and the movie theaters (with three-quarters of their audience now comprised of teenagers) began to show far more sexually risqué films. Proclaiming the message that the single woman could enjoy all the same joys of the bedroom as the single man, Helen Gurley Brown's *Sex and the Single Girl* (1963) became an instant best-seller.

Long aware that sex sells products and given to sweeping conclusions, the mass media announced in the early sixties that the nation was in the midst of a "sexual revolution." Sex-starved coeds, they suggested, were shedding their virginity en masse. Margaret Mead, who was by now a senior sage of modern ways, abandoned all semblance of careful judgement when she declared that "we have jumped from puritanism to lust." "The Puritan ethic, so long dominant in the U.S., is widely considered to be dying, if not dead," pontificated *Time* magazine in 1965, "and there are few mourners."

While change in actual sexual behavior never approximated the wild claims of the media, historian Susan Douglas has made the more important point that "imposing one's own sexual standards on others was now as anachronistic as a Jonathan Edwards sermon; sophisticated tolerance was in." By the early 1970s few restraints were left on the media. Frontal nudity, simulated or actual sexual intercourse, and sexual acts previously considered unnatural could now be seen in frontline movie houses, and what was once considered to be illegal pornography could be found in corner drugstores or in public libraries. That many more couples began living with one another outside of marriage occasioned far less public criticism than in the past. Perhaps nothing reflected the growing sexual tolerance more than the American Psychiatric

Association's decision in 1973 to no longer classify homosexuality as a disease. Like the youth revolt, the sea change in sexual tolerance was not limited to the United States. It swept through the entire Western world.

As the feminist movement soon brought to the attention of the public, the sexual revolution was not an unmixed blessing for women. While women enjoyed far more freedom to experience sexual pleasure than in the past, abetted by the popular culture and consumer society, the revolution seemed to encourage men to look upon women more exclusively in terms of sexuality than they had earlier. Male novelists frequently depicted women who enjoyed being raped, and in the popular media incidences of violence, rape, and even mutilation of females increased. Fearful of being classified as frigid, faked orgasms by females became a metaphor for their exploitation. Paradoxically, the revolution also potentially added to male anxieties. "Our findings show that women have completely abandoned the role of passive sexual partner," wrote sociologist Robert J. Levin. Unlike in the past, sensitive, modern men now found themselves confronted with growing demands that they aid in the achievement of sexual fulfillment of their partners.

UNLEASHING ART

Dramatists, literati, painters, architects, and musicians—all explored in the long 1960s the outermost reaches of their respective genres. Long before the sixties, modernist doubts about the existence of a superintending God, an orderly universe, the human capacity for reason, and a set of absolute truths had opened up a seemingly limitless realm of possibilities for individual creativity and artistic expression. No longer obligated to elevate the spirit, to educate, or to promote morality, modern artists had been cast free of all external references and restraints. Art no longer needed to imitate life; art could be done merely for its own sake. Such an unshackling encouraged radical experimentation in form, the bridging of traditional polarities, and the heightening and savoring of all varieties of experience. In short, it encouraged what George Roeder, Jr., has described as the "modernist urge to see, experience, and express everything."

Nonetheless, until the 1960s modernist artists had accepted some restraints on their work. Much of it was self-imposed. For they carried in their heads, as Robert Hughes has observed, "an invisible tribunal" of their predecessors who sat "in judgment" of the quality and style of their work. Artists also saw themselves as engaged in something—though they would be hard-pressed to define precisely what this something was—far more important than gratifying the tastes of the masses or in making money. Indeed, the modernist artistic commitment can be likened to that of a religious calling. An overt hostility to what was variously described as "puritanism," "Victorianism," "bourgeois," and/or "mass" culture frequently served as a defining characteristic of the modernist artist. While ostentatiously renouncing materialism and condemning hypocrisy, conformity, and sexual repression, they sought truth in the medium itself or the elements (in painting, for example, color, composition, and dimensions) that defined their medium. As testimonials to the seriousness that they attributed to their work, they consciously exiled themselves from mainstream society, cultivated a bohemian lifestyle, and frequently took pride in living a hand-to-mouth daily existence.

By the 1960s artists (sometimes labeled in hindsight as postmodernists) came to openly reject, or at the least to compromise, even these modernist constraints. For one thing, their pose of alienation and a bohemian self-exile became far more difficult to sustain when the artists found their lifestyles and attitudes embraced by the nation's rebellious youth. Imitating the artists, literally millions of youth also took drugs, engaged in sexual experimentation, rejected materialism, and condemned conformity. In effect, co-option by the young, as David Steigerwald has written, "enlarged bohemia, commercialized it, and destroyed its artistic soul." Eventually a bohemian-like lifestyle extended far beyond the rebellious young; by the early 1970s, even Wall Street brokers were sporting long hair and sideburns and were wearing brightly colored clothes.

For another thing, many artists sought to reestablish connections of their work to society. Art, they said, could be employed to usher in the new Age of Aquarius. In order for art to become "an instrument for modifying consciousness and organizing new realms of sensibility," essayist Susan Sontag even urged the suspension of criticism. Artistic and literary criticism, she said, stifled creativity and repressed the passions. Without criticism, no one could claim that one piece of art was superior to another and no longer could formal art be separated from popular culture.

By collapsing ages-old distinctions between art and life, feelings and expressions, and high culture and popular culture, artists in the sixties further eroded the last of the modernist constraints. Perhaps no "work of art" succeeded quite so well in this regard as John Cage's 1952 recording of $4'33"$, which consisted of four minutes and thirty-three seconds of total silence. While regaling in the sounds around them, listeners to Cage's recording completely escaped the "tyranny" that composers traditionally imposed on their audiences. Since art no longer had to be "something," it could be anything. As depicted in Andy Warhol's silk screens of Campbell's Soup cans and pictures of Marilyn Monroe, art could even be the objects of consumer society. With alienation now "in" or fashionable and with all standards in shambles, art as traditionally understood seemed indeed to be in the throes of its final demise.

On the other hand, the unleashing of art may have also opened up new realms of art and artistic understanding. Defenders of the "artistic revolution" observed that art was no longer restricted to museums or a limited preserve of elites. Art could be anything and everything. It could be psychedelic T-shirts, a hydroelectric dam, an atomic explosion, or "Carhenge" (a piece of "art" in Nebraska that consisted of used cars with their noses buried in the ground in a configuration resembling England's ancient Stonehenge).

THE LONG SIXTIES' IMPACT ON RELIGION

Neither did religion escape the tumultuous cultural upheavals of the long sixties. Not only did the decade's unrest affect all traditional religious groups, but the rebellion itself can be seen as something of a religious revival. Traditional religions, the cultural rebels frequently concluded, were part of the "establishment" and therefore complicit in the failures of American society. In a quest for a less contaminated spirituality, in the late 1960s and early 1970s many of the rebels turned from Western to Eastern faiths; some even journeyed to far-off India to consult with Buddhist monks and gurus. While most of the so-called new-age religions demanded a total commitment from their adherents, these religions downplayed a rule-oriented morality in favor of opening one's self up to the combined wisdom of multiple cultures.

One product of this widespread spiritual quest reached far beyond the corps of those who had been converted to a new faith. That was transcendental meditation. By the mid-1970s, millions of Americans of varying religious persuasions or none at all tried to set aside a special time in which they could concentrate their thoughts on transcending the daily cares of their immediate world. Likewise, experimentation with Eastern religions convinced many young Americans to alter their lifestyles; they frequently renounced meat-eating in favor of vegetarianism and sought to dress and live more simply than other Americans.

In the meantime, mainline Protestant groups such as the Methodists, Presbyterians, Congregationalists, and Episcopalians sought to adjust themselves to the cultural rebellion. Since the 1920s, "modernists" or "liberals" within these groups had preached tolerance, social inclusiveness, and sometimes pacifism. With the long sixties, modernist ministers frequently moved to the forefront of the civil rights and antiwar movements. And on college campuses one could find ministers wearing blue jeans and beads while conducting religious services that included guitar-playing, hugging, and endless talk of universal love.

Critics argued that the efforts by the mainline groups to make themselves more amenable to the cultural rebellion backfired. Rather than accommodating to modern ways, the young were in fact seeking more overt and distinctive forms of religious experience. Hence, by the end of the sixties, not only were many of the cultural rebels turning to Eastern religions but others were becoming "Jesus freaks." While the Jesus freaks shared with the counterculture an enthusiasm for communal living and a simper lifestyle, they supported strict moral standards and biblical revelation. Whether due to a failure to comprehend the spiritual yearnings of the young or other causes, beginning in the long sixties and continuing into the twenty-first century, the mainline Protestant churches no longer commanded the same power and prestige that they had once enjoyed.

Far more dramatic and profound than changes in mainline Protestantism was a far-reaching "revolution" in American Catholicism. Directions from the top of the Catholic hierarchy triggered the revolution. In order to bring the church into closer accord with modern ways, Vatican II, which was called by Pope John XXIII in 1962 and completed its work in 1965, abandoned the ages-old quest to employ the power of the state on behalf of making Catholicism the universal faith. The council renounced religious intolerance and recognized Protestants as "separated brethren." By permitting mass to be conducted in the vernacular, calling for greater congregational participation in services, and emphasizing the sermon, Vatican II demystified the church's ancient liturgy. While most Catholics seemed to welcome these radical departures from the past, the reforms weakened the church's distinctive identity and may have contributed, as conservative Catholics argued, to a sudden drop in attendance at mass during the late 1960s and early 1970s. Still, nearly half of all Catholics reported regular attendance at mass, a figure far higher than anywhere in western Europe (except Portugal).

In the meantime, other divisions developed within American Catholicism. While overwhelmingly supporting the church's opposition to abortions and homosexuality, by 1970 a staggering nine of ten American Catholics endorsed artificial methods of birth control. Influenced by the women's movement, growing numbers of Catholic women took umbrage with the male domination of the church; the number of women entering nunnery orders declined sharply. As with Protestants, Catholics divided over the Vietnam War; two of the best known opponents of the war, the brother priests Fathers Daniel and Philip Berrigan, gained notoriety by burning their draft cards and making raids on draft board records. "Liberation theology," which fused a religious concern for the poor with a Marxian analysis of poverty, also divided Catholics. Throughout the last quarter of the twentieth century, the fissures opened by these and other issues continued to divide Catholics into opposing camps.

Unlike Catholic and mainstream Protestant churches, evangelical Protestant denominations (as well as a broadly based religious conservatism that cut across denominational lines) experienced rapid growth in the long sixties and afterwards. Well before the sixties, evangelical churches had been the fastest growing religious organizations in the country. Between 1940 and 1960, the Southern Baptist Convention doubled its membership, and in the late 1960s Baptists overtook the United Methodists as the largest Protestant body in America. Perhaps reflecting the general impulse of the day to unleash personal feelings, a so-called "charismatic" movement spread rapidly—not only through evangelical churches but also into mainline Protestant denominations and even into the American Catholic church. In worship services and small groups the charismatics, similarly to earlier and present-day Pentecostals, expressed a range of strong spiritual emotions that could include speaking in tongues, weeping, and swooning in ecstasy.

Evangelical Protestants stood at the forefront of those most disturbed by the rights revolution and the sixties' outbursts of expressive individualism. In particular, the U.S. Supreme Court's decisions on school segregation in 1954, school prayers in 1962, and abortions in 1973 horrified evangelicals; they saw these decisions as frontal assaults by modernists on religion, on biblically based morality, and on traditional America. Unlike many mainline Protestant leaders, nearly all the evangelicals condemned both the antiwar protestors and hippies as well. These were the opening salvos in a new campaign by traditionalists against some but not all modern ways, a counterattack that picked up momentum during the last quarter of the century.

THE NEW INDIVIDUALISM

While individualism had long been at the very core of American society and culture, in the past it had always been caged in by widely agreed-upon constraints. For example, the founders of the republic loudly proclaimed the principles of individual freedom, but at the same time they insisted that a virtuous citizenry—a citizenry that exercised self-restraint—was essential to the new republic's survival. Similarly, all of the nation's major religious communities generally defended individual autonomy, but they invariably allowed such freedom only within the limits imposed by obligations to God, the community, and a divinely ordained system of personal morality. Consequently, the pursuit of material welfare, for example, never exempted the individual from obeying the Ten Commandments. In addition, the unequal rights and obligations embedded in the nation's social and economic ways had long limited the individual freedom of women, African Americans, and working-class people.

As we have seen, the growing acceptance of modern ways weakened each of these traditional constraints on the individual. Cultural pluralism challenged the inequalities built into the nation's social ways, secularization eroded support for transcendental moral authority, and a consumer-centered economy encouraged Americans to abandon the middle-class Victorian emphasis on self-control. The sixties' revolution for rights and the dismissal of all traditional forms of cultural authority, when combined with the continuing imperatives of consumer capitalism, gave even freer reign to the individual.

In the 1970s and beyond, ever larger numbers of Americans came to embrace an even more radical form of individualism, a *new individualism* that included not only the rights revolution but also, equally important, a view that individual happiness was the main end of life. Above all else, the achievement of happiness required the freedom to choose. When asked in a Gallup Poll to rate a series of values, Americans gave the highest ranking to "freedom to choose," placing it before "following God's will," "high income," or "a sense of accomplishment." No longer was freedom limited to choices of religion or politics, but also it was increasingly understood to mean the freedom to buy consumer goods of one's own choosing, to earn as much money as one possibly could, to do what one wished in one's private life (and to a substantial degree in one's public life as well), and to make or break personal ties freely. In its ultimate formulation, the new individualism took as its primary commandment that people should "do their own thing."

CONCERN FOR THE INDIVIDUAL PSYCHE

At first glance peace, equality, and social justice—as goals of the long sixties' cultural rebels and rights advocates—seem far removed from the new individualism. But in fact the rebels frequently employed a psychological yardstick to evaluate the social evils of their day. Those social institutions that dehumanized and warped the individual personality should be reformed, they said. In their places should be built institutions that cared for the individual and that allowed each individual to realize his or her own potentialities. Most of the cultural rebels of the day applauded popular humanistic psychologist Abraham Maslow when he wrote that "after the need to satisfy one's hunger and thirst, man needed love, belongingness, self-esteem, and ultimately self-actualization."

While concern for the psyche had always been a major preoccupation of modernists, it became even more central to the mainstream culture of the 1970s and afterward. Rather than wealth, public recognition, or reputation for high moral character, happiness now emerged as *the* ultimate life goal. Unhappiness arose not so much from one's class, race, ethnic, or religious position, but mainly from treatable psychic inadequacies. Given this premise, little wonder then that a huge personal therapy industry began to flourish in the post–World War II era; the number of psychologists doubled and then tripled. By 1976, 26 percent of the American public had at one time or another been treated by a professionally trained therapist. Therapists, emotional-support groups, and countless self-help books advised Americans to rid themselves of hang-ups, free their emotions, and discover their true selves. Only then, the therapeutic industry promised, could individuals achieve happiness.

Millions of Americans (and not just the cultural rebels), believed they could take a long stride toward the achievement of happiness by reinventing the self. "All sorts of people," wrote a journalist, "suddenly appeared as other than they were: stockbrokers dressed up as for safari; English professors looked like stevedores; grandmothers in pant suits, young girls in granny dresses." Hair no longer was a symbolic issue; by 1979, even the Des Moines, Iowa, police officers sported long hair, beards, and mustaches. Americans widely embraced a looser code of personal conduct; traditional notions of decency, civility, dress, and restraint gave way to a new informality. "Even those who had never been hippies, or never even liked hippies," explained historian Bruce J. Schulman, "displayed a willingness to let it all hang out."

Illustrative of the efforts to reinvent the self included the growing popularity of unorthodox marriage ceremonies. Rather than in houses of worship, couples chose to get married in underground subway stations, around swimming pools in their trunks, or in the open spaces of city parks. Couples who retained traditional vows explicitly connected themselves to earlier generations; they kept intact a long chain of custom. But couples who wrote their own vows insisted on expressing their own individuality. They believed that they should shape the institution of marriage to fit their own individual needs. They were saying, in effect, "Thou shalt construct thine own identity."

Restraints on language previously considered profane or vulgar gave way to much freer expression. Four letter words no longer commanded the same shock value as they once had. By the 1980s, to describe their negative attitudes toward somebody or something, even preteenagers of both sexes began to routinely employ such words as "suck" in their daily conversations. The greater freedom of expression seemed to grow more lax with time. In 2004, even Vice President Richard Cheney was able to advise a senator to "Go f_ _ _ yourself" in a public forum with hardly a murmur of public protest. Cheney offered no apologies; indeed, he exulted, "I felt better afterwards." However, *Newsweek* columnist Anna Quinlan did note a double standard at work. She wondered what would have been the public response had Hilliary Clinton or any other female politician used the same words.

Hot Air Balloon Wedding, 1981. By taking traditional vows and marrying in houses of worship, couples in earlier times not only kept intact a long chain of custom but also implicitly agreed to conform in their married life to ages-old expectations. But, as this photo suggests, couples in the long sixties and afterward frequently chose to write their own vows and marry in nonreligious settings. They thereby expressed their own individuality and in effect sought to construct their own identities without reference to family, church, community, or the past. However, in the late 1980s and afterward, millions of couples returned to formal weddings.

THE QUEST FOR SELF-SUFFICIENCY

During the 1970s a waning of public confidence in government, the economy, and expertise furnished an additional impetus for the new individualism. With immoral behavior in high places, raging inflation, setbacks in Vietnam and elsewhere in the world, the hidden or indirect costs of the Industrial Revolution, and limits on scientific expertise now daily revealed on the evening news, Americans increasingly turned away from society or the community. They sought greater sufficiency in the self. *Looking Out for #1* became the best selling self-help book of the decade. Labeled by commentator Tom Wolfe as the "Me" decade and by historian Christopher Lasch as an age of "narcissism," millions of Americans (but especially those in the white-collar classes) looked for greater control over their lives and greater personal fulfillment in arenas other than their jobs or in social involvement. They became converts to charismatic religions; experimented with vegetarianism, hallucinatory drugs, or psychotherapy; or became apostles of a new physical fitness cult. The popular culture also furnished them with forceful images of individual potency. For instance in sports, by reducing the size of the strike zone, baseball increased its offensive output; television glamorized the bone-crunching game of professional football; and spectators were even introduced to what was described as "power" golf and "power" tennis.

Perhaps nothing so revealed the dynamics of the seventies' quest for greater self-sufficiency than what may be described as the new strenuosity. "I am a nervous, shy non-combatant who has no feeling for people," Dr. George A. Sheehan, the self-appointed chief philosopher of the nation's running cult, said in a remarkable confession. "I do not hunger or thirst after justice. I find no happiness in carnival, no joy in community." In exceptionally demanding individual physical activities, Sheehan, like millions of others in the professional and business classes, sought and claimed to find greater self-sufficiency. Physical fitness, its advocates asserted, not only served to counter the ravages of cardiovascular disease and cancer—two ailments against which modern medicine had made little headway—but also offered the individual feelings of satisfaction and greater personal potency.

In the end, there was reason to doubt that the new individualism's fervor for self-expression, self-actualization, self-acceptance, and any number of other self compounds led back to an authentic or perhaps even a happier self. For each of us, no matter how much energy we devote to the quest for a true inner self, is to one degree or another a product of culture. What may have distinguished the "new individualists," then, was not so much their special propensity for expressing and realizing their inner selves, but that they rejected or gave little weight to such traditional sources of cultural authority as the family, religion, ethnicity, and the past.

Instead of these, the new individualists tended to conform to directions for living their lives provided by experts or by the closely intertwined worlds of commerce and entertainment. More than ever before images and messages from advertising, the movies, popular music, the Net, sports, and above all else television furnished millions of Americans with a map for daily living. Studies repeatedly found that late twentieth-century Americans frequently "knew" personalities on television better than they did their neighbors, their workmates, or sometimes even members of their own families. These kinds of cultural authority, as Alexis de Tocqueville recognized with respect to public opinion long ago, could be just as demanding, tyrannical, and inimical to individual freedom as the past, family, religion, ethnicity, hereditary hierarchies, or monarchies.

CONCLUSION

From the perspective of the twenty-first century, the era spanning the 1960s and the early 1970s can be seen as a culminating moment in the history of modern ways. It was then that the modern values of cultural pluralism and toleration found expression in a rights movement that forever changed the nation's racial and gender hierarchy. While neither African Americans nor women gained full equality during the long sixties, henceforth few would seek a complete restoration of the earlier inequalities that had existed between blacks and whites or women and men. As in no previous era of American history (except perhaps the 1920s), the long sixties challenged all traditional sources of cultural authority. No longer did the church, the family, customs, or institutions command the same respect that they had earlier enjoyed. While rejecting nearly all authority except that arising from the self or from within their own ranks, many of the nation's rebellious youth yearned for and experimented with new kinds of community. But in the end the most enduring result of this aspect of the cultural rebellion was a new individualism, one that placed individual happiness before concern for character or community and prized a view of life as one long array of unrestrained and ever-changing individual choices.

COMING TO TERMS
WITH MODERN WAYS

During the last quarter of the twentieth century and the first years of the twenty-first century, coming to terms with the momentous cultural upheavals of the long sixties and an expanding consumer capitalism occupied much of the nation's attention. Few Americans wanted to turn back the clock completely to the ways of the 1940s and 1950s. Not only did most Americans accept the extension of additional rights to African Americans and women, but by 2000 public opinion polls revealed far greater racial and gender tolerance than had been the case a half century earlier. Americans continued to embrace another legacy of the long sixties, the *new individualism*. The new individualism held that the chief end in life was personal happiness. In pursuit of that goal, there was a widespread tendency to turn away from social ties and commitments and toward the self.

Turning inward brought with it a weakening of older social adhesives. Declines in voting, membership in civic organizations, the public's trust of its leaders, marriage rates, civility, and the depth of personal friendships—in these and other respects Americans retreated from earlier engagements with one another and with their communities. Neither did the nation's common or core culture hold firm. Late twentieth and early twenty-first century society witnessed continuing and sometimes heightened regional, ethnic, racial, and religious divisions. The nation's shared popular culture splintered into dozens of niche cultures. At the same time, a new campaign in the cultural war between modernists and traditionalists, one reminiscent of the 1920s, divided the country into hostile camps.

Yet not all evidence pointed toward division, strife, and civic disengagement. The nation had persevered through deep social divisions before; indeed, it had even survived the fighting of a bloody civil war. Historical experience suggested that it was possible for white southerners, African Americans, feminists, gays, Baptists, Catholics, and any number of other groups to cultivate their distinctive identities while at the same time continuing to embrace the major ingredients of the nation's core or mainstream culture. And even in the very midst of the widespread separatist tendencies of turn-of-the-twenty-first-century life, millions of Americans continued to seek ties beyond the self. Furthermore, mass consumption and the mass media seemed paradoxically to possess capacities for both dividing and bonding Americans. What remained to be seen by future generations was whether these apparent countercurrents could successfully stem the powerful forces of social and cultural fragmentation.

TURNING INWARD

While there were abundant signs of a hungering for ties beyond the self in the late twentieth- and early twenty-first centuries, the dominant impulse of the American people everywhere and in all aspects of their lives was to turn inward, to turn away from formal and enduring associations with others, with the past, with everything outside the self. The unsatisfactory resolution of the Vietnam War, stagflation, revelations of wrongdoing at the highest levels of government, a disillusionment with the Great Society's social programs, a growing recognition of the "hidden costs" of industrialization, and the discovery of the limits of modern medicine—these and other developments of the 1970s encouraged a turning inward. So did the growing economic autonomy of women; with greater job opportunities women were no longer so dependent on men for their livelihoods. Further reducing the time and energy available to civic enterprises, especially among middle- and upper-class women, was the growth in the number of two-income families. Simultaneously extending and expanding on urges that had been present in modern ways from the outset and seizing the opportunities for personal pleasures made available by an expanding consumer economy, more and more Americans looked to the self for personal fulfillment.

DISENGAGEMENT

"My wife is safe, my children are safe, so screw you and your Metro," read an ominous bumper sticker on a sports utility vehicle in 1999. At every level of American society and in every significant group, temptations and pressures mounted for individuals to disengage from one another and from the larger society.

Reflective of the inclination to turn inward was a startling decline in the nation's associational life. The large-scale protest movements of the long 1960s no longer compelled large, active grassroots followings. As early as 1970, the organized civil rights movement had receded in importance and, with the defeat of the Equal Rights Amendment in 1982, the revived feminist movement began a sharp decline. The only exception seemed to be the environmental movement; membership in the Sierra Club, the Audubon Society, Greenpeace, and the National Wildlife Federation continued to grow phenomenally until the 1990s. But these organizations seldom generated the kind of intense civic or interpersonal relationships that in the long sixties had brought thousands of students, African Americans, women, and gays and lesbians into the streets. The activism of the membership of such groups usually entailed nothing more than a positive response to mail solicitations for money.

Likewise, political participation declined. Americans voted less frequently than in the past; beginning in 1968 rarely more than half of the qualified voters went to the polls, one-third less than the figures in the 1940s and 1950s. Identification with, and membership in, political parties declined. Widespread disengagement apparently reduced the power of ordinary citizens to affect government decisions. Without unpaid volunteers and with local media outlets reducing their coverage of politics, political candidates had to resort more and more to expensive media campaigns. To pay the added campaign costs, they increasingly turned to special interest groups, who, in repayment, often expected and received special favors from government.

No imagery more vividly captured the tendency to disengage than the title of political scientist Robert Putnam's influential 1993 essay, "Bowling Alone: America's Declining Social Capital." While the total number of bowlers increased nearly 10 percent between 1980 and 1993, Putnam found that league bowling decreased by 40 percent. Lest this be considered a trivial example of the decline in the nation's associational life, Putnam observed that almost eighty million Americans went bowling at least once in 1993, almost a third more than voted in the 1994 congressional election and about the same number that claimed to attend church regularly.

Participation in voluntary associations, especially those that served their local communities, also fell. Between the 1960s and the 1990s, membership in Parent-Teacher Associations and the League of Women Voters dropped more than 40 percent. So did membership in such traditionally male civic groups as the Lions, the Masons, and the Elks. In 1999, Welcome Wagon, long a symbol of 1950s suburban neighborliness and congeniality, officially announced its demise.

Work no longer linked people to one another or to their communities as firmly as it had in the past. In the wake of the New Deal and through the 1960s, labor unions had bound working people together and to their communities, but by 2000 union membership as a percentage of the workforce had fallen to half of what it had been in the 1950s. The reconfiguration of white-collar work spaces reflected a growing isolation of the individual at work. To encourage employee unity, the Miesian model of the 1950s and 1960s had called for the elimination of interior barriers in employee workplaces, but in the 1980s and 1990s corporations replaced open spaces with individual cubicles or offices. Increasingly driven by the "bottom line" (short-term profits), corporations

David Butow/Corbis Saba

Security Entrance to a Gated Community, Palm Desert, California. In the late twentieth century, many of the nation's wealthy retreated to gated and privately guarded neighborhoods. This strategy reflected a growing civic disengagement, especially at the local level, among the nation's more economically successful citizens.

were less loyal to employees than in the past. Even capable and conscientious workers could no longer be assured of lifetime employment with the same firm. White-collar professionals also saw work more exclusively in personal rather than in social or familial terms. Corporate volatility encouraged placelessness among white-collar employees, particularly among those at the top of the corporate pyramid. In their lives away from the job, the new, more peripatetic wealthy retreated behind the walls of alarm-protected condominiums or into gated and guarded neighborhoods where they were likely to build what critics called large "McMansions" or "trophy" houses. Except for issues that directly affected their personal welfare, elites less frequently involved themselves in local civic affairs than their counterparts of the past.

OPPOSITION TO GOVERNMENT

Congruent with the decline in associational life was a sharp fall in trust. In 1964, 77 percent of the public said that they "always" or "most of the time" trusted the decisions of the national government; by 1980 the figure had plummeted downward to less than 25 percent. Polls revealed a similar collapse of

trust in lawyers, doctors, teachers, ministers, journalists, and business leaders. To the question "can people be trusted generally?" the percentage of positive answers fell in a descending curve from 58 percent in 1960 to less than
40 percent in the 1990s. The percentage of Americans with unlisted telephone
numbers grew by two-thirds and call-screening tripled from the late 1980s to
2000. Nationwide, the numbers of policemen, guards, and watchmen soared.
"Road rage," a term coined in the 1980s to describe the increasing expressions
of anger on the nation's streets and highways, reflected a general erosion
of civility.

Accompanying the declining trust in government was a resurgence of
political conservatism. With the Great Society programs of the sixties, "liberals" (understood here as those who endorsed an expanded social safety net
provided by government and the use of the state to expand the rights revolution) achieved their greatest triumphs since the New Deal. But during the
balance of the twentieth century, "conservatives" (understood here as those
favoring a reduction in government regulation, either limiting or abolishing
the safety net, and general opposition to using the state to expand individual
rights) returned to prominence. On the national level, conservatives won
their greatest symbolic and perhaps substantive victory by electing Ronald
Reagan to the presidency in 1980. Although a product of the world of commercial entertainment (Hollywood), divorced, and not religiously active, the
president championed traditional values and institutions. He condemned
explicit sexuality in the media and permissive child-rearing and sought to
restore respect for the family, the flag, and religion.

While achieving limited gains on behalf of his conservative cultural
agenda, Reagan enjoyed far more success in his campaign against big government. "Government is not the solution to our problem. Government *is* the
problem," he announced in his first inaugural address. He denounced affirmative action on behalf of women and minorities. While not successful in
decreasing the overall growth of government (indeed, the defense budget
and the national debt grew enormously), he obtained from Congress large
tax cuts and a sharp reduction in welfare expenditures.

To be sure, elected officials continued to make demands on government
for benefits on behalf of their specific constituencies, but by the 1990s virtually all politicians adopted a rhetorical stance against "big government."
Nearly everyone, it seemed, accepted the premise that government, especially the federal government, was inherently evil. Even President Bill Clinton,
a Democrat, renounced his party's longtime association with an expanded
role of government. "The era of big government is over," he announced. The
election of George W. Bush to the presidency in 2000 brought yet another
round of income tax cuts and the potential repeal of the inheritance tax,
which, apart from shifting a larger percentage of the nation's taxes from the

rich to other income groups, were intended to reduce the size and role of the national government. Yet, ironically, the "war on terrorism" fought after the tragedy of September 11, 2001, an expensive farm bill, and a drug bill for senior citizens not only increased spending and the size of the national government but also brought with them record-shattering deficits.

The combined effects of welfare cuts for the poor and tax cuts for the rich was to encourage a massive redistribution of wealth and income. In proportions similar to the closing decades of the nineteenth century, the income gap between the rich and the remainder of the population widened. By the mid-1990s the top 1 percent of American families owned 40 percent of the nation's wealth, a figure twice as high as twenty years earlier. In the same period the top 1 percent doubled their income after taxes while the real income of other groups increased slightly, stagnated, or even declined. As the rich got richer, the poor got poorer. Poverty struck hardest unmarried women with families; by 2000 about two out of three poor adults were women. The number of the homeless increased sharply. "Get off the subway in any American city," reported a group concerned with low-income housing, "and you are stepping over people who live on the streets."

Perhaps equally disturbing was the status of the middle class. In order for middle-class families to maintain or slightly improve on earlier income levels, increasingly both husbands and wives had to work. Such families faced the "two-income trap," one that required additional money for child care, help with sick children, and ownership of a second car. In the meantime, the costs for health care, housing, and college soared. No longer did labor unions or government programs offer middle-class families as much protection from financial disaster as they once had done. According to a study by political scientist Jacob Hacker in 2004, middle-class family incomes were "two or three times more unstable . . . even for well-educated workers and two-earner families" than they had been in the 1950s and 1960s. Nonetheless, fewer Americans seemed as concerned as they once had been that the nation was taking these huge steps away from a major premise of the nation's founders—that the success of a republican society required a roughly equal distribution of wealth among its citizenry.

At the local level, the zeal for cutting back on government was equally strong. Many states imposed lids on taxation. In particular, these measures adversely affected education and hence the future of the nation's youth. To offset reduced financial assistance from the states, tuition at public colleges and universities soared. Coming at a time when the better jobs were increasingly found in a knowledge-based economy, rising costs made it more difficult for low income groups to turn to education to improve their lot. Simultaneously both the states and the national government rushed to privatize what in the past had been considered public services. Not only did "user" fees rise sharply for public parks both locally and nationally, but also governments frequently contracted out to private enterprise the services offered by these parks. In Lincoln, Nebraska, in exchange for providing the county sheriff's department with financial assistance, local businesses plastered the sheriff's official car with advertisements. All over the nation, except for expanded road building, publicly controlled spaces gave way to privately controlled spaces.

At its most radical fringes, hostility to the state spawned a host of groups—militias, freedom fighters, and other self-proclaimed patriots—who armed themselves to fend off governmental authority. Millions of Americans seemed to believe that the right to bear arms was the only safeguard against state tyranny. "We're here because we love freedom," declared a demonstrator in a 1995 rally against legislation proposing a ban on semiautomatic assault weapons. Antistatism seemed to reach its ultimate and certainly its ugliest expression in the bombing of the federal building in Oklahoma City in 1995.

The almost reflexive antistatism of the eighties and nineties reflected a growing veneration of "free enterprise" or what was increasingly abbreviated as simply "the market." Reinforced by the collapse of the USSR in 1989 and an upwardly spiraling stock market in the 1990s, enthusiasm for the market as an all-solving mechanism knew few bounds. Echoing the acquisitive individualism of the nineteenth century, the more extreme of the market fundamentalists even argued that nothing needed to be or should be done by the state to counter poverty, inner-city ghettos, violence, racial or gender discrimination, declining educational performance, and pollution. Nothing was so efficacious in solving these problems, they said, as a free and unfettered market. Any efforts to inhibit it or control its vagaries were artificial, detrimental to the general welfare, and undemocratic. Market fundamentalism and an enthusiasm for consumer culture was not limited to the United States; in the 1990s and beyond they achieved striking triumphs throughout the world.

THE REMOVAL OF RESTRAINTS ON MONEY

In the late twentieth century, the loosening of restraints on the making, spending, and flaunting of money were integral components of the new individualism. "The Great Inflation" of the 1970s encouraged new attitudes toward borrowing and spending. While advertisers had long urged everyone to buy now and save later, until the 1970s most Americans still considered thrift a cardinal virtue. But, then, as prices rocketed upward more than 10 percent annually, delaying purchases no longer seemed to make sense. Why not borrow and buy now, before prices went up? Then you could pay for the goods later with inflated dollars that were worth less. While parents whose memories had been shaped by the Great Depression continued to admonish their children and younger couples to "never buy what you can't afford," explained Paine Webber economist Christopher Rupkey, "today the statement has been changed to, 'you can't afford not to buy it.'" In response to this kind of thinking, entrepreneurs invented the consumer credit card; a "credit card revolution" allowed consumers to borrow money instantaneously and without the hassle of obtaining loans from their local banks. The Great Inflation may have permanently altered American attitudes toward savings and consumer debt. Even when inflation was tamed in the decades following the 1970s, the nation's per capita consumer debt continued to balloon each year.

Encouraged by the relaxation of government regulation, tax reductions, and a soaring stock market, in the 1980s and the 1990s individual money-making moved to the forefront of the quest for greater self-fulfillment. With an enthusiasm never before equaled in American history, the mainstream culture lent its approval to individual avarice. "Greed is not a bad thing," declared junk bond dealer Ivan Boesky in 1988. "You shouldn't feel guilty."

Ed Bock /Corbis

Young Asian American Woman Making an Online Purchase with a Credit Card. This photo illustrates the enduring significance of the "credit card revolution" that began in the 1970s. As an easy way of borrowing money, the use of credit cards encouraged a fundamentally new attitude toward personal savings and consumer debt.

Rather than those who were responsible for making things or even those selling them, it was the young money managers on Wall Street who became the heroes of the popular culture. Madonna's "Material Girl" climbed to the top of the pop music charts. The yuppies, as young urban professionals whose lives were absorbed in money-making were dubbed by the media, flaunted their wealth in a manner reminiscent of no group so much as the nouveau riche of the late nineteenth century. A new class of the well-to-do embarked on a new orgy of consumption. They not only built huge homes with aircraft-carrier-sized kitchens and high-end vacation homes but also bought expensive luxuries. By 2000, in the nation's most affluent neighborhoods, there were more cars than there were residents.

By the end of the twentieth century, consumer capitalism and the long sixties' rebel culture were inseparable. Advertisers had coopted the iconography of the rebel culture; they tied their products to immediate gratification, individualistic lifestyles, youthfulness, uninhibited instinct, and liberation of the libido. "We consume not to fit in, but to prove, on the surface at least, that we are rock 'n' roll rebels, each of us as rule-breaking and hierarchy-defying as our heroes of the 60s, who now pitch cars, shoes, and beer," observed Thomas Frank in 1995. A rule-defying individualism even swept into the once-staid corridors of corporate power. *First Break All the Rules* was the title of a 1999 best-selling book based on in-depth interviews by the Gallup organization of over eighty thousand managers in over four hundred companies. According to the new management mavens, corporate bosses needed to forget the wisdom of the past, ignore rules, and encourage "thinking outside the box."

FAMILIES AND FRIENDS

Despite the tidal wave of the new individualism, millions sensed that reaching out beyond the self might be a beneficial or necessary strategy for the achievement of personal fulfillment. When asked what they valued most in life, Americans continued to place the family at the top of the list. Beginning in the late 1980s, and continuing through the 1990s and into the twenty-first century, millions of couples returned to formal, ever more expensive and elegant weddings. The enormous popularity of multimedia lifestyle entrepreneur and advisor Martha Stewart indicated that equal numbers were happy to have Stewart lecture them on how to maintain "family" and "tradition." Stewart's insistence that her largely female audience still wanted to "iron, to polish silver, to set a sensible table, [and] to cook good food" suggested a widespread yearning for the idealized close-knit family of the past. Many Americans also sought to establish or reestablish more direct linkages with their ancestors. In quest of family roots, *The Financial Times* reported in 1999, fifty million people attempted within a single hour to enter the genealogical Web site of the Mormon Church.

The institution of marriage remained popular albeit far less so than in the past. The number of marriages per thousand women age fifteen and older dropped 40 percent between 1960 and 2000. Couples also divorced, entered short-term relationships, and experimented with unorthodox family-like relationships more frequently than in the past. By 1996 nearly half of the people ages twenty-five to forty reported that at some point in their lives they had set up a joint household with a member of the opposite sex outside of marriage. Surveys revealed that traditional family life weakened in other ways. No longer did family members spend as much time as in the past in eating, watching television, visiting, or vacationing together.

Television sitcoms reflected the changing nature of the family. While popular sitcoms such as *The Simpsons* and *Roseanne* frequently mocked the idealized fifties' family, family ties remained important to the lives of each member of both of these working-class families. Late twentieth-century television also offered viewers several series based on "mismatched families"; in *Full House* a widower, his three daughters, his deceased wife's brother, and his best friend all live in the same house and in *Different Strokes*, an equally if not more improbable family consisted of a white widower, his daughter, and two adopted black sons. Apparently unable to find satisfaction in traditional families, in *Cheers* even a neighborhood bar "where everybody knows your name" served as a surrogate family for an astonishingly diverse array of people. (In fact, *Cheers* was at best something of a period piece; whether single or married Americans were patronizing bars less frequently than they had in the past.) Of equal importance, such shows as *Cheers*, *Friends*, and *The View* offered lonely television viewers vicarious participation in surrogate families.

As the popular television series suggested, friendships could potentially serve as partial substitutes for traditional families. In 2000, Americans were twice as likely to visit with friends as they were to join with others in a civic enterprise. Yet, increasingly confronted with longer working hours, constraints on time imposed by two-income family members, and obligations arising from after-school activities of their children, Americans spent less time on friendships than in the past. Suggestive of the decline was the fact that between 1970 and 1998 the number of full-service restaurants dropped by one quarter while the number of fast-food outlets more than doubled. Rather than sit a while and talk, more and more Americans opted to grab a bite and run. The incidence of card-playing exploded in the 1950s, but plunged downward beginning about 1970. While video games emerged as substitutes for card-playing among younger Americans, frequently the games were played alone. On the basis of this and other evidence, Robert Putnam concluded in 2000 that "friendship . . . ties are measurably more feeble than a generation ago."

EMOTIONAL-SUPPORT GROUPS

While conceding that both friendship and family ties had weakened, some observers took consolation from the rapid growth of emotional support groups. In 1994, sociologist Robert Wuthnow even went so far as to conclude that "the small-group movement has been effecting a quiet revolution in American society." Wuthnow and his team of investigators found that 40 percent of American adults claimed involvement in at least one small group that met regularly. Many of the groups sought to aid their members in overcoming such specific problems as alcohol, drug, sex, and overeating "addictions." Other self-help groups met to deal with loneliness, spousal abuse, and "personal growth." Still other groups were less serious; they met to play games, read books, exercise, or share a meal. Regardless of their ostensible purpose, nearly all of the small groups offered their members at least some interpersonal ties and emotional support. Four of five of those interviewed by Wuthnow and his team said that their group made them "feel like [they] weren't alone."

The burgeoning of emotional-support groups sprang mostly from a growing belief in what historian Eva Moskowitz has described as the "therapeutic gospel." Rather than economic, social, or cultural problems, according to the therapeutic gospel, the absence of individual happiness sprang mainly from psychological causes. The good news was that the causes were treatable.

Treatment at first consisted mainly of one-to-one counseling, but, beginning with the pioneering work of Alcoholics Anonymous (formed in 1935 and led by ex-alcoholics themselves rather than professionally trained therapists), group therapy became increasingly popular. Based on the assumption that the expression of feelings in a group setting was more therapeutic (or perhaps cheaper) than individual counseling, in the 1960s young adults organized dozens of "encounter groups" and the cultural rebels of the day met in thousands of informal "bull sessions." At about the same time, to give their employees opportunities to discuss personal and work-related problems with their cohorts, businesses began to sponsor training or "T-groups." Religious organizations soon followed; small-group retreats, they found, could encourage spiritual renewal. By the 1980s, retreats had become something of a national mania. Not only did members of religious groups gather regularly in places remote from home or work, but so did groups ranging from military officers to the chairs of academic departments of the nation's universities. In the 1990s and beyond, therapy "went public"; in popular television shows such as *Donahue* and *Oprah*, guests presumably received psychic relief through nationwide public confessions.

The fastest-growing religious groups at the turn of the twenty-first century were especially adept in offering their members a rich mix of opportunities for group therapy, emotional support, entertainment, and theological certainties. At the forefront of this religious development were the nondenominational megachurches. Scattered across the nation's suburbs, Sunday services included all of the latest electronic wizardry, Christian rock music, and a short, passionately delivered sermon by a charismatic preacher. At the door of the North Point Church in suburban Atlanta, a church of seventy-five hundred members, a small cadre of women in skirts and heels welcomed newcomers as members of "our family." "It's the first time in my 47 years that I've gone to church not because it's the right thing to do . . . but because I'm really looking forward to Sunday," exclaimed a former Baptist who had recently joined the North Point Church. The North Point Church, like other megachurches, offered its members far more than modern entertainment and warm greetings. Affiliated with the church were dozens of emotional support groups.

Yet, American religion, like the larger culture, was on the whole, in the words of historian George Marsden, "highly individualistic." Whereas in the past Americans had turned to religion to understand the mysteries of the universe and for solace in the face of tragedies, modern Americans tended, as they did in other aspects of their lives, to look for emotional support and self-fulfillment in their religious experiences. "Need a Friend?" read a sign on the Southview Christian Church building in Lincoln, Nebraska. Rather than generating feelings of anguish, finitude, or sorrow, religious groups usually sought to provide their adherents with a wide array of psychic satisfactions.

Even Robert Wuthnow, an enthusiastic supporter of church-related and other emotional-support groups, acknowledged that they were inadequate substitutes for more traditional kinds of personal attachments. Unlike the family, they did not share an imagined heritage or physical or personality characteristics; nor did they provide shelter, clothing, and food. Unlike the traditional neighborhood, members did not necessarily live in close proximity, see each other informally, nor identify with local history or long-standing physical edifices. Attachments among group members were more fluid; one could easily join or leave a group. For example, members of the fast-growing Red Hat Society, an organization of older women, did not have to make treats, serve on committees, or organize fund-raisers; all they did was to join others in a common activity such as sharing dinner and conversation. Rather than grassroots organizations that brought Americans face-to-face with their neighbors—the agreeable and disagreeable alike—to engage in common civic discourse and enterprises, the emotional-support groups represented the narrower interests of like-minded people.

Catherine Karnow/Corbis

Interior View of Crystal Cathedral, Completed in 1980, Garden Grove, California. The Reverend Robert Schuler, a popular television minister, employed renowned architect Philip Johnson and his partner John Burgee to design this mammoth structure. Without any manifest religious symbols or icons but in some respects resembling the nation's shopping malls, the cathedral towered twelve stories high and contained 12,000 panes of glass. Within the auditorium, which seated 3,000 worshipers, was a huge television screen and an electric fountain with a stream of water running down the central aisle. Telecast across the nation, Sunday services at the cathedral featured such Hollywood celebrities as Glen Campbell, Arnold Schwarzenegger, and Charlton Heston. As with other megachurches, the Crystal Cathedral offered worshipers not only entertainment but also opportunities to participate in a wide variety of emotional-support groups.

Other signs of apparent engagement could be equally deceptive. "Being alone together" was the way that Robert Bellah and his associates described those individuals who were involved in some of the fastest growing organizations of the late twentieth century. For instance, membership in AARP (American Association of Retired Persons) grew spectacularly, but, while its members had common interests, they had no genuine interactions with one another. Neither did the Internet, a much-ballyhooed technological means of building "virtual" communities, live up to its promise. A 1998 study sponsored by the computer industry itself found that people who spent even a few hours a week online experienced higher levels of depression and loneliness than they would have had they used the computer network less frequently.

NICHE CULTURES

Niche cultures, while providing at best ephemeral connections with others, may have also represented something of a countercurrent to the forces of disengagement. "Television in the old days made it [the United States] a smaller community," observed Norman Lear, the producer of *All in the Family*, a weekly sitcom watched by more than a third of American homes as recently as the 1970s. But, by the 1980s, technology was splintering the nation's mass culture into an endless array of niche cultures. Cable television destroyed the grip over the public long enjoyed by the Big Three—CBS, NBC, and ABC—networks. Programmers could now tailor their shows to special audiences. MTV led the way; designed to appeal to preteenagers, teenagers, and young adults with lots of money, MTV showed music videos around the clock. Soon there seemed to be a niche for everyone: CNN for news junkies, Nickelodian for children, Black Entertainment Television for African Americans, and the History Channel for history buffs. Studies showed that blacks and whites, men and women, and the young and the old now watched completely different shows.

Television was only the most striking example of the shift from a national culture to niche cultures. Use of the Internet exploded in the 1990s and the early years of the twenty-first century. Millions of Americans logged onto specialized websites where they could participate in an astonishing array of specialized chat groups, play games with others or themselves, or even view pornography (the most popular male Internet pastime). Specialized magazines replaced the mass-circulation periodicals; readers now had available to them more than thirty automotive magazines, at least twenty-five devoted to computers, and dozens more to physical fitness, food, and other forms of self-help. Specialized marketing also grew in popularity. Perhaps nothing illustrated the growth of niche marketing more than the successes of chains of stores selling only coffee or ice cream.

Special lifestyle enclaves grew in popularity. Unlike communities that shared a history, acted together politically, or featured strong interdependencies, the lifestyle enclaves grew out of leisure activities. They brought together people who sought to express their individuality in similar ways. Without giving up the rewards of expressive individualism, lifestyle enclaves, in the apt words of Robert Bellah and his associates, celebrated "the narcissism of similarity." For example, individuals otherwise divided by ethnicity, religion, gender, and age might join one another in an enthusiasm for golf, taste for exotic foods, jazz, foreign travel, and any number of other spare-time activities.

Niche cultures developed around an interest in history. In the 1990s enthusiasm for Victorian culture soared. Across the country, Americans refurbished Victorian homes and watched the dramatizations on television or in the movies of Jane Austen's nineteenth-century novels that featured the manners and morals of the early English Victorians. Victoria's Secret, a lingerie store, successfully transformed the idea of repressed Victorian sexuality into salable commodities. For the professional classes, visiting historical sites, whether in the United States or in Europe, became a popular vacation rite. A renewed enthusiasm for baseball seemed to reflect a nostalgia for an earlier, presumably simpler past; recognizing this, the major league club owners began to replace their modernistic, multipurpose stadiums with facsimiles of earlier ball parks. But nothing reflected the yearning for ties with the past and for a larger, more noble way of life more than a mammoth outpouring of enthusiasm for the fiftieth anniversary of World War II. Each of the major television networks prepared huge, expensive, sprawling documentaries and Steven Spielberg's movie *Saving Private Ryan* (1998) drew record-breaking crowds.

CONCLUSION

Not all evidence in late twentieth and early twenty-first-century American life pointed inward. Millions of Americans continued to identify with a particular ethnic or religious group or with a region. There was still a substantial minority—indeed sometimes a majority—of Americans who voted. Neither did civic groups and other activities designed to promote the common welfare of local communities totally disappear. Millions exhibited an enthusiasm for history, kept abreast of the latest sporting events, and sought to "go with the flow" by participating in current fads. Membership in small emotional-support groups actually mushroomed. Perhaps equal numbers joined together to resist what they considered to be the immoral aspects of the long sixties' cultural revolution. And, finally, the terrorist assault on the World Trade Center and the Pentagon on September 11, 2001, ignited a nationwide surge of patriotism whose dimensions had been unequalled since World War II.

Yet it would be a mistake to see this evidence of turning outward as a rejection of the new individualism or as the blossoming of new forms of community. In some instances, it was indeed that. There was a tiny minority who tried to counter the splintering forces of the new individualism by seeking to build more civil and caring local communities. But these were exceptions. On the whole, the quest for ties beyond the self was an inward-looking, personal enterprise. One joined an emotional-support group in order to achieve greater individual happiness or fulfillment, not to strengthen the sinews of community. The most energetic and fast-growing religious groups of the day were also more inward than outward looking. Rather than being involved in the wider community, they spent most of their energy on providing help to their own members or on drawing even firmer boundaries between themselves and those outside their own group.

24

"A VERY STEWPOT OF SEPARATE IDENTITIES"

Many observers expected the forces unleashed by modern industrial-urban society and the mass media to wipe out regional, racial, ethnic, and even significant religious differences. During the twentieth century, as we have seen, Americans were increasingly buying the same kind of goods, listening to similar radio programs, watching the same movies, and reading the same or similar books, periodicals, and national wire-service news stories. Regional accents seemed to be giving way to a common American accent. Scholars gathered evidence that third-generation immigrants from southern and eastern Europe were rapidly assimilating into American life. The federal government contributed to national homogenization; in the twentieth century, it set about establishing nationwide standards in dozens of areas—from what constituted poverty to proper legal procedures for handling those accused of committing felonies. Some observers believed that the forces of modernity, especially the mass media and consumer capitalism, were even creating a common global culture. At the level of popular culture nothing supported the plausibility of this argument more than adolescents everywhere listening to the same music, adopting the same hair and clothing styles, and in countless other ways resembling one another.

Yet, in the last quarter of the twentieth and in the early years of the twenty-first century, all over the globe ethnic, religious, and regional conflicts were becoming more pronounced. They sometimes erupted into open warfare and in some places tore nations apart. The United States was not immune to the worldwide impulse towards separatism. "American culture in the late twentieth century is a very stewpot of separate identities," observed Todd Gitlin with only slight exaggeration in 1995. "Not only blacks and feminists and gays declare that their dignity rests on their distinctiveness, but so in various ways do white Southern Baptists, Florida Jews, Oregon skinheads, Louisiana Cajuns, Brooklyn Lubavitchers, California Sikhs, Wyoming ranchers." The anonymity of industrial-urban society, the new individualism, the rights revolution, the dominance of political conservatism, and the growing acceptance of the modern values of cultural pluralism and diversity all seemed to heighten rather than reduce regional and group self-awareness.

THE SUNBELT

As in the past, no major region within the United States was more self-conscious, distinctive, nor commanded greater loyalty from its residents than the South. A more stratified social order, lower per capita incomes, a predominance of agriculture, a biracial society, a hostility to institutions, high homicide rates, a special religiosity—these and other markers had long distinguished the South from the remainder of the country. Even as late as 2000 large pockets of the rural South remained essentially unchanged; for example, eighty-four of the nation's poorest counties were still in the Deep South. Yet, in the last half of the twentieth century, across much of the region, the "redneck" stereotypes of racism, sexism, and backwardness began to give way to the long-awaited "New South," an urban-industrial South, one featuring entrepreneurial buccaneers, sprawling cities, happier race relations, and a new, fast-growing middle class.

In the second half of the twentieth century, the balance of national regional power began to shift from the Frostbelt or Rustbelt states (as pundits now began to describe the industrial tier of states extending from the Northeast to the Midwest) to the Sunbelt (a term coined in 1969 by Kevin Phillips to explain the increasing significance in national elections of the former slave states plus New Mexico, Arizona, and southern California). Fed by massive transfusions of federal dollars into the defense and space industries, by warmer weather that was now tamed by air conditioning, and by a hostile climate toward labor unions, in the post–World War II era jobs and people (including a large influx of retirees) fled from the North to the Sunbelt. Reversing a half-century trend, by the 1970s even African Americans joined more than a million people a year who were flocking southward and westward. By 2000 seven of ten Sunbelters lived in metropolitan areas and, with a rapidly growing Latino population, the Sunbelt contained a higher percentage of immigrants than any other region in the nation.

These sudden changes did not necessarily mean the Sunbelt's amalgamation into the nation's mainstream culture; indeed, substantial evidence supported the argument that they just as often reinforced regional distinctiveness. While the sexist, racist, free-drinking, white "Bubba" of the older South passed into oblivion, a new "faux Bubba," as he was hailed by cartoonist Doug Marlette, was taking his place. Even those most responsible for the modern Sunbelt—the white bankers, defense contractors, engineers, oil company personnel, military personnel, and northern retirees—felt a strong connection to the Old South. As did less successful white Sunbelters, they frequently drove pickup trucks, listened to country music, wore cowboy boots, watched stock car races, and flew Confederate flags. They continued to admire "the good old boys," those white southerners who were presumably more authentic, friendly, and trustworthy than their northern counterparts. The Sunbelt remained religiously orthodox; no other region in the nation approached its degree of pervasive religiosity.

The regional shift in economic power soon manifested itself in nearly every other phase of American life. The Sunbelt pioneered in the construction of a new kind of sprawling city; fast-growing cities such as Atlanta, Houston, and Los Angeles had no downtown and no one walked on the streets. Their real centers were suburban shopping malls. Sunbelt power extended to the national political scene. While the overwhelming dominance of one party (the Democratic) in the region and Congress's seniority system had long given the South a disproportionate influence in the national government, the Sunbelt elected every president from Lyndon B. Johnson in 1964 to George W. Bush in 2004. Seizing on a widespread regional backlash against the rights revolution and the cultural rebellion of the long sixties, the Republicans in the 1980s cracked open the once "solid Democratic South." And it was from the Sunbelt that the "religious right" arose and began successfully to impose its traditionalist cultural agenda—opposition to abortion, the equal rights amendment, affirmative action, the school prayer decision, and gay rights—on the platform of the national Republican party.

The sunbelting of America was not limited to politics. Apart from the Sunbelt's economic boom, the very successes of modern ways increased the region's influence on the national culture. To those Americans everywhere who were most disturbed by the changes wrought by the economy, the Supreme Court, the federal government, and the popular culture in the late twentieth century, the Sunbelt seemed to offer a clear-cut alternative, a far more traditional way of life. Without giving up the wonders of modern technology nor the satisfactions of mass consumption and expressive individualism (observe that the region had the highest divorce rate in the nation), the Sunbelt, according to its own proclamations, stood in sharp contrast to the remainder of the nation. It continued to value religion, friendliness, civility, trust, honor, patriotism, and traditional gender roles.

Nothing concretely illustrated how the Sunbelt functioned as a national counterweight to modern ways more vividly than the Dallas Cowboys football team of the 1970s. In the midst of the antiwar movement and cultural unrest of the day, the Cowboys, who became the most-watched professional team on television, called themselves "America's Team." They wore silver and blue uniforms and featured as their quarterback Roger Staubach, who had attended the Naval Academy, served as an officer in the Navy, wore his hair short, and publicly proclaimed his religiosity. Their coach, Tom Landry, was equally "straight." Perhaps the Dallas Cowboys Cheerleaders also reassured those Americans anxious about the nation's departures from the past. While scantily clad and flaunting heaving cleavages, their cheerleaders were said by Cowboy spokesmen to be the quintessential representatives of the girl-next-door southern wholesomeness.

A similar set of traditionalist images accompanied the astonishing growth of stock-car racing. Emerging in the 1990s as the country's most popular sporting spectacle, an outlaw, working-class southern mystique surrounded the origins of stock-car racing. According to legend, the sport's first heroes were drivers such as Junior Johnson, who had earlier won renown by eluding federal authorities while delivering bootleg whiskey from the hill country to the coastal cities. Stock-car racing's heroes—the drivers—climbed from the bottom to the top through a Darwinian world in which such traditional southern male behaviors as courage and assertiveness counted for everything. Given the similarities in the external appearance of its cars, the sport was also able to perpetuate the myth that stock cars were essentially the same vehicles anyone could buy from their local dealer. They were everyman's cars, the opposite of

David Madison/New Sport/Corbis

EA Sports 500 NASCAR Race Gets Underway at the Talladega Speedway, Alabama, 2003. Identified with the South but spreading in popularity nationwide in the 1990s, stock-car racing emerged as an allegorical counterweight to modern ways. While conspicuously embracing modern advertising and consumption, the power, speed, violence, and risk taking involved in the sport seemed to affirm traditional manliness and individualism. In 2001 millions of Americans in all parts of the country mourned the tragic death of champion driver Dale Earnhardt, who was known as "The Intimidator" for his aggressive, no-holds-barred style of driving.

the souped-up, specially built streamlined racing cars that the better-off watched at the Indianapolis Motor Speedway.

The sunbelting of America extended to popular music. Long before the late twentieth century, distinctively southern forms of popular music had spread far beyond the Sunbelt. By the 1920s, accompanying the migration of black musicians from New Orleans to the North, jazz had become a national and then shortly even an international fad. African Americans were also responsible for rhythm and blues which morphed into rock and roll. By way of Alabama and Tennessee, white singer Elvis Presley not only brought rock and roll to the attention of the nation's white youth but also to the entire world.

In the 1920s and 1930s southern "country" music, a genre that combined elements of earlier North Britain, gospel, and African American popular music, began to invade the North and the West (where a derivative form was frequently called "cowboy music"). But country really took hold nationally only with the Sunbelt boom of the late twentieth century. Country's sympathy for the "little guy," its nostalgia for "the good old days," its hostility to urban America, and its enthusiasm for the more relaxed pace of life resonated with all those Americans, regardless of region, who were most troubled by cultural change. While continuing to challenge modern life, country paradoxically departed from its traditional roots. No longer exclusively twangy vocals accompanied by fiddles, banjos, or guitars, it even included full orchestras and the mixing of traditional forms with various genres of popular music. By 2000 not only did country music regularly occupy the top spots on the sales charts, but Branson, Missouri, which featured a glittering array of country entertainers, outdistanced Las Vegas, Nevada, as the nation's most popular entertainment destination.

AFRICAN AMERICANS

In the heady atmosphere of the mid-1960s few anticipated the degree to which race would continue to separate the American people. With the passage of the civil rights acts, administrative initiatives, affirmative action, and favorable court decisions, most modernists assumed that blacks would make rapid progress toward assimilation into the larger society. As one possible indicator of assimilation, interracial marriages did increase by nearly fivefold. By 2000, about 10 percent of all black males outside the South married nonblack women. Polls also revealed a growing acceptance by whites of changes wrought by the rights revolution of the long sixties. Nationwide, blacks nearly doubled their percentage of white median income. African Americans made even bigger gains in politics. For example, the number of elected black officials—the majority of whom were in the Deep South—jumped from about fifteen hundred in 1970 to more than nine thousand by 2000. Several of the nation's largest cities elected black mayors.

Black successes were especially conspicuous in the entertainment industry. By the 1990s even a casual glance at the television screen revealed the presence of large numbers of African Americans; indeed in team sports blacks were overrepresented in terms of their proportion of the population. Once one of the most controversial and divisive figures in America, by 1996, in a rite of expiation, the entire nation applauded former heavyweight champion prizefighter Muhammad Ali, whose body was now wracked with Parkinson's disease, as he carried the torch and lit the cauldron opening the Olympic Games at Atlanta. Such black athletes and entertainment figures as Michael Jordan, Tiger Woods, Oprah Winfrey, and Bill Cosby crossed over racial boundaries to become among the best-known and highest paid performers in the world.

Yet these successes masked a more complex reality. While there were a growing number of African Americans who were able to seize the opportunities opened up by the rights revolution, others slid more deeply into poverty. In the 1940s and 1950s, more than two million blacks had moved from the South to northern and western cities to take blue-collar jobs, but at the very moment that legal segregation's walls were tumbling down, jobs for unskilled workers in inner cities began to evaporate. In the 1970s and 1980s, whole neighborhoods, observed one scholar, shifted from "working-class to hard-core poverty." There one could see block after block of graffiti, youth gangs, drugs, and boarded up, rundown, unoccupied buildings. Schools reflected the increasing physical separation of the races. Inner-city school classrooms, observed the *Boston Globe*, "are a sea of black and brown faces interrupted only by the occasional white child." In the more prosperous 1990s, inner-city conditions improved slightly, but deep chasms continued to separate poor blacks from not only whites but middle-class blacks as well.

Blacks and whites were divided in other respects. By 1990, polls revealed that a majority of whites believed that racial discrimination no longer existed in America; indeed, many whites thought that there was reverse discrimination in favor of blacks. Blacks held exactly the opposite view. In election after election, by whopping majorities, African Americans cast their ballots differently than whites. Blacks watched different television programs than whites. The races held sharply opposing views of the American justice system. Based on their collective experience with the police and the courts, a substantial majority of African Americans applauded when Johnnie Cochran, O.J. Simpson's defense attorney in a sensational 1994 murder trial, urged a mostly black jury to "do the right thing" and set Simpson free as a message to the world against racism. "Blacks and whites looked at the case through race-tinted glasses," explained historian Steven Gillion. Almost twice as many whites as blacks believed that

Simpson was guilty while African Americans were three times more likely than whites to think that Simpson was innocent. Blacks and whites did, however, agree on one point; there was a different system of justice for those who had money and those without money.

A growing disillusionment with the dream of racial inclusion encouraged the cultivation of a distinctively black identity. Among blacks in the 1990s, it was not the martyred Martin Luther King, Jr., but the martyred Malcolm X who emerged as the most admired African American. In the 1990s, membership in the Nation of Islam and other Black Muslim groups increased. The quest for racial pride included a widespread interest in African ancestry and culture. In many black communities, colorful West African dress became popular. On college campuses, African American studies programs frequently promoted one or another version of Afrocentrism, which held that black people everywhere shared a rich, distinctive culture. More and more blacks celebrated Kwanzaa, a week-long event invented in the 1960s that specifically acknowledged the African heritage of African Americans.

Within the inner city, the separatist impulse found expression in hip hop. In the tradition of the 1950s beats and the 1960s hippies, hip hop was a rebel culture. To vent their rage against "the system," young male hip hoppers turned to a special art form (graffiti), a special dance form (break dancing), special clothing that mocked successful Americans (baggy pants, baseball caps worn backwards or sideways, loose polo shirts, and expensive sneakers), and a special music (rap). Rap, the linchpin of hip hop culture, accentuated race and the issues of the urban underclass. By unrelentingly promoting sex, derogating women and homosexuals, and glorifying violence (especially against the police), the rappers horrified black and white adults alike.

Appealing to rebellious youth everywhere, in the 1990s hip-hop culture flooded across racial, ethnic, and national boundaries. In 1998 rap even topped country as the nation's top-selling musical format. But, while a force in separating generations, as rap became more commercialized, tamed its message, and included many nonblack and women artists, it was less an agency of racial and gender separation. Among youth worldwide it became a dominant style and ethos. Everywhere it provided a familiar soundtrack for advertising, television, film, and the newest digital and multimedia channels of communication.

WOMEN

Alongside African Americans, Todd Gitlin in 1995 included "feminists" (notice he does not use the word *women*) as an ingredient in the stewpot of separate American identities. If by feminists, Gitlin was referring to those

Reuters/Corbis

Ludacris and His Posse Posing for Pictures at the Source Hip-Hop Music Awards, Miami, Florida, 2001. In the tradition of the 1950s beats and the 1960s hippies, hip-hop culture began as a rebel culture in the 1970s (and to a degree remained so, into the twenty-first century). Initially, its young black male performers derogated women and homosexuals, extolled sexual conquest, and glorified violence (especially against the police). In the 1990s, however, hip hop tamed its message, became more commercialized, and crossed racial boundaries. It then became a popular style and ethos among youth worldwide.

involved in organized campaigns on behalf of women, then their numbers by 1995 were quite small. As an organized grassroots movement, feminism never recovered from the setbacks and internal divisions of the 1970s and early 1980s. By the 1990s, to many women, it seemed that the battle against gender discrimination had been won and that feminism was a label that restricted their individuality. Anyone calling themselves a feminist, explained Paula Kamman in 1991, faced a twisted logic embedded in negative stereotypes: "If you stand up for women, you must hate men. Therefore, you must be angry. Thus, you must be ugly and can't get a man anyway. Hence, you must be a dyke." By the 1990s, active feminism was limited mostly to those in staff-run organizations and to the feminists in the academy. Both of these groups reflected mainly the concerns of upper-middle-class white women.

Yet, as Barbara Epstein observed in 2001, "a feminist perspective, or identity [is] spread widely and a diffuse feminist consciousness is now found nearly everywhere." Millions of American women who were not involved in any feminist organizations per se regularly talked to each other and with men about women's issues. Employing the vocabulary of feminism, women across the country continued to raise such issues as discrimination in the workplace, sexual harassment, domestic violence, rape, reproduction rights, and female poverty. On public issues ranging from gun control, abortion, education, and welfare, opinion polls also revealed differences between women and men. Though the divisions were not nearly as great as those separating blacks and whites, presidential elections in the 1990s and in the 2000 (but not the 2004) election suggested that the "gender gap" might be widening.

One controversial branch of feminist thinking, sometimes labeled "difference feminism," offered women *as* women a source of pride and group identity. While agreeing with other twentieth-century feminists in denying that women's destiny should be determined by biology, the difference feminists sought to reclaim a distinctive women's identity. Carol Gilligan, the best-known proponent of this position, argued that women shared "a different voice, different moral sensibilities—an ethic of care," all of which separated them from men. The distinctively feminine moral sensibilities embodied in an ethic of care, the difference feminists contended, partially offset and countered modern (masculine produced) social pathologies. Stepping considerably beyond Gilligan, John Gray in *Men Are from Mars, Women Are from Venus* (1993), a book that sold more than fifteen million copies, popularized the idea that men and women differed sharply on a wide range of other fronts. To critics, theories that emphasized differences between the sexes reflected and frequently reinforced traditional notions of women and men as well as the continuing patriarchal domination of American society.

In terms of the kingdom of images created by the mass media, what it meant to be a feminist shifted from involvement in a shared "sisterhood" to being a "superwoman." Superwoman enjoyed all the pleasures of sexual freedom, marriage, and motherhood. Donning a "power woman's" jacket with padded shoulders and with hair flying, attaché case in hand, and baby in arms, she allegedly "had it all and did it all." Superwoman was a quintessential example of the new individualist. Instead of demanding general social equality or a strengthening of community bonds, she was driven by the pursuit of her own individual success. Not only did a career offer her opportunities for fulfillment and liberation, so did consumption. By smoking Virginia Slims cigarettes, a popular advertising slogan promised, a woman could make a statement of personal freedom—"You've Come a Long Way, Baby." As a full partner in capitalistic enterprise and the quest for individual acquisitiveness, Superwoman could no longer, as her middle-class predecessor had presumably done in the past, act as a counterweight to marketplace values.

Superwoman. While in the idealized suburbs of the 1950s the wife saw her husband off to work, this striking photo taken in the 1990s indicates a complete reversal in gender roles. According to the popular media, the modern "superwoman" "had it all and did it all." However, studies revealed that working mothers frequently continued to do a disproportionate amount of the family's child care, cooking, and housework.

THE NEW IMMIGRANTS

In the late twentieth and early twenty-first centuries, immigration reemerged as an important contributor to the nation's "very stewpot of separate identities." As of 2000, well over half of the newcomers came from just seven countries: Mexico, China (including Taiwan), the Philippines, Vietnam, India, Cuba, and the Dominican Republic, none of which were European. Between 1965 and 2000, the nation's Asian population jumped from one million to ten million while those of Latino or Hispanic origins increased from some four million to thirty-five million. By 2000, the fast-growing Latinos comprised about 13 percent of the nation's population; by 2005, the Census Bureau predicted that Latinos would overtake African Americans as the nation's largest minority group.

In terms of income and wealth, the profile of the Asian population resembled that of an hourglass. Most Asian-Americans were either relatively affluent or relatively poor. The better off were frequently the beneficiaries of the Immigration Act of 1965, which extended preferences to reuniting the families of those already resident in the United States—so much so that some observers nicknamed it the "brothers and sisters act." "My brother-in-law left his wife in Taiwan and came here as a student to get his Ph.D. in engineering," explained Subi Lin Felipe. "After he received his degree, he got a job in San Jose. Then he brought in a sister and his wife, who brought over one of her brothers and me." Apart from the Chinese, family chain migration also encouraged the immigration of Asian Indians, about two-thirds of whom already had college degrees.

And even though most Asians came with modest means and experienced at least some discrimination, they soon made their mark in American society. By 1990, Asian Indians, who were prominent in computer science and medicine, moved ahead of all other groups, including even all categories of old-stock Americans, in per capita income. By 2004, nearly half of all Ph.D. candidates in the sciences had been born abroad. Academically, the children of Asian immigrants far outperformed other American children. In 2004, of the forty finalists in the Intel Science Talent Search (the "Junior Nobel Prize"), 60 percent were the children of immigrants. "If we had blocked these people from coming in [i.e., the parents]," explained Stuart Anderson, the director of the Foundation of American Policy, "two-thirds of the top future math and science [people] wouldn't be here." But the future flow of talented immigrants into the United States was in jeopardy. In 2003, the National Science Foundation reported that in the wake of the 9/11 tragedy the denial of high-skilled visa applications by the Immigration Service had nearly doubled.

Not all Asians prospered. There were at least an equal number of Asians at the bottom of the hourglass. These included a new wave of Chinese immigrants, who usually worked in restaurants or sweatshops, and more than a million refugees from war and revolution in southeast Asia, who were also employed mostly at menial tasks.

Rather than an hourglass, a bell shape more accurately described the social profile of the Latino population. At the narrow top of the bell shape were a small number of Latinos whose ancestry extended back to earlier generations or to exiles from Fidel Castro's Cuba. Nearly all the Cuban refugees settled in the greater Miami, Florida, area. While better educated than most immigrants and mostly from Cuba's upper and middle classes, they initially were forced to take menial jobs. Yet they quickly moved up the occupational ladder; by 1990 Cuban-American family median income exceeded that of the nation as a whole. At the bottom of the bell were the less successful Latinos: Puerto Ricans (who as American citizens were not technically immigrants), Central Americans, peoples from the Caribbean Islands, and Mexican immigrants. While having exceptionally high employment rates, these Latinos frequently toiled at low wages in the nation's most physically demanding jobs.

In terms of preserving a distinctive cultural identity, the Latino population enjoyed resources that had been unavailable to earlier immigrants. True, as with earlier immigrants, the Latino newcomers were not homogeneous; their numbers comprised a medley of social classes, nationalities, and ethnicities. But unlike the immigrant mix of earlier times, nearly all Latinos had a shared language (Spanish), a shared religion (Roman Catholicism), and to one degree or another a shared Spanish cultural heritage. Strengthening these potential bonds of unity was the spatial concentration of the Latino immigrants. More than half of all Latinos lived in only two states—California and Texas. By 1990, Los Angeles ranked next to Mexico City as the home of the second-largest Spanish-speaking population in North America. Following jobs in the construction, service, meat, and poultry industries, Latinos also established substantial pockets of settlement in such far-flung states as Illinois, Georgia, Arkansas, and North Carolina. Nearly all the newcomers crowded into barrios that were overwhelmingly comprised of fellow Latinos. Regular transfusions of large numbers of new immigrants, many of whom were illegal aliens, into concentrated areas also helped to keep alive Latino separateness.

Other resources aided Latinos in preserving their cultural identities. Sustaining ties with the homeland was much easier than in the past. Seizing on the advantages of geographical contiguity and relatively cheap transportation, for example, more than a million Mexican Americans per year returned to their homeland for the Christmas season. Weekly and sometimes even daily phone calls across national boundaries kept up family ties and friendships. Spanish-speaking radio stations and television networks in the United States not only helped to preserve the native language of the immigrants but also provided them with aural and visual reinforcements of their traditional ways. Because of their extraordinary intercourse across national borders, which included substantive remittances of money to relatives, American Latinos have been labeled as "hemispheric citizens."

Perhaps even more than for immigrants in the past, religion served Latinos as a powerful agency of cultural conservatism. The Roman Catholic Church, to which some two-thirds of all Latinos were in some way affiliated, permitted and sometimes encouraged Latinos to remain ethnically apart from other American Catholics. The reforms of the Second Vatican Council, the emergence of ethnic pride generated from the long sixties' rights revolution, and liberation theology gave rise to what one scholar has described as a distinctive "Latino religion that could not be absorbed into the Euro-American experience." Apart from the more formal services of the church itself, at the core of Latino life were popular religious practices such as home altars, pilgrimages, lighting candles in church, and family prayers. Large numbers of Latinos also participated in small fellowship and prayer groups.

Preserving a Mexican American Identity in the Basilica of Our Lady, San Juan, Texas. In addition to religion, sheer numbers, a shared cultural heritage, and residence mostly in concentrated areas near Mexico aided Mexican Americans in preserving their traditional identities.

Concentrations in places of residence, sustenance of ties with homelands, the persistence of traditional ways, outright bigotry—these and other considerations spurred a growing concern about the effects of Latino immigrants on American society and culture. Prominent intellectuals, both traditionalists and modernists, called attention to the differences between present and earlier immigration experiences. Without additional restraints placed on Latino immigration, they even warned of the possibility of the southwestern United States becoming an American Quebec, a region similar to French Canada whose language and other ways were sharply at odds with the dominant culture.

Ordinary citizens expressed similar concerns but often more bluntly. In Miami, cryptic bumper stickers read, "Will the last American out of Miami please take the flag." Responding to such thinking as well as complaints that immigrants were taking jobs away from old-stock Americans, Congress in 1986 passed a new immigration law that offered legal status to aliens already in the country, tightened the border between Mexico and the United States, and imposed fines on employers who hired illegal aliens (a provision not rigorously enforced). The concern about Latinos also spawned a powerful "English only" movement. In 1986 California voters overwhelmingly supported a referendum that outlawed bilingualism and endorsed "English as a unifying force in the United States." By the end of the decade, seventeen other states had passed similar English-only laws.

THE DEBATE OVER MULTICULTURALISM

An aspect of the debate spilled over into the nation's educational system. In the past, the schools had been committed to the task of molding Americans of all backgrounds into a single people, but in the 1980s and 1990s, the values of "multiculturalism" and "diversity" emerged as the educational establishment's reigning orthodoxy. Whatever else it meant, the advocates of multiculturalism insisted that far more attention ought to be given to the roles and contributions of women, blacks, Latinos, and other minority groups to American society. Only through a greater knowledge of its own group and its contributions, the advocates of multiculturalism reasoned, could the minorities fully realize their individual potentialities. Consistent with this premise, universities and colleges across the country redoubled their efforts to hire minorities and many established special programs in women's studies, African American studies, Latino or Hispanic studies, gay studies, and a few even set up "white" studies and men's studies.

Traditionalists launched a counterattack. In his *Closing of the American Mind*, a book that remained on the *New York Times* best-seller list for seven weeks, Allan Bloom in 1987 defended "the great books" of western civilization; he lamented, "You can't talk about Chaucer without someone saying 'What's the woman's perspective?, 'What about the Third World perspective?'" At its most extreme, critics said, the multiculturalists even rejected the existence of a common American culture. Supportive of their contention was a Lake County, Florida, teacher who said, "we regard American culture as very diverse, and we're not sure what values they [the opponents of multiculturalism] see as American values." Other multiculturalists simply charged that the writings of such white men as Thomas Jefferson or the authors of *The Federalist Papers* had nothing important to say to women or minority groups. To the critics, such thinking encouraged a cultural balkanization that jeopardized the republic's very existence.

Whether the worries of those who questioned multiculturalism and the possibility of assimilating the nation's new immigrant population were justified remains to be seen. But, in the instance of immigration assimilation, it is worth noting that the percentage of foreign-born people in the United States in 2000 was still considerably below the nation's high-water mark set in 1910 and that, in the long run, the nation had been able to absorb the earlier immigrants without ill effects. Furthermore, in an age of greater tolerance, intermarriage between ethnic groups was higher than ever before in American history. A study in 1994 revealed that about half of all Asians and one-third of all Latinos married outside their ethnic groups. Moreover, strident affirmations of separate identities may in fact have masked waning ethnic differences. Popular and consumer cultures were powerful agents of assimilation. They worked to make all Americans alike.

THE RENEWAL OF CULTURAL WARFARE

Race, gender, ethnicity, and region were not the only cleavages in turn-of-the-twenty-first-century America. Echoing many of the same concerns that divided Americans in the 1920s, a new cultural war pitted those variously labeled as traditionalists, conservatives, or the religious right on the one side against those variously called modernists, liberals, progressives, or secularists on the other. The war's campaigns revolved around a wide range of issues: affirmative action, abortion, gay rights, environmentalism, funding for the arts, the public school system, multiculturalism, censorship, and the role of religion in American life, all of which took new shapes in the wake of the cultural tumult of the long sixties. But, while these issues provided an agenda for the new cultural war, the war itself was about something far deeper and more significant.

The new war revolved around the ultimate sources of moral authority. That is, where did people turn to determine whether something was good or bad, acceptable or unacceptable? While the majority of Americans occupied a vast middle ground between the polarizing tendencies of the cultural war, conservatives, whether Protestant, Catholic, Jewish, or Muslim, turned to external, definable, and transcendental sources of authority for guidance. Specifically, they looked to the Bible, the church hierarchy, the Torah, or the Koran. Authority came from on high and its dictates were true for all time, they believed. Their opponents, on the other hand, found their moral authority primarily in secular sources. Specifically these might include a hodge-podge of convictions arising from religion, personal experience, scientific knowledge, popular culture, and the Western tradition of humanism. Truth to them was tentative and contingent, and moral direction arose from a dialectic between tradition and the contemporary world. Such opposing sources of moral authority inevitably led to conflicts about the meaning of America. "What ultimately should America be all about?" asked combatants on both sides of the cultural war.

Though not normally spilling over into the political arena, divisions between religious conservatives and modernists had been evolving well before the late twentieth century. As we have seen, Protestants had long been split into two major camps: evangelicals and fundamentalists on the one side

and mainline or liberal religionists on the other. Within Judaism, a continuum extended from Orthodoxy (with Conservatives somewhere in between)
to Reform Judaism, and within Catholicism, especially after Vatican II, there
was a basic cleavage between "liberals" and "conservatives." Polls docu-
mented two distinctive cultural orientations that cut across these three major
faiths; for example, a 1987 survey revealed striking agreement among evangelical Protestants, conservative Catholics, and Orthodox Jews on the locus of
authority in the family (the husband/father), the proper roles of women,
political party preference, and the role of the marketplace in the nation's
economy. Regardless of denominational affiliations, religious conservatives
joined in a rising opposition to specific (but not all) aspects of the general
drift of American life toward modern ways.

FIELDS OF CONFLICT

One major field of conflict was education. Rather than teaching religion, conservatives accused the public schools at all levels of indoctrinating their
charges with a pernicious "secular humanism." Secular humanism, said the
Reverend Jimmy Swaggart, "is education without God." Whether Catholic,
Orthodox Jew, or evangelical Protestant, conservatives fixed much of the
blame for the teaching of secular humanism on the Supreme Court ruling in
1962 that had prohibited prayers in the public schools. In the wake of that ruling, they said, the schools increasingly taught "values clarification" and
"moral relativism" rather than an absolute morality originating in religious
beliefs. Sex education in the schools was an especially hot-button issue.
Conservatives objected to courses in family and sex education; instead of
promoting the values of premarital chastity, the critics said, such courses, by
teaching students how to use contraceptives, encouraged sexual promiscuity.
Apart from launching rhetorical assaults on the public schools, conservatives
argued that parents should have the right to choose the schools that their children attended. As alternatives, in the 1980s and 1990s home schooling and
private religious schools grew in popularity, though even as late as 2000 less
than 20 percent of the nation's children attended such schools.

A second major field of conflict was the family. What was at stake, as sociologist Robert Davison Hunter has cogently argued, was the very definition
of the family. The religious conservatives called for the preservation, or perhaps more accurately the creation, of the idealized nineteenth-century,
middle-class family, one that was male-dominated and nuclear, sentimentalized childhood and motherhood, and saw domestic life as a refuge from the
harshness of modern life. Such a family, they believed, was ordained by God.
"Much of the conflict in the modern family," wrote an evangelical, "is caused

CONCLUSION   387

either by misunderstanding of or by the refusal to accept the role each [family] member was designed by God to fulfill." On the other side, the modernist saw this kind of family as a source of inequality and the oppression of women.

No family issue divided the warring sides more sharply than abortion. Conservatives saw legalized abortion as an assault on both a woman's obligation to fulfill her destiny as ordained by God and as the very source of her identity while modernists insisted that "the right to choose" was essential to a woman's autonomy and self-fulfillment. Without that option, they said, she was handicapped in competing in the workplace with men as well as in escaping potential tyranny in her domestic life. Next to abortions, conservatives saw homosexuality as the biggest threat to the traditional family.

The cultural war spilled over into electoral politics. While elections might have little to do with actually altering family life, education, or the contents of popular culture, elections frequently did offer voters opportunities to embrace symbols of what they thought the country is or should be about. The candidates themselves became representatives of these symbols. Appealing to cultural conservatives, Ronald Reagan seized such symbols in the election of 1980 when he asserted that "America is a land of destiny created by some divine plan" and that "law must be based on a higher law." He pledged to appoint federal judges "who respect family values and the sanctity of innocent life." The result was that evangelicals, conservative Catholics, and Orthodox Jews fled the Democratic party in droves. The cultural war extended to the local political level as well. The cultural war encouraged the taking of sides and the exclusion of political power from those who were in between. Elected officials increasingly found themselves hostages to one side or the other. Such obligations intensified partisanship, making compromise and cooperation across party lines more difficult.

CONCLUSION

For much of the late twentieth and early twenty-first centuries, modern ways continued to hold the center stage of American life. In particular, as we have seen in our examination of recent American history, no one could deny the enormous power and popularity of the new individualism. The achievement of fulfillment and happiness, it was said, required a world of unrestrained individual choices—choices in jobs, consumption, and affiliations. The new individualism encouraged a turning inward, a severing of many of the older ties that Americans had had with one another and with their communities as well as a retreat from the long sixties' concern for community and for racial, gender, and class equality. It encouraged a growing opposition to government and the veneration of money, individual money-making, and private consumption. Whatever ties one did make beyond the self were frequently casual and nonbinding. Their main intent was the achievement of greater personal satisfactions—an intent consistent with the new individualism—rather than the forging of stronger community bonds.

While virtually no one escaped the lure of the new individualism, probably an overwhelming majority of Americans experienced some uneasiness with its more radical manifestations. Polls suggested that most Americans yearned to live in warmer and more caring communities and that they would like to experience greater civility, restraint, and comity in their daily lives. Millions also worried about the nation's stewpot of separate identities and the apparent erosion of the nation's common or core culture. And then there were those who stridently waged war against what they considered to be the immoral legacies of the long sixties. Their war did *not* include campaigns against the consumer-centered, market-driven economy; indeed they for the most part warmly embraced these. Nor did they completely reject the rights revolution and its consequences. But instead, these cultural traditionalists warred against what they considered to be violations of a set of explicit moral rules laid down by higher authority.

No one can yet confidently say whether the predominant trends of the late twentieth and early twenty-first centuries were part of an older cultural paradigm or the constituents of a new one. As events unfold, scholars may decide that it was, like the late nineteenth and early twentieth centuries, a transitional age, one that heralded both the final stage of modern ways and the beginnings of a new cultural era. Regardless, it is clear that Americans in the late twentieth century carried modernist impulses about as far as they could possibly be taken. No earlier age in American history prized more fully the idea that each individual should be given nearly unlimited discretion in fulfilling his or her own distinctive needs. What remains to be seen, however, is whether the new individualism will continue to occupy a central position in the American ways of the twenty-first century.

A SELECTIVE BIBLIOGRAPHY

GENERAL

While there are literally hundreds of works that treat aspects of the history of American ways, useful reference books include Mary Kupiec Cayton and Peter W. Williams, eds., *Encyclopedia of American Cultural and Intellectual History* (2001); Mary Kupiec Cayton, Elliott J. Gorn, and Peter W. Williams, eds., *Encyclopedia of American Social History*, 3 vols. (1993); Richard W. Fox and James T. Kloppenberg, eds., *A Companion to American Thought* (1995); Charles Lippy and Peter W. Williams, eds., *Encyclopedia of the American Religious Experiences*, 3 vols. (1988); Stephan Thernstrom, ed., *Harvard Encyclopedia of American Ethnic Groups* (1980); and Charles Wilson and William Ferris, eds., *Encyclopedia of Southern Culture*, 3 vols. (1989). For the place of cultural history within the discipline of history, see Joyce Appleby, Lynn Hunt, and Margaret Jacob, *Telling the Truth about History* (1994). For more in-depth treatments of specific topics, examine such books as Thomas Bender, *Community and Social Change in America* (1978); Jon Butler and Harry S. Stout, eds., *Religion in American History: A Reader* (1998); William H. Chafe, *The Paradox of Change: American Women in the 20th Century* (1991); Clifford Clark, Jr., *The American Family Home, 1800–1960* (1986); Paul Conkin, *Puritans and Pragmatists: Eight Eminent American Thinkers* (1968); Carl Degler, *At Odds: Women and the Family in America from the Revolution to the Present* (1980); John d'Emilio and Estelle Freedman, *Intimate Matters: A History of Sexuality in America* (1988); Roger Fiske and Rodney Stark, *The Churching of America, 1776–1960* (1994); Eric Foner, *The Story of American Freedom* (1998); George M. Fredrickson, *Racism: A Short History* (2000); Paul R. Gorman, *Left Intellectuals and Popular Culture in Twentieth Century America* (1996); David Hollinger and Charles Capper, eds., *The American Intellectual Tradition*, 2 vols. (3d. ed., 1997); Robert Hughes, *American Visions: The Epic History of Art in America* (1997); James L. Huston, *Securing the Fruits of Labor: The American Concept of Wealth Distribution, 1765–1900* (1988); Joseph Kett, *Rites of Passage: Adolescence in America, 1790 to the Present* (1977); Lawrence Levine, *Black Culture and Black Consciousness: Afro-American Folk Thought from Slavery to Freedom* (1977); Lawrence Levine, *The Unpredictable Past: Explorations in American Cultural History* (1993);

George Marsden, *Religion and American Culture* (1990); Steven Mintz and Susan Kellogg, *Democratic Revolutions: A Social History of the American Family* (1988); Lewis Perry, *Intellectual Life in America* (1984); Benjamin Rader, *American Sports* (4th ed., 1999); Daniel Rodgers, *The Work Ethic in Industrial America* (1978); Robert H. Wiebe, *Self-Rule: A Cultural History of American Democracy* (1995); and Gwendolyn Wright, *Building the Dream: A Social History of Housing in America* (1981).

THE WAYS OF THE MIDDLE CLASS, 1865–1930

The quantity of the literature treating middle-class Victorian ways is enormous. To obtain an overview of middle-class culture, read David W. Howe's remarkable essay, "Victorian Culture in America," *American Quarterly*, Special Issue, 27 (Dec. 1975), 507–32. While dated and focused on England, Walter E. Houghton, *The Victorian Frame of Mind* (1957), is rich in detail and remains insightful. An invaluable memoir is Henry Seidel Canby, *The Age of Confidence* (1934). William L. Barney, *The Passage of the Republic* (1987), offers a useful synthesis of research in nineteenth-century social history.

Works of a more specific nature include Cindy Aron, *Working at Play: A History of Vacations in the United States* (1999); Gunther Barth, *City People: The Rise of the Modern City Culture in Nineteenth Century America* (1980); Gail Bederman, *Manliness and Civilization: A Cultural History of Gender and Race in the United States, 1880–1917* (1995); Stuart M. Blumin, *The Emergence of the Middle Class* (1989); Paul Boyer, *Urban Masses and Moral Order in America, 1820–1920* (1978); Ann Douglas, *The Feminization of American Culture* (1977); John Gillis, *A World of Their Own Making: Myth, Ritual, and the Quest for Family Values* (1996); John Henry Hepp IV, *The Middle-Class City: Transforming Space and Time in Philadelphia, 1876–1926* (2003); John Kasson, *Rudeness and Civility: Manners in Nineteenth-Century Urban America* (1990); Lawrence W. Levine, *Highbrow/Lowbrow: The Emergence of Cultural Hierarchy in America* (1988); Karen Lystra, *Searching the Heart: Women, Men, and Romantic Love in Nineteenth-Century America* (1989); Timothy R. Mahoney, *Provincial Lives: Middle-Class Experience in the Antebellum Middle West* (1999); Michael McGerr, *The Rise and Fall of the Progressive Movement in America, 1870–1920* (2003); Stephen Nissenbaum, *The Battle for Christmas* (1998); Shelia M. Rothman, *Women's Proper Place: A History of Changing Ideals and Practices, 1870 to the Present* (1978); Mary Ryan, *Women in Public: Between Banners and Ballots, 1825–1880* (1990); Carroll Smith-Rosenberg, *Disorderly Conduct: Visions of Gender in Victorian America* (1985); Louise Stevenson, *The Victorian Homefront: American Thought and Culture, 1860–1880* (1991); a book of sources edited by Alan Trachtenberg, *Democratic Vistas: 1860–1880* (1970); and Trachtenberg's *The Incorporation of America: Culture and Society in the Gilded Age* (1982).

The Ways of Others, 1865–1930

For the ways of the "outsiders"—those outside the dominant northern middle-class culture—during the 1830–1930 era, primary sources include Abraham Cahan, *The Rise of David Levinsky* (1917, many editions); John G. Neihardt, *Black Elk Speaks* (1996); Charles Reznikoff, *By the Waters of Manhattan* (1930); and Jacob Riss, *How the Other Half Lives: Studies Among the Tenements of New York* (1890, many editions).

For secondary accounts, see, among other books, Edward L. Ayers, *The Promise of the New South: Life after Reconstruction* (1992); Robert F. Berkhofer, Jr., *The White Man's Indian* (1978); John Bodnar, *The Transplanted: The History of Immigrants in Urban America* (1985); John C. Burnham, *Bad Habits* (1993); W. J. Cash, *The Mind of the South* (1941); Howard Chudacoff, *The Age of the Bachelor* (1999); Angie Debo, *And Still the Waters Run: The Betrayal of the Five Civilized Tribes* (1991); Vine Deloria, Jr., *Custer Died for Your Sins: An Indian Manifesto* (1988); Jay Dolan, *The American Catholic Experience* (1985); Eric Foner, *Politics and Ideology in the Age of the Civil War* (1980); Gary Gerstle, "Liberty, Coercion, and the Making of Americans," and the responses to this essay in *Journal of American History*, 84, No. 2 (Sept. 1997), 524–80; Elliott J. Gorn, *The Manly Art: Bare-Knuckle Prize Fighting in America* (1986); Herbert Gutman, *Work, Culture & Society in Industrializing America* (1977); Jacqueline Jones, *Labor of Love, Labor of Sorrow: Black Women, Work, and the Family from Slavery to the Present* (1985); Joy Kasson, *Buffalo Bill's Wild West: Celebrity, Memory and Popular History* (2001); Kenji Kawano, *Warriors: Navajo Code Talkers* (1990); Bruce Laurie, *Artisans into Workers: Labor in Nineteenth-Century America* (1989); Lawrence Levine, *Black Culture and Black Consciousness: Afro American Folk Thought from Slavery to Freedom* (1977); Patricia Nelson Limerick, *The Legacy of Conquest: The Unbroken Past of the American West* (1987); Alessandra Lorini, *Rituals of Race: American Public Culture and the Search for Racial Democracy* (1999); J. Carroll Moody and Alice Kessler-Harris, eds., *Perspectives on American Labor History: The Problems of Synthesis* (1989); Charles R. Morris, *American Catholic* (1997); Ted Ownby, *Subduing Satan: Religion, Recreation, and Manhood in the Rural South, 1865–1920* (1999); Kathy Piess, *Cheap Amusements: Working Women and Leisure in Turn-of-the-Century New York* (1986); Madelon Powers, *Faces Along the Bar: Love and Order in the Workingman's Saloon, 1870–1920* (1998); Roy Rosenzweig, *Eight Hours for What We Will: Workers and Leisure in an Industrial City* (1983); Richard Slotkin, *Gunfighter Nation: The Myth of the Frontier in Twentieth-Century America* (1992); Henry Nash Smith, *Virgin Land: The American West as Symbol and Myth* (1950); Ronald T. Takaki, *Stranger from a Different Shore: A History of Asian Americans* (1989); Elliott West, *The Contested Plains: Indians, Goldseekers, and the Rush to Colorado* (1998); Richard White,

"It's Your Misfortune and None of My Own": A New History of the American West (1991); and David Wishart, *An Unspeakable Sadness: The Dispossession of the Nebraska Indians* (1994).

The Origins of Modern Ways, 1890–1930

There are no satisfactory overviews of modern ways, but see Norman F. Cantor with Mindy Cantor, *The American Century: Varieties of Culture in Modern Times* (1998). Opinionated and provocative, the book looks at high culture throughout the Western world. Eric Foner's *The Story of American Freedom* (1998), while examining the concept for the entirety of American history, is especially insightful for the modern era. See also Michael G. Kammen, *American Culture, American Tastes: Social Change and the 20th Century* (1990) and *The Tastes of Leisure: Popular Culture and Social Change in America* (1999); Eva S. Moskowtiz, *In Therapy We Trust: America's Obsession with Self-Fulfillment* (2001); David J. Singal, ed., *Modernist Culture in America* (1988), especially Singal's essay "Towards a Definition of American Modernism"; Christine Stansell, *American Moderns: Bohemian New York and the Creation of a New Century* (2000); Peter N. Stearns, *Battleground of Desire: The Struggle for Self-Control in Modern America* (1999); and Warren Susman, *Culture as History: The Transformation of American Society in the Twentieth Century* (1984).

For the origins of modern ways, consider George Cotkin, *Reluctant Modernism: American Thought and Culture, 1880–1900* (1992); Nancy Cott, *The Grounding of Modern Feminism* (1987); Carl N. Degler, *In Search of Human Nature: The Decline and Revival of Darwinism in American Social Thought* (1991); Lewis Erenberg, *Steppin' Out: New York Nightlife and the Transformation of American Cluture* (1981); Susan A. Glenn, *Female Spectacle: The Theatrical Roots of American Feminism* (2000): John Higham, "The Reorientation of American Culture in the 1890s," in Higham, ed., *Writing American History* (1970); David Horowitz, *The Morality of Spending: Attitudes Toward Consumer Society in America, 1874–1940* (1985); John Kasson, *Amusing the Millions: Coney Island at the Turn of the Century* (1978); James T. Kloppenberg, *Uncertain Victory: Social Democracy and Progressivism in European and American Thought, 1870–1920* (1986); William Leach, *Land of Desire: Merchants, Power, and the Rise of a New American Culture* (1993); T. Jackson Lears, *No Place of Grace: Antimodernism and the Transformation of American Culture, 1880–1920* (1981); Susan J. Matt, *Keeping Up with the Joneses: Envy in American Consumer Society, 1890–1930* (2003); Henry F. May, *The End of American Innocence* (1959); Lary May, *Screening Out the Past: The Birth of Mass Culture and the Motion Picture Industry* (1980); David Nasaw, *Going Out: The Rise and Fall of Public Amusements* (1993); Kathy Piess, *Cheap Amusements: Working Women and Leisure in Turn-of-the-Century New York* (1986); Julie A. Reubin, *The Making of the Modern University* (1996); Dorothy Ross, *The Origin of American*

Social Science (1991); Robert W. Rydell, *All the World's a Fair: Visions of Empire at America's International Expositions, 1876–1916* (1984); Cynthia Russett, *Darwin in America: The Intellectual Response, 1865–1912* (1976); Gilbert Seldes, *The 7 Lively Arts* (1923); Robert B. Westbrook, *John Dewey and American Democracy* (1991); Robert Wiebe, *The Search for Order, 1877–1920* (1967); and Oliver Zunz, *Why the American Century?* (1998) and *Making America Corporate, 1870–1920* (1990). Also examine the writings of such influential people of the day as Henry Adams, Jane Addams, Charles A. Beard, Edward Bellamy, Randolph Bourne, Charles Darwin, John Dewey, Henry George, Charlotte Perkins Gilman, William James, Elizabeth Cady Stanton, Frederick Jackson Turner, and Thorstein Veblen.

The Coming of Age of Modern Ways, 1920–1960

Primary sources are an equally good way to look at modern culture from the 1920s to the 1960s. See for example the writings of Ruth Benedict, Malcolm Cowley, John Dewey, W. E. B. DuBois, Sigmund Freud, Joseph Wood Krutch, Walter Lippmann, Margaret Mead, Reinhold Niebuhr, George Santayana, and Edmund Wilson.

Also see the secondary works of Charles Alexander, *Here the Country Lies: Nationalism and the Arts in the Twentieth Century* (1980); Beth Bailey, *From Front Porch to Back Seat: Courtship in Twentieth Century America* (1988); Christopher Brookeman, *American Culture and Society since the 1930s* (1984); Paul Carter, *The Twenties in America* (1968) and *Another Part of the Twenties* (1977); George Chauncy, *Gay New York: Gender, Urban Culture, and the Makings of the Gay Male World, 1890–1940* (1994); Lizabeth Cohen, *Making a New Deal: Industrial Workers in Chicago, 1919–1939* (1990); Paul Conkin, *The New Deal*, 2d. ed. (1975); Terry A. Cooney, *Balancing Acts: American Thought and Culture in the 1930s* (1995); Robert Crunden, *From Self to Society, 1919–1941* (1972); Ann Douglas, *Terrible Honesty: Mongrel Manhattan in the 1920s* (1995); Susan J. Douglas, *Listening In: Radio and the American Imagination* (1999); Lynn Dumenil, *The Modern Temper: America in the 1920s* (1995); Melvin Ely, *The Adventures of Amos 'n' Andy: A Social History of an American Phenomena* (1991, 2001); Lewis Erenberg, *Swingin' the Dream: Big Band Jazz and the Rebirth of American Culture* (1998); Neil Foley, *The White Scourge: Mexicans, Blacks, and Poor Whites in Texas Cotton Culture* (1997); Conal Furay, *The Grass-Roots Mind in America: The American Sense of Absolutes* (1977); William Graebner, *The Age of Doubt: American Thought and Culture in the 1940s* (1990); James Gregory, *American Exodus: The Dust Bowl Migration and Okie Culture in California* (1989); Anthony Heilbut, *Exiled in Paradise: German Refugee Artists and Intellectuals in America from the 1930s to the Present* (1983); David Hollinger, "Ethnic Diversity, Cosmopolitanism, and the Emergence of the American Liberal Intelligentsia," in Hollinger, *In the American Province: Studies in the History and Historiography of Ideas* (1985); Nathan Huggins, *Harlem Renaissance* (1971); John F. Kasson, *Houdini, Tarzan, and the Perfect Man: The White Male Body and the Challenge of Modernity in America* (2001); David Levering Lewis, *When Harlem Was in Vogue* (1981); Roland Marchand, *Advertising and the American Dream: Making Way for Modernity, 1920–1940* (1985); Joanne Meyerowitz, ed., *Not June Cleaver: Women and Gender in Postwar America, 1945–1960* (1994); Nathan Miller, *New World Coming: The 1920s and the Making of Modern America* (2003); Eric Sandeen, *Picturing an Exhibition: The Family of Man and 1950s America* (1995); Warren Susman, ed., *Culture and Commitment, 1929–1945* (1973), a source book; and Stephen J. Whitfield, *The Culture of the Cold War* (1991).

THE CULMINATION OF MODERN WAYS AND COMING TO TERMS WITH MODERN WAYS, 1950–PRESENT

For modern ways since about the mid-twentieth century, consult the influential writings of Daniel Bell, Robert Bellah, Betty Friedan, Clifford Geertz, Paul Goodman, Will Herberg, Richard Hofstadter, Kenneth Keniston, Martin Luther King, Jr., Alfred Kinsey, Christopher Lasch, Russell Kirk, Norman Mailer, Margaret Mead, David Riesman, Richard Rorty, Carl Sagan, Susan Sontag, Benjamin Spock, Lionel Trilling, Cornell West, George Will, E. O. Wilson, Gary Wills, and Tom Wolfe. European writers who have particularly influenced the history of American ideas in recent times include Simone de Beauvoir, Michel Foucault, Jean Paul Sartre, C. P. Snow, Claude Levi Strauss, and E. P. Thompson.

In addition, as secondary works, see James L. Baughman, *The Republic of Mass Culture: Journalism, Filmmaking, and Broadcasting in America since 1941* (1992); Paul S. Boyer, *By the Bomb's Early Light: American Thought and Culture at the Dawn of the Atomic Age* (1986, 1994); Taylor Branch, *Parting the Waters: America in the King Years* (1988); Howard Brick, *The Age of Contradiction: American Thought and Culture in the 1960s* (1998); David Brooks, *Bobos in Paradise: The New Upper Class and How They Got There* (2000); Joan Jacobs Brumberg, *The Body Project: An Intimate History of American Girls* (1997); Peter Clecak, *America's Quest for the Ideal Self: Dissent and Fulfillment in the 60s and 70s* (1983); Susan J. Douglas, *Where the Girls Are: Growing Up Female with the Mass Media* (1994); Sara M. Evans, *Tidal Wave: How Women Changed America at Century's End* (2004); David Farber, *The Age of Great Dreams: America in the 1960s* (1994); Thomas Frank and Matt Weiland, eds., *Commodify Your Dissent: The Business of Culture in the New Gilded Age* (1997); Mark Gerson, *The Neoconservative Vision: From the Cold War to the Culture Wars* (1996); Todd Gitlin, *The Twilight of Common Dreams: Why America is Wracked by Cultural Wars* (1995); Pete Hamill, *Why Sinatra Matters* (1998); D. G. Hart, *That Old Time Religion in Modern America: Evangelical Protestantism in the Twentieth Century* (2002); David A. Hollinger, *Postethnic America: Beyond Multiculturalism* (1995); Robert D. Hunter, *Culture Wars: The Struggle to Define*

America (1991); Andreas Huyssen, *After the Great Divide: Modernism, Mass Culture, Postmodernism* (1986); John Leland, *Hip: The History* (2004); David Marc, *Comic Visions: Television Comedy and American Culture*, 2d. ed. (1997); Arthur Marwick, *The Sixties: Cultural Revolution in Britain, France, Italy, and the United States* (1998); Elaine Tyler May, *Homeward Bound: American Families in the Cold War Era* (1988); Mark Oppenheimer, *Knocking on Heaven's Door: American Religion in the Age of Counterculture* (2003); Robert D. Putnam, *Bowling Alone: The Collapse and Revival of American Community* (2000); Tricia Rose, *Black Noise: Rap Music and Black Culture in Contemporary America* (1994); Ruth Rosen, *The World Split Open: How the Modern Women's Movement Changed America* (2000); Bruce J. Schulman, *The Seventies: The Great Shift in American Culture, Society, and Politics* (2001); David Steigerwald, "The End of Culture," in his *The Sixties and the End of Modern America* (1975); Juan Williams, *Eyes on the Prize: America's Civil Rights Years, 1954–1965* (1988); Robert Wuthnow, *The Restructuring of American Religion: Society and Faith since World War II* (1988); and Robert Wuthnow, *Sharing the Journey: Support Groups and America's New Quest for Community* (1994).

PHOTO CREDITS

Chapter 23 P. 359, Gated community entrance, Palm Desert, CA, © David Butow/Corbis Saba; p. 363, Woman making online credit purchase © Ed Bock/ Corbis; p. 368, Crystal Cathedral, Garden Grove, CA, © Catherine Karnow/Corbis.

Chapter 24 P. 374, NASCAR racing, Talladega, AL, © David Madison/New Sport/Corbis; p. 378, Ludacris and posse, Miami, FL, 2001, © Reuters/ Corbis; p. 380, Woman saying goodbye to stay-at-home husband and baby, © Michael Krasowitz/Taxi/Getty Images; p. 383, Mexican American parishioners praying, Basilica of Our Lady, San Juan, TX, © Bob Daemmrich/ The Image Works.

INDEX

Page numbers in italics refer to illustrations.